KANT:

Disputed Questions

KANT:
Disputed Questions

EDITED WITH AN INTRODUCTION

AND NEW TRANSLATIONS BY

Moltke S. Gram

CHICAGO

Quadrangle Books

1 9 6 7

Library of Congress Catalog Card Number: 67-12355

Preface

There are three issues central to Kant's *Kritik* which have guided the organization of this anthology. The first concerns the Transcendental Deduction: does it represent a single argument or is it in fact only a medley of different arguments? Until this question has been answered, we will be in no position to ask about the success of the central task of the first *Kritik*. For until we know whether the argument in the Deduction is sound, we will not know whether Kant has shown how a set of concepts which we cannot derive from experience can apply to experience.

The second issue represented here concerns Kant's critique of ontology. Does he, for example, succeed in showing that the claims of traditional ontology are empirically meaningless? Or does he merely propound one more ontological position?

There is, finally, the issue of whether Kant has shown that there are such things as synthetic judgments *a priori*. This last issue appears here in several different forms. Can the general account which Kant gives of the logical character of a synthetic judgment *a priori* be assimilated to what Leibniz and Wolff had called necessary propositions, which, on Kant's account, would really be only analytic judgments? And, more particularly, even if we grant that Kant has successfully distinguished his synthetic judgments *a priori* from Leibniz's necessary propositions, has Kant really succeeded in giving us a way to demonstrate the truth of such claims in metaphysics? This question is raised here in the context of Kant's proof of the Second Analogy. These are the issues which the papers in this anthology are meant to illuminate.

I am indebted to Messrs. Henry Veatch and Robert Browning, both of whom gave a critical reading to sections of the book.

MOLTKE S. GRAM

Evanston, Illinois, 1967

Acknowledgments

Hans Vaihinger's "The Transcendental Deduction of the Categories in the First Edition of the *Critique of Pure Reason*" was originally published in *Philosophische Abhandlungen* (Halle, 1902), pp. 24-98, and appears here for the first time in English translation. I have omitted the third part of the essay, which is a discussion of Kant's posthumous works as they relate to Vaihinger's thesis.

H. J. Paton's "Is the Transcendental Deduction a Patchwork?" first appeared in *Proceedings of the Aristotelian Society* (1929-1930), pp. 143-178, and was reprinted in Paton's *In Defence of Reason* (Hutchinson's University Library, 1951). His article "The Key to Kant's Deduction of the Categories" appeared first in *Mind* (1931), pp. 310-329, and was also reprinted in *In Defence of Reason*. Both of these articles are reprinted here by permission of the author.

Arthur O. Lovejoy's "Kant's Antithesis of Dogmatism and Criticism" first appeared in *Mind* (1906), pp. 191-214; his "Kant's Classification of the Forms of Judgment" appeared in the *Philosophical Review* (1907), pp. 588-603; and his "On Kant's Reply to Hume" appeared in the *Archiv für Geschichte der Philosophie* (1906), pp. 380-407.

Ernst Cassirer's "Kant and the Problem of Metaphysics" appears here for the first time in English translation. It was previously printed in *Kant-Studien* (1929), pp. 10-26, and is reprinted here by permission of the editor of that journal.

Heinz Heimsoeth's "Metaphysical Motives in the Development of Critical Idealism" appears here for the first time in English. It was previously printed in *Kant-Studien* (1924), pp. 121-159, and is reprinted here by permission of the editor.

Lewis White Beck's "Kant's Theory of Definition" and his "Can Kant's Synthetic Judgments Be Made Analytic?" are from *Studies in the Philosophy of Kant*. The former article first appeared in the *Philosophical Review* (1956), pp. 179-191; the latter first appeared in *Kant-Studien* (1955), pp. 168-181.

Contents

PREFACE   5

PART I: THE PATCHWORK THESIS

*The Transcendental Deduction of the Categories in the
First Edition of the* Critique of Pure Reason:
    HANS VAIHINGER   23
Is the Transcendental Deduction a Patchwork?
    H. J. PATON   62

PART II: KANT AND THE PROBLEM OF METAPHYSICS

Kant's Antithesis of Dogmatism and Criticism:
    ARTHUR O. LOVEJOY   105
Kant and the Problem of Metaphysics: ERNST CASSIRER   131
*Metaphysical Motives in the Development of Critical
Idealism:* HEINZ HEIMSOETH   158

PART III: KANT'S THEORY OF THE SYNTHETIC-ANALYTIC DISTINCTION

Kant's Theory of Definition: LEWIS WHITE BECK   215

Can Kant's Synthetic Judgments Be Made Analytic?
    LEWIS WHITE BECK   228
The Key to Kant's Deduction of the Categories:
    H. J. PATON   247
Kant's Classification of the Forms of Judgment:
    ARTHUR O. LOVEJOY   269
On Kant's Reply to Hume: ARTHUR O. LOVEJOY   284

INDEX   309

Part I

The Patchwork Thesis

VAIHINGER gave us what was to become one of the most sustained defenses of the view that the Transcendental Deduction in the first edition of the *Kritik* is not a unified argument at all but rather a composite of four different layers or levels, each of which represents a different view. Vaihinger begins by pointing out discrepancies in Kant's account of the subjective sources of knowledge. From A94 to A95 of the *Kritik,* Kant reduces the conditions of the possibility of experience to three components—the three functions of sensibility, imagination, and understanding. But from A97 to A98 Kant gives us a different account. While the three functions had been sharply separated in the first account, now the main distinction is between receptivity and spontaneity. And, further, in the first account synthesis was only a function of imagination, while the functions of sense and understanding were not called functions of synthesis. In the second account not only imagination but also sense and understanding are called functions of synthesis. Moreover, in the second account all three of these functions are assigned to spontaneity. This was not the case in the first account. And, finally, in the second account the transcendental faculty of imagination is called both productive and reproductive. In the first account this faculty was only productive.

But this is not the only discrepancy which Vaihinger finds in Kant's account of the subjective sources of knowledge. There is, according to Vaihinger, yet a third account of these sources which must be separated from both of the foregoing accounts. The third account extends from A115 to A128. At this point, however, Kant calls all of the three functions empirical—a claim that allegedly runs counter to his characterization of them as transcendental in both the first and second accounts. And, as if to compound the confusion, Kant now divides the functions of synthesis into apprehension, reproduction, and recognition, claiming that all of them are functions of imagination—a claim which runs counter to both the first and the second accounts.

This, as I understand it, is Vaihinger's main evidence for the view that Kant is not giving us a unified argument in the Deduction. For, according to Vaihinger, this radical divergence shows that Kant is advancing conflicting theories of the subjective sources of knowledge. In the face of this, Vaihinger proposes not to repair Kant's argument but only to explain what is alleged to be a series of clear discrepancies by making the hypothesis that they betoken different theories which arose at different times in Kant's development. Vaihinger distinguishes four different layers or levels in the argument, each of which is said to correspond to a different period of composition. Briefly, they are as follows. There is, first, the layer which Vaihinger considers to be the oldest because (1) the layer contains no discussion of the productive imagination (a notion which is central to the Deduction); (2) there is here a discussion of the object of representation (a notion that is elsewhere taken for granted) and how we relate our representations to objects; (3) there is no mention of the categories as such but only of some concepts or other (be they empirical or pure) which give synthetic unity to the manifold; and (4) space and time are called *a priori concepts* which give objective unity.

In the second layer distinguished by Vaihinger, pure concepts are said to be applicable to the transcendent world, the categories are said not to represent the conditions under which objects are given to us, and there is no mention of productive imagination. This second layer is separated from the first because, according to Vaihinger, it is only in the second layer that Kant asks about the right we have to apply categories to sensuous representations. And this is a new problem, for the first layer treated only the relation of sensuous representations to objects.

The third layer of the argument is seen in those passages which introduce productive imagination and ascribe to it the entire task of uniting the manifold. There is, moreover, no distinction drawn in the third layer between the various kinds of transcendental activities.

The fourth and last layer in the Deduction is distinguished from the foregoing layers in that it contains an analysis of the imagination into a threefold synthesis, makes the claim that apprehension is a kind of synthesis which does not belong to sensibility but to understanding, and adds the reproductive imagination to the general analysis of imagination.

Vaihinger's position about the structure of the Deduction raises two questions. For one thing, what is Vaihinger's justification for the chronological distinctions he wants to make regarding the four layers? For another, even assuming that Vaihinger is right in believing that the layers he distinguishes were in fact written at different times in Kant's development, does the distinction Vaihinger makes help us to explain the discrepancies in Kant's account of the subjective sources of knowledge?

I take the latter question first. According to Vaihinger, the passage from A94 to A95 belongs to the third layer. The discrepancy which must be explained here is why Kant divides the subjective sources of knowledge into three components (something he did not do at A97), why Kant does not call sense and understanding functions of synthesis (something he did do at A97), why he did not assign all three functions of synthesis to the capacity of spontaneity (something he did do at A97), and why he limits imagination to the productive imagination (which he extended to include the reproductive imagination at A97). How does Vaihinger's assumption that A94 to A95 belongs to the third layer help explain any of this? What Vaihinger says is that one of the distinctive features of the third layer is that the threefold distinction of apprehension, reproduction, and recognition is just assimilated to the activity of the productive imagination. But if this is the case, then it would be evidence for excluding the passage from the third layer, for the passage in question contains an explicit distinction between the three subjective sources of knowledge. And even if we just waive this point, what must be explained is precisely how the information Vaihinger gives us about the third layer can explain why Kant does not call sense and understanding functions of synthesis, or why he talks only of the productive imagination, or yet why he assigns all three subjective sources of knowledge to the capacity of spontaneity.

Let us now consider the passage from A97 to A98, which contains the second account of the subjective sources of knowledge and which Vaihinger assigns to the fourth layer. The second account, it will be remembered, is based solely on the distinction between receptivity and spontaneity, contains an account of the three subjective sources of knowledge in which all of them are called functions of synthesis, assigns all three of them to the faculty of spontaneity, and introduces the distinction between productive and reproductive imagination. Here, again, what is said about the fourth layer does not explain what is said about the account that Kant gives of the subjective source of knowledge. For all we are told is that the fourth layer contains an analysis of the imagination into a threefold synthesis (which has nothing to do with anything said about the second account), that apprehension belongs to the understanding and not to sensibility (which merely repeats part of what is said about the second account), and that the reproductive imagination is added to the analysis (which again repeats part of the second account of the subjective sources of knowledge). The weight of the entire argument must, then, be borne by whatever evidence Vaihinger has to suggest that the fourth layer is really a different layer from the third. For it is only on the assumption that they are very different layers that the discrepancies between Kant's first and second accounts of the subjective sources of knowledge can be explained. The evidence which Vaihinger gives to distinguish the third from the fourth layer is in large part the evidence he gives to show that the first and the second accounts of the subjective sources of knowledge are at variance with each other. Thus the entire question of whether Vaihinger is right in thinking that there are two layers here arises only after it has been shown that there are the discrepancies in the argument that he alleges. The rest of the evidence Vaihinger cites for the distinction can be found in the characterization he gives of the third and the fourth layers. And whatever is in the characterizations that is not due to the discrepancies between the first and second accounts of the subjective sources of knowledge does not itself suffice to show that we are dealing with two different layers in Kant's development.

Consider, lastly, the passage from A115 to A128, which, in Vaihinger's opinion, belongs to the third layer. This passage contains what Vaihinger takes to be Kant's third account of the subjective sources of knowledge. Here Kant claims both that all three functions of synthesis are empirical and that they are all functions of the imagination. Why did Vaihinger assign this passage to the third layer? Perhaps because the third layer contains a theory according to which the productive imagination has the entire task of uniting the manifold. But this theory bears only a superficial resemblance to the claim of the third account of the subjective sources of knowledge that all functions of synthesis are functions of imagination. To say the latter is not to make any claim about whether the productive or the reproductive imagination is solely responsible for synthesizing the manifold. And once this superficial resemblance is exposed for what it is, there is no other reason for assigning the passage in question to the third layer. For the claim, contained in the passage, that all functions of synthesis are empirical is not explained by anything which Vaihinger says about that layer. Thus my general conclusion is this: the hypothesis that there are various layers in the Deduction rests mainly on the evidence Vaihinger gives to show that there are discrepancies in the accounts which Kant gives of the subjective sources of knowledge.

Here the work of H. J. Paton has particular significance. For Paton has undertaken to show that the evidence adduced by Vaihinger to point out discrepancies in Kant's argument does not survive examination. Paton's general strategy is to take up the alleged inconsistencies and to show that Vaihinger has confused different stages in a unified argument with different arguments. Paton argues that we should expect a difference between the second and third layers, because what Vaihinger calls the second layer is the objective part of the Deduction, while Vaihinger's third layer is the subjective part of the Deduction. Yet Vaihinger has argued that there is an inconsistency in the two layers: the second layer mentions sense and understanding and ignores imagination. Paton's answer to this is that the passage (A92-93) in which this is done is really meant to be an introduction to the objective deduction, which, on Kant's own admission, does not concern the subjective machinery by which we apprehend the manifold; hence we are justified in expecting Kant to omit imagination in this context and deal only with the more general distinction between sense and understanding.

The next problem Paton discusses is the alleged distinction between the first and the fourth layers. Vaihinger has argued that the fourth layer has absolutely nothing to do with the first layer. Vaihinger's way of explaining this is to hypothesize that the first layer is tacked onto the fourth because the fourth layer was developed by Kant on the eve of the publication of the *Kritik*, then abandoned, and was finally supplanted by an argument which was written years before but was hastily inserted into the Deduction. Apart from this attempt to explain how Kant could have apparently thrown together such mutually irrelevant positions, Vaihinger adduces several minor arguments to prove that the two layers have nothing to do with each other. For one thing, the first layer contains no mention of the productive imagination, while the fourth layer discusses it at length. For another, the first layer contains the only discussion of the notion of an object to be found in the Deduction. And, finally, the whole of the first layer is concerned with the relation of empirical concepts and their objects, while the fourth layer repeats the claim that all empirical activities of the mind presuppose corresponding transcendental activities.

Paton answers this argument by first pointing out the gratuity of Vaihinger's hypothesis and then answering the more specific arguments *seriatim*. The difference between the two layers is to be explained, Paton argues, by looking upon the first layer as part of a unified argument, the total results of which are then summarized in what Vaihinger calls the fourth layer. This would easily explain why the two layers appear to have nothing to do with each other. But what about the more specific points of divergence between the two layers? These can be easily disposed of. It is true, for example, that the first layer contains no mention of the productive imagination, because Kant is not concerned there to give an account of the subjective side of the Deduction. It is also true that the first layer contains the only discussion of the notion of an object in the Deduction; but this is to be expected, for this layer is concerned to expound the objective side of the Deduction. And, finally, it is true that the first layer deals with empirical concepts; but this is to be expected, too, for Kant has just finished trying to show that every concept is a principle of unity and also involves a necessity. And that Kant chooses an empirical concept to illustrate this view does not license the inference that Kant has not yet recognized that all empirical concepts presuppose categories for their application. Hence there is no inconsistency between the first and fourth layers.

The last major point that Paton treats is Vaihinger's claim that there is a contradiction between the fourth layer and other parts of the Deduction. Vaihinger points out that, in the fourth layer, the synthesis of imagination is described as reproductive, while everywhere else it is called productive. Vaihinger takes this to prove that

Kant first wrote the fourth layer, then retracted it; for Vaihinger holds that Kant first made the productive imagination transcendental, then the reproductive, and finally reverted to the productive imagination again. But Paton gives us two very good reasons for rejecting this hypothesis. In the first place, the change which Vaihinger signals in Kant's views of the imagination can be equally well explained by assuming that Kant was not very clear about the place of the imagination in relation to understanding and sensibility. And, in the second place, there is a strong philosophical reason for rejecting Vaihinger's hypothesis. Kant holds that the productive imagination is necessary for the apprehension of the pure synthesis of imagination. We must, that is, be able to combine spatial-temporal relations before we can reproduce our percepts of things in space and time. But, once anyone has held this view, how could he have then said that the reproductive, not the productive, imagination is transcendental?

This concludes Paton's answer to Vaihinger. If Paton is right, then Vaihinger is simply wrong in holding that there is no internal connection between the first and the fourth layers as well as between the second and the third layers. And by showing how the layers fit together, Paton has shown how the discrepancies which Vaihinger alleges in the various accounts of the subjective sources of knowledge are illusory. Paton does not, to be sure, extend his argument to show how the three different accounts are consistent. The question to ask Paton is, accordingly, how his attempt to fit together the layers of the Deduction helps remove the alleged contradictions between the three accounts. Let us consider each account in turn, asking how Paton either does or might seek to remove the discrepancies.

1. In the first account (A94 to A95), the various conditions of the possibility of experience are separated; in the second (A97 to A98), they are not. The key to answering this can be found by relating the third layer to the fourth layer, because the first account belongs to the third layer and the second to the fourth layer. But on this matter Paton is silent. He points out only that both the third and the fourth layers belong to the subjective side of the Deduction; and this leaves the discrepancy unexplained. An argument can, however, be constructed to remove the discrepancy. At A97-98 Kant says only that spontaneity is the ground of the threefold synthesis.

And this is not to obliterate the distinctions between kinds of synthesis which he makes at A94. Thus the discrepancy here is not between parts of Kant's text but only between the text and Vaihinger's gloss.

2. Another discrepancy that Vaihinger mentions is that, at A94-95, synthesis is restricted to imagination; but at A97 the term is extended to cover both understanding and sense. Here, too, Paton is silent; but what Vaihinger has found is not a real discrepancy. Instead of inferring, as Vaihinger does, that the accounts are at variance, why should we not infer that "synthesis" has both a broad and a narrow sense? Construed broadly, synthesis is any process of unification or combination. And this is the way in which Kant uses it at A97, where the three faculties he mentions are taken to be modes of combination. Yet there is also a narrower sense of "synthesis," according to which the term denotes a particular mode of combination which is to be distinguished from a synopsis on the one hand and from the unity of the combination on the other. This narrow sense would fit the passage at A94, where Kant specifically distinguishes between the synopsis of apprehension, the synthesis of imagination, and the unity of the synthesis in the concept.

3. Vaihinger also argues that, in the second account of the subjective sources of knowledge, all three functions are assigned to spontaneity, while they were not so assigned in the first account. This alleged discrepancy is explained once it is realized that Kant is completely silent about spontaneity at A95, from which it cannot be inferred, as Vaihinger does, that Kant therefore refuses to assign all three functions of synthesis to spontaneity.

4. In A97-98, Vaihinger tells us, the transcendental faculty of imagination is both reproductive and productive. In A94-95, however, imagination is solely productive. Now Paton does not speak to this discrepancy except to say that Kant is probably confused about the place of imagination. But there is a stronger argument against Vaihinger's interpretation. It is false to say that Kant denies both productive and reproductive functions to imagination at A94-95. The only difference between the two passages is this: in A97-98 Kant does not distinguish between the two functions of imagination; but this is very far from explicitly denying that the imagination is in fact reproductive as well as productive.

What remains now is to raise the same question about Paton's answer in the context of what Vaihinger calls Kant's third account of the subjective sources of knowledge that we have just been raising in the context of the first and second accounts. What about the discrepancies Vaihinger alleges to obtain between the third account (A115 to A128) and the other two?

1. Beginning at A115, Kant is said to call all three modes of synthesis empirical, while they were called transcendental throughout the other parts of the argument. Paton does speak to this when he points out that Kant is merely arguing here that *all* concepts involve functions of synthesis. And that Kant is in fact holding that there are two levels on which the threefold synthesis works—the empirical and the transcendental—can be shown by his own words at A115:

> There are three subjective sources of knowledge. . . . Each of these can be viewed as empirical, namely, in its application to given appearances. But all of them are likewise *a priori* elements or foundations, which make this empirical employment itself possible.

2. Another discrepancy which distinguishes the third account from the other two is found in the relation between the threefold synthesis and imagination. Vaihinger claims that, on Kant's third account, the functions of synthesis are first divided into apprehension, reproduction, and recognition, and are then called one and all functions of imagination. In neither of the first two accounts was the threefold synthesis derived from imagination. Although Paton does not speak to this issue, an examination of the text from which Vaihinger derives the discrepancy will give us the answer. The only passage in A123 to A126 which even appears to support Vaihinger's interpretation occurs at A123 and runs like this:

> That the affinity of appearances, and with it their association, and through this, in turn, their reproduction according to laws, and so [as involving these various factors] experience itself, should only be possible by means of this transcendental function of imagination, is indeed strange, but is none the less an obvious consequence of the preceding argument.

But exactly how does imagination make this possible? Kant's answer is given at A124, where he says that imagination mediates between sensibility and understanding, "otherwise the former [sensibility], though indeed yielding appearances, would supply no objects of empirical knowledge, and consequently no experience." What Kant says here is not, as Vaihinger holds, that the threefold synthesis is a function of the imagination, but rather that imagination is an indispensable part of an account of how we come to know objects. Hence there is no textual foundation for the discrepancy Vaihinger finds between Kant's third account and the first two.

What I have been urging here is that Vaihinger's thesis depends almost entirely upon his ability to show that the discrepancies he finds in Kant's view of the subjective sources of knowledge are genuine. The existence of such discrepancies is the main motive and the principal source of evidence for the layers which Vaihinger sees in the argument of the Deduction. Although Paton's reply succeeds in removing the main discrepancies, it does not, I think, extend to all of them. That this does not weaken Paton's case has, I believe, been shown by the arguments which can be given to account for the remaining discrepancies.

THE TRANSCENDENTAL DEDUCTION OF THE CATEGORIES IN THE FIRST EDITION OF THE *CRITIQUE OF PURE REASON*

Hans Vaihinger

§

INTRODUCTORY

Attentive and sharp study of the Deduction in A tells us at every turn that we are not dealing with a unified discussion: Kant cannot possibly have written it at one time; but also that he should have written it in individual paragraphs but nonetheless in the present order of sections is hardly possible. The repetitions and the contradictions in the order are rather such that we must assume not only merely successive levels but even levels that have been thrown together. The publication of the *Lose Blätter,* the *Reflexionen,* and the *Opus Postumum* from Kant's posthumous works has instructed us in Kant's method of working: everywhere we find individual shorter or longer discussions in which Kant tries to master the unyielding object in ever new attempts; and with these new attempts he hardly ever refers to his own earlier discussions. He almost always begins anew without referring to the older notes at hand.

This explains not only the ever new treatment of the same topic but also the conspicuous divergences of these treatments from one another. Thus the apparently strictly unified Deduction in A dissolves into a series of loose notes which may date from very different times and which Kant himself brought only into a loose, external connection at the final redaction, without internal interpenetration and unity.

That this is really the case did not escape earlier, more attentive observers. As early as 1876 Riehl (in his *Philos. Kriticismus,* I, 377, 386) advanced the thesis: "The Deduction is taken up and carried out not less than three times from three different perspectives"; "The line of thought is repeated in various formulations." In 1878 B. Erdmann [1] directed attention especially to this situation: *Kants Kriticismus* (p. 24ff.): "The sequence of proof of the Deduction does not constitute a continuous sequence but rather a four-time repetition of one and the same argument.

"First order of proof: Apprehension; reproduction; recognition (apperception, object of representations); categories. A98-112.

"Second order of proof: Association; affinity; apperception; laws. A112-114.

"Third order of proof: Apperception; imagination; understanding; categories; appearances. A116-119.

"Fourth order of proof: Perception; apprehension; reproduction; association; affinity; apperception (recognition); laws. A119-128.

"These four presentations are not only distinguished from one another in that the third, which is less detailed, reverses the direction of the argument, but also in that the first is richer by one element (the relation to the object of representations) than the others. These latter, however, introduce two elements—association and affinity—that do not exist as separate elements without its being possible precisely to determine their place within that first row. . . . Even within the individual arguments the various elements are not intelligibly related. Especially in the first argument the discussion of the relation of representations to their object enters quite

1. Cf. B. Erdmann's edition of the *Prolegomena* which appeared at the same time, *Einleitung* IV-V, XXXII-XXXIX, LXXIX sq. Especially at XXXVI the "contradictions" between the various presentations are pointed out. Regarding the composition of the Transcendental Deduction cf. further B. Erdmann's discussion in the *Philosophische Monatshefte* (1883), pp. 140ff.; (1884) pp. 89ff.

perfunctorily and inexplicably into the proof despite all the material solidarity with the last element."

Those four individual lines of proof are "only loosely joined together, at times even so that it seems as if a later interpolation had taken place, as with the second order of proof, which attaches itself to the first without reason." The "divisive presentation, which everywhere arouses the impression of the incomplete," is then expressly emphasized: "It is a task of the history of Kant's development to explain this strange composition of the section."

Eleven years later Adickes made a new start in this direction. In his edition[2] of the *Critique of Pure Reason* (1889, pp. 139, 653-684) he tried quite sharply to analyze the Deduction in A into its individual components: "The Deduction in A is artificially put together from various earlier independent deductions which were separated from one another in point of time and content" (139). The Deduction is "a mosaic-like assemblage and combination of various thoughts from various times." Adickes believed that he could sharply separate the various lines of thought from various times. The individual paragraphs of every new attempt at the Deduction in A do have, to be sure, the common rationalistic principle "that only in virtue of the categories is combination of representations and the resulting unity of experience possible." But here arise "various points of view, according to whether the one or the other of the factors which produce experience is placed in the foreground and referred to the categories. These differences and contradictions . . . yield sufficient clues in order to separate the individual components with comparative certainty" (139). Accordingly, Adickes separated seven different deductions in which he found as many different variations of the same principle.[3] The principle of

2. Concerning the great merit of this edition, I refer to my review of it in the *Archiv für Geschichte der Philosophie* (IV, 723-729), where I have made a few inessential corrections. Cf. also Busse, *Kantstudien*, II, 127.

3. Adickes spoke with considerably greater caution about the chronological sequence of the individual sections; he believed that "an exact dating of the individual sections cannot be carried" (p. 683). But Adickes ventured a few conjectures about how he conceives the relation of the ages of the individual sections (pp. 683-684, compared with XXV-XXVII of his introduction): the most important of them I have included in the table which follows later. Nevertheless, Adickes gave essential supplements to these in his *Kantstudien* (1895), pp. 173ff., and in the *Kantstudien* (1896), I, 244ff., about which greater details are given later.

their distinction is the different manner in which one and the same fundamental idea is varied. But then Adickes finds that, in almost each of these seven deductions, insertions from the others are found, and in these insertions other insertions, in addition to harmonizing sections for the unification of the various presentations. Thus, in Adickes' view, not only the synthesis of the individual sections but also their analysis has been necessarily very artificial—like a system of cycles and epicycles.[4]

The following analysis of the Deduction in A will perhaps appear no less artificial; but it has arisen in complete independence of Adickes and arrives in its details at completely different results. What is common is perhaps the main result of both of the analyses —that the Deduction in A consists of levels that are different in time and in content; but the principle of their division is different. My principle of separation is the following: Kant gives in the various presentations different accounts of the "subjective sources of knowledge"—sense, imagination, understanding, and the like. Geologists, who prefer to distinguish various levels of the earth's surface, use in part the designation of various "guide shells" where these levels have later been interlarded: various Neptunic shells are distinguished according to the shells that are enclosed in them; and the diversity of these shells is the guideline for the distinction of levels. Such "guide shells" for the various levels of the Deduction in A are the presentations of the subjective sources of knowledge which diverge radically from one another and whose diversity (which was remarked already by B. Erdmann) Adickes had indeed seen without making this into the real principle of separation. But for us that distinction is the sole and decisive principle of division of the individual levels.

We shall analyze first the individual presentations in the present sequence in Kant, according to the principle of division developed above. Thereafter we shall be in the position of attempting to re-

---

4. G. Thiele, in his *Philosophie des Selbstbewusstseins* (Berlin, 1895, p. 255), makes differences in the Deduction in A. He contents himself, however, with the hint that Kant, in the Deduction, "struggles with his thoughts and presents them no fewer than four times in succession"; namely, first A98-114; second, A115-119; third, A119-128; fourth, A128-130. (Moreover, as Thiele correctly remarked, A76-79 and A84-94 belong here, too.) Thiele did not go into the differences of the four presentations in more detail.

turn the individual presentations to their chronological order, in which they were probably conceived by Kant.

Before we proceed to this, there is still a technical difficulty to be overcome: it concerns a convenient and short characterization of the individual sections which we distinguish through easily recognizable numbers. Adickes, too, found it expedient to supply the individual presentations which he distinguished with definite numbers (cf. the last heading of the following table); but he had in this a great advantage over us: he could introduce in the margin of his edition the relevant distinguishing sign and explain his theory in short footnotes at the bottom of the text. We must, however, express the wish that the reader enter the code we have chosen for the individual presentations in his copy of the text; for, without this external but nonetheless indispensable aid, the reader will not be in a position to form an independent judgment. The code we have selected is taken from the source itself: the three sections into which Kant himself divided the Transcendental Deduction in A are designated by I, II, III. In the first section, which is also incorporated in the second edition, the paragraph divisions of the second edition (¶13, ¶14) have been retained by us; the rest of the first section, which was not incorporated in B, is designated as "I conclusion." In the second section the introduction was first separated into two parts (a and b); Kant himself distinguishes four numbers in the section. We believe that, shortly after the beginning of the third number (after the second paragraph), a sharp division is to be made. Thus we had to divide the third number into a and b. Finally, the individual divisions that we thought necessary to make in the third section have been designated, with the exception of the introduction, as a, b, c, d, e. The designation of the "summary presentation, etc." by S is self-explanatory. The first half of ¶10, which belongs to the "Clue to the Discovery, etc.," stands in very close relation to the Deduction: this explains the code L 10.

As an aid to a synoptic survey, I am attaching a table. Under the first heading are the page numbers of the first edition, which are given in the margins of the editions of B. Erdmann, Adickes, and Vorländer and are at the bottom of the Kehrbach edition. Wherever it appeared necessary, the beginning or concluding words of the divisions are cited here. The second heading provides a short characterization of the content of the relevant sections (so far as possible, in Kant's own words). The third heading gives the numbers which I have selected for the individual sections, the choice of which I have just justified. The Roman numerals which follow give the four levels (that is, the chronological sequence) in which I believe that I can organize the parts which I distinguish for the reasons that appear in the following discussion. Finally, the last heading gives the designation which Adickes chose for the individual sections; the first six sections coincide with the divisions I have made; the other seven "deductions" that he distinguished do not agree with the ones I have distinguished; but the mutual relation of Adickes' division and mine is made easily recognizable through the brackets. The last heading contains, at the same time, the most important references which Adickes made in his edition concerning the relation of the individual divisions and especially concerning their chronological relations (cf. his edition of the *Critique*, pp. 683-684 and XXV-XXVII).

COMPARATIVE TABLE

PAGINATION OF *The Critique of Pure Reason*	CHARACTERIZATION OF THE CONTENTS	VAIHINGER NUMBER	LEVELS	ADICKES (1889 EDITION OF TI *Critique*)
A76-79 =102-104 (¶10)	The categories as concepts of the unity of the pure synthesis (Clue to the Discovery of All the Concepts of the Understanding, 3rd section)	L ¶10	III/IV	B.S. 102-104a; later ac tion at this place; belo to the IV. Deduction

The Deduction of the Pure Concepts of the Understanding
First Section (I)

A84-92 =B116-124 (¶13)	"Principles of a Transcendental Deduction in General"	I ¶13	I/II	¶13 added later; the last t paragraphs are the la of all

COMPARATIVE TABLE (Cont.)

AGINATION OF The Critique f Pure Reason	CHARACTERI- ZATION OF THE CONTENTS	VAI- HIN- GER NUM- BER	LEVELS	ADICKES (1889 EDITION OF THE Critique)
A92-94 =B124-127 (¶14)	"Transition to the Transcen- dental Deduc- tion of the Categories"	I ¶14	II	¶14 the latest added
A94-95	First Table of Subjective Sources	I conclu- sion	III	B.S. 127, footnote I; be- longs behind the passage A. (pp. 95-96a) as the conclusion of the intro. to the IV. Deduction
Second Section (II)				
A95-97	"Concerning the *A priori* Grounds of the Possibility of Experience" (Introduction)	II Intro. a	II	A.S. 95-96a; belongs to IV. Deduction *als ets* original intro. B.S. 127 was attached to this earlier
A97-98	Second Table of Subjective Sources (conclu- sion of the II Intro. b Intro- duction)	II Intro. b	IV	A.S. 97/98 belongs to the I. Deduc- tion as its intro. and serves as the intermediary be- tween the I. and the IV. Deduction (esp. B.S. p. 127 and ft. I)
A98-104 ". . . knowl- ge of objects quite impos- le."	1. "Synthesis of apprehension in Intuition" 2. "Synthesis of Reproduction in Imagina- tion" 3. "Synthesis of Recognition in the Con- cept"	II, I-3a	IV	I. Deduction from the ear- liest period but with many inserts under the influence of the V. and also the IV.
A104-110 n: "and here is necessary . " to the clusion of the d number	—Theory of the Object	II, 3b	I	Deduction; the original conclusion of the I. Deduc- tion is absent

COMPARATIVE TABLE (Cont.)

PAGINATION OF *The Critique of Pure Reason*	CHARACTERIZATION OF THE CONTENTS	VAIHINGER NUMBER	LEVELS	ADICKES (1889 EDITION OF T. *Critique*)
A110-114	4. "Preliminary Explanation of the Possibility of the Categories as *A priori* Cognitions"	II, 4	II	II. Deduction from the liest period, but with serts under the influe of V. III. Deductior inserted to connect with IV/V

Third Section (III)

A115-116	Third Table of Subjective Sources	III Intro.	III	IV. Deduction
A116-119 from: "now we shall . . ." to: ". . . have to the understanding."	Presentation from above: beginning with pure apperception	III a	III	from the earliest perie but with later additio under the influence of
A119-123 from: "Now we shall . . ." to: ". . . would flow together."	Presentation from below: beginning with the empirical	III b	III	V. Deduction has similarity on the hand to I and on the hand to IV; contains additions that are enced by I.
A123-126 from: "For the permanent ego" to: ". . . to recognize an object in experience"	Development of the doctrine of the productive imagination and introduction of recognition	III c	III	
A126-128 from: "We have the Understanding . . ." to: the conclusion of the third section	The Understanding as source of the laws of nature	III d	III	VI. Deduction beginning on p. 125 the words: "The orde . . .," inserted later nevertheless related t IV. Deduction

COMPARATIVE TABLE (Cont.)

GINATION OF The Critique Pure Reason	CHARACTERIZATION OF THE CONTENTS	VAIHINGER NUMBER	LEVELS	ADICKES (1889 EDITION OF THE Critique)
	Summary Presentation			
A128-130	Short repetition of the argument but without the doctrine, developed in the second section, of the three kinds of synthesis	S	III	VII. Deduction inserted at the last

I. SHORT ANALYSIS OF THE INDIVIDUAL SECTIONS ACCORDING TO THEIR SEQUENCE IN KANT

L. ¶10

While Kant had set intuitions and concepts, sensibility and understanding, over against each other without further explanation at the conclusion of the general introduction, at the beginning of the Transcendental Aesthetic and at the beginning of the Transcendental Analytic another presentation appears for the first time in the third section of the "Clue (L) to the Discovery of all Pure Concepts of the Understanding" (=2nd. ed. ¶10). In the first paragraph the spontaneity of thought is more closely designated as "synthesis" and attributed to the understanding; in that synthesis "going through," "taking up," and "combining" are distinguished.[5] In the third paragraph, however, this same synthesis is represented as a matter of an unconscious faculty of imagination ("as we shall see further on," it is said here with reference to the Transcendental Deduction). Now only in the fifth paragraph are the following sharply distinguished: 1. pure intuition (=sensibility) yields the manifold; 2. imagination accomplishes the synthesis of the mani-

5. The two former functions will later, A98 (=II, 1), be ascribed to apprehension under the names "running through" and "taking together"; only the third is later the affair of the understanding, which is identical with apperception.

fold; 3. the understanding adds the concepts of unity. This preliminary presentation in the "Clue"—apart from its inner dis-
cordance—is unnecessary at that point and produces confusion,
especially because of the strange shift according to which the manifold is said to be primarily *a priori* and not *a posteriori*. (Concerning this there are more details below.)

1. ¶13

The first part of the first section, "Concerning the Principles of
a Transcendental Deduction in General," that is designated as ¶13
in B, stands in opposition to L ¶10 by mentioning only the old
dichotomy of sensibility and understanding. It arrives at the problem or task of the Deduction and presupposes that the categories of
the understanding are not necessary for the objects of intuition.
This presupposition, however, is later in fact taken back.

1. ¶14

The second half of the first section, "Transition to the Transcendental Deduction of the Categories," that is designated by ¶14
in B, likewise mentions only the dichotomy of sensibility and understanding but goes far beyond the content of ¶13; for now it is seen
that the categories are necessary for thinking intuitions as objects
and for combining them into a unified experience.

1. *Conclusion*
FIRST TABLE OF THE SUBJECTIVE SOURCES OF KNOWLEDGE

Now after the old, familiar dichotomy of sensibility and understanding has constantly recurred, at the conclusion of the first section of the Transcendental Deduction (=I) the new division is to
be found of the "three original sources that contain the conditions
of the possibility of all experience": 1. the *a priori* synopsis of the
manifold through sense; 2. the synthesis of this manifold by the
imagination; 3. the unity of this synthesis by original apperception.
In all three the empirical use is distinguished from the transcendental. "Of this [latter] we have spoken with respect to the senses
above in the first part [in the Transcendental Aesthetic]; but we
want now to try to understand the nature of the other two." Thus
only these latter are to be discussed in what follows. It should be
remarked that synthesis occurs not only in the second but also in

the third, just as, in L ¶10, the understanding is that which gives unity to the synthesis.

II. *Introduction a*

According to the preparation of the first section, the Deduction proper should begin with the second section; but now there follows first a new introduction in four paragraphs, which repeats the requirements of ¶14: it must be shown that only "in virtue of the categories can an object be thought." Here, too, the discussion concerns only the understanding in general in opposition to the sensibility. The matter turns out quite differently in the fifth paragraph. This latter constitutes an independent passage as

II. *Introduction b*
SECOND TABLE OF THE SUBJECTIVE SOURCES OF KNOWLEDGE

Beginning anew, the author explains that a unity must be made out of the isolated representations through synthetic operations. Sense has, to be sure, a synopsis of the manifold; but this consists, as it appears from the context, in a passive, receptive, external intuition of things together. To be sure, this is also a kind of synthesis; but it is a quite inferior synthesis, a purely external sequence and juxtaposition. A genuine internal combination and interconnection arises only through synthesis as a spontaneous act. Now there is a threefold synthesis distinguished: the apprehension of representations in intuition, the reproduction of them in imagination, and the recognition of them in the concept. "These lead the way to three subjective sources of knowledge which even make the understanding . . . possible." This presentation diverges significantly from the ones that have gone before. While in L sense, imagination and understanding (which was replaced in "I Conclusion" by apperception) were set over against one another, here receptivity (=sense) and spontaneity stand over against one another. Spontaneity is then divided into three functions of synthesis, while in L and in "I Conclusion" synthesis was represented formally only as one function (that being imagination) and materially as a matter of understanding or apperception. Hence, while earlier there were only one formal and two material synthetic functions distinguished, here three material functions appear, since apprehension is added as the third or, rather, is placed before the two others. These three together "make the understanding possible"; they are thus components and factors of the understanding or, as Kant himself later says, "elements." (Below, in III a, the understanding is reduced to two factors of imagination and apperception.)

Thus here sensibility and understanding are opposed to each other and only the understanding is divided into three special elements. These three elements "give a direction toward the three subjective sources of knowledge"; these factors are designated as "intuition, imagination, and concept." This special division of the understanding into three parts reminds one formally of the general threefold division discussed above: sense, imagination, and understanding; but that first and this second table of the subjective sources of knowledge should absolutely not be confounded with each other (one of the main reasons for this will be given below).

Since "recognition in the concept" points to the understanding, this understanding in the narrower sense which shows itself only in recognition would have to be distinguished from the understanding in a wider sense, which comprehends those three partial functions. The presentation is also confusing because there is no mention made of the apperception which was mentioned above in "I Conclusion." Such divergences allow only one explanation: that Kant has just put together papers from very different periods without editing them thoroughly—an explanation to which we shall be forced by the further contradictions of the following presentations. One should, however, remember that we have so far arrived at the following divisions: first, the twofold division into sensibility (I) and understanding (II); then, in its place, the threefold division into sense (I), imagination (II), and understanding (III); then the first twofold division into sensibility (I) and understanding (II) returns; but here the understanding in a wide sense is divided into three partial functions: intuition (1), imagination (2), and concept (3) (and this last element must be reduced to the understanding in a narrower sense). Thus we have first a twofold division, then a threefold division, and then a confused and confusing combination of the twofold division and the threefold division.

II. 1-3 a

The complete presentation of the three synthetic functions in the three successive numbers of the second section (=II, 1-3) begins with the synthesis of apprehension. This is an "activity which is directed toward intuition," which is apparently ascribed to no special capacity, in the invention of which Kant was not sparing, standing as he was in the grip of the psychology of the time.

As a result of later passages (III b), one would ascribe apprehension to the faculty of imagination; but here that is excluded by the context.

In apprehension an empirical and a transcendental function are distinguished—if not expressly then implicitly. But the transcendental employment in fact disappears completely in the later discussions and apprehension is then used only as an empirical function.

The second synthetic function is the synthesis of reproduction. Here Kant tortures himself and the reader with a very contrived and involuted proof that the usual empirical-psychological reproduction presupposes a transcendental synthesis of reproduction (while, in the case of apprehension, the pure function was only juxtaposed with the empirical function). To be sure, the transcendental activity, analogically to the empirical activity which is treated by psychology, is designated as reproductive and, as such, ascribed to "the transcendental faculty of imagination." Later Kant omitted this and designated the transcendental function of imagination exclusively and expressly as productive, in doing which Kant himself takes back this entire section in A—all of which does not heighten clarity and lucidity. But even before this (that is, in "I Conclusion," the first table of the subjective sources and in the presentation that is related to it in L ¶10), transcendental imagination is only to be understood, according to the whole context, as productive. The reproductive imagination as a transcendental function belongs only to the second table of the subjective functions. For this main reason the second table of the subjective sources is essentially distinguished from the first as it is from the third.

The third synthetic function is the synthesis of recognition. One should now expect that an empirical and a transcendental recognition be distinguished; but this does not happen. To be sure, an empirical and a pure apperception, into which empirical and pure recognition must divide themselves, would have to be distinguished later; but this does not happen either; recognition does not return in this section III at all and only later as an empirical function.

II. 3 *b*

The following presentation which, together with the third section, begins with the words, "and here it is necessary, then," shows a quite different character. It is a completely different path, a different style. Proceeding from the concept of object, Kant shows that the "formal unity of consciousness" is its subjective counterpart. The formal unity of consciousness is the ground of all unity of the manifold and this unity is the object. That "formal unity of consciousness" together with conceptual rules of unity which express themselves in this unity are then traced back to transcendental apperception. Here those rules of unity are, conspicuously enough, empirical concepts. Reproduction and apprehension are mentioned here—and this is very important—only as empirical functions; and they are mentioned only in passing. It is obvious that, especially because of the latter fact, this section is separated like a chasm from the section that has gone before.

II. 4

A presentation that diverges fundamentally from the preceding ones is given by the fourth number of the second section. In this number only apperception is discussed, which is distinguished as "original" and "transcendental" without there being a discussion of a corresponding empirical apperception. In the fourth section, where transcendental apperception is first introduced, the "synthesis according to rules" is subordinated to it *a priori* without further explanation. This synthesis of the manifold according to *a priori* concepts is later called "transcendental affinity" of appearances, out of which the empirical affinity of appearances which is universally verified in experience later accounts for itself. To this empirical affinity of phenomenal objects corresponds the "empirical rule of association" in the subject. In this way the entire deployment of this line of thought is entirely independent of the previous presentations —and thus obviously originates at a completely different time. There is no discussion of those three synthetic functions, either as transcendental or as empirical in character. Only the apprehension of appearances as a purely empirical reception of them and thus as a purely empirical synthesis stands here over against apperception as the source of the original "synthesis according to concepts." The empirical synthesis of reception must naturally be thoroughly in accord with these *a priori* syntheses of appearances according to pure concepts; that is, from the transcendental affinity of appearances follows its empirical affinity, which we establish through empirical apprehension. What is most conspicuous is this: not one word is said about imagination, which in L ¶10 and in "I Conclusion" played such a great role as productive, and in "II Introduction b" as well as II, 1-3 a played such a great role as reproductive.

III. *Introduction*
THIRD TABLE OF THE SUBJECTIVE SOURCES OF KNOWLEDGE

This section returns again to the "three subjective sources of knowledge" and, more particularly—corresponding to the presentation in "I Conclusion"—to sense, imagination, and apperception. But here the "empirical employment" of these sources, which were only briefly mentioned there, is thoroughly depicted: "Sense represents appearances empirically in perception; the faculty of imagination, in association (and reproduction); apperception, in the empirical consciousness of the identity of these reproductive representations with the appearances through which they were given in recognition."

We may briefly call attention here to the conspicuous divergences of II, 3 b in the determination of "recognition." What is conspicuous, however, is especially the absence of "apprehension," which is here passed by with silence. The transcendental employment of those three sources of knowledge follows the empirical employment: pure intuition, pure imagination, and pure apperception. That only the last two belong here is not said but is self-explanatory. We do not discover anything in this preliminary presentation.

III. *a*

First the presentation from above follows—which proceeds from pure apperception. All appearances must be brought together in the unity of consciousness. But this synthetic unity of apperception presupposes a synthesis through the pure productive imagination which goes hand in hand with it; the reproductive imagination is only mentioned in passing here; and there is no discussion at all in the entire section of apprehension and recognition. Apperception "in relation to the imagination" is identified later with the understanding; "in relation to . . ." is a somewhat mysterious term. At any rate, the faculty of imagination is subordinated here to the understanding; for "in the understanding there is pure *a priori* knowledge, which retains the . . . synthesis of the pure faculty of imagination." The role of co-ordinator, which the faculty of imagination otherwise plays between sensibility and understanding, is not expressly mentioned and practically disappears here.

III. *b*

Now the presentation "from below" follows. The first sentence was, in all probability, inserted later; then the original presentation began with the words: "The first thing that is given to us is appearance." Appearances consist of a manifold whose connection sensibility cannot itself provide. There is "an active power" which is necessary: the imagination. Apprehension (that is, "reception of impression in its activity") is designated as the first function of this active faculty of imagination. Does this apprehensive activity belong to the empirical or to the transcendental employment of imagination? Does it, that is, belong to the reproductive or the productive imagination? Kant says nothing explicit about this. According to the context here one could at first be tempted to ascribe apprehension as primary function to the productive imagination, since in the footnote it is said about the faculty of imagination that it fashions images of objects out of the impressions of the senses. That footnote, which probably refers to the productive imagination, seems, however, to have been added to the text only later; for in the following paragraph of the text only the reproductive power of imagination is mentioned, "which is also only empirical." One could emphasize the "also" and so interpret it that it refers back to apprehension as the first empirical function. But even if one leaves the "also" unemphasized, apprehension must be conceived as work which is preliminary to an empirical function itself. Empirical reproduction is then depicted even more accurately and, as "reproduction according to rules," is identified with "association." But it is only empirically active—like the apprehension which appears again. But a synthetic unity which has come about through transcendental imagination is now set over against both empirical functions (or, rather, it provides their foundation). This "productive imagination" is later accurately described in addition to its activity, which presents itself as synthesis according to *a priori* rules. This synthesis produces "the affinity of appearances"; and this in turn makes possible and justifies empirical association and reproduction (in addition to apprehension).

III. *c*

The following three paragraphs show a somewhat different character—which makes it necessary to set them apart. The productive imagination and its *a priori* synthesis is, as it is now depicted, still sensuous; only the intrusion of apperception lends it an intellectual character; that is, the unifying function of apperception with its categorial forms of unity gives the productive imagination substance and direction. If these remarks show a divergent character, this is even more the case in what follows: genuine experience now consists, in addition to apperception and association (reproduction), of "recognition of appearances"; and this "final and highest of the purely empirical elements of experience" includes—in a completely unclear way—the *a priori* concepts. The same enumeration of the factors "of the empirical employment of imagination" is then once more repeated in reverse order. One should not let oneself be led astray through the remainder of the presentation of II, 1-3 a, where, in addition to the empirical employment, a transcendental employment was established. The presentation here is both in substance and time a completely different one: here apprehension, association, reproduction, and even recognition are only empirical functions; and all three—even the last one—are functions of imagination; and only in the last one are the *a priori* factors contained in some very unclear way. And this last element is due to the transcendental imagination which, according to the same paragraph, mediates between sensibility and understanding, projecting the intellectual concepts of the latter into the sensuously given manifold.

III. *d*

In the four following concluding paragraphs of the third section, the discussion no longer explicitly turns on the cooperation of the pure imagination. But, on the other hand, in the first of the four paragraphs "the original sources of knowledge of our understanding" are presented as "subjective conditions" of experience in a way that includes the imagination. In the following three paragraphs the "rules" are again traced solely back to the understanding; and it is identified again with transcendental apperception. The basic idea is this: that "the understanding is the source of the laws of nature." This idea is varied in different forms.

s.

The "Summary Presentation" does not go any further into the "subjective sources of knowledge" which have already been discussed. "Pure imagination" and "original apperception" are only mentioned.

II. CHRONOLOGICAL RECONSTRUCTION

This comparative analysis enables us to assert that the Transcendental Deduction in A is absolutely not a unified presentation but rather a very loosely composed juxtaposition and confusion of different and contradictory presentations from various times. The determination of the chronological sequence of the individual presentations is naturally not possible with certainty; but one can venture the following conjectures about it, the hypothetical character of which is conceded at the very outset. They are perhaps able to solve the many puzzles of the Deduction in A to a certain extent.

1. *The Level of the Transcendental Object (Without the Categories)*
The oldest presentation is perhaps II, 3 b. That it is old is attested, first of all, by the conspicuous fact that there is no mention there of the productive imagination, although the argument would have demanded its mention if it had even entered Kant's thought at that time. Because of its importance this point could not be passed by silently. Thus Kant had not at that time grasped the role which the productive imagination was later to play in the Deduction.[6] But this absence of the productive imagination is shared by the presentations in II, 3 b and II, 4 just as it is shared, as we shall see, by "II Introduction, a" and I ¶14. What is it then that gives evidence

6. The reproductive imagination is introduced only insofar as reproduction is mentioned three times without express mention of "imagination." Apprehension is introduced expressly as an empirical function and, moreover, is designated as "synthesis." Apprehension here is thus the empirical synthesis of sensations. Cf. above.

for saying that II, 3 b is the oldest of these presentations? The topic: the "object of a representation." In none of the other presentations is this concept considered; rather, it is everywhere taken for granted. This concept, however, is just the topic of the much-discussed letter to Herz of February 21, 1772. There the question of two ways of relating the representation to the object is introduced. For us only the first way is relevant here: "If the representation contains only the way in which the subject is affected by the object, it is easily understood how it [the representation] [7] accords with the latter [the object] as an effect of its [the representation's] causation, and how this determination of our understanding can represent something; that is, can have an object. Passive or sensuous representations thus have a conceptual relation to objects. . . ." The same topic is treated in our section II, 3 b in a more advanced way, but still connecting with the passage from the letter and, at the same time, apparently pointing to the Transcendental Aesthetic as immediately preceding. For II, 3 b begins with the words, "We have said above that appearances are themselves nothing but sensuous representations . . ." But the problem with which the entire section is concerned is this: on what rests "our conception of the relation of all knowledge to its object?" (fourth section). But "knowledge" is in this entire context—what has so far been overlooked completely—only empirical in character. It does not concern the question of why pure concepts, pure cognitions, can be related to an object. Rather, it concerns only that "which in all our empirical concepts can provide . . . a relation to an object" (last section); or, as it says there, it concerns "all appearances insofar as they are to give us objects." Similarly, in the penultimate section, it is said to be a matter of "determining an object of their [of phenomena's] intuition." In short: "To think some kind of object to our intuitions" (seventh section).

In the letter of February 21, 1772, Kant still finds this question "easy to understand." But soon thereafter he must have come to the conclusion that this question was to be taken more seriously; and the result of this renewed consideration we have before us in II, 3 b: the insight that the unified "object" of a sensuous, empir-

---

7. In the text there are "er" and "seiner" (also in the new edition of Kant X, 124). The above change [reading "sie"] appears necessary. As I have afterwards discovered, Arnoldt (*Krit. Excurse*, p. 116) also demanded this change.

ical representation is nothing save the opposite pole of the unity of the subject, of transcendental apperception in such a way that we exhibit our "formal unity of consciousness" "in the synthesis of the manifold of representations or of intuitions." In the sensuous representations of this tree, of that house, there is, in addition to a passive element, an active, synthetic factor, a beam of the unity of our ego; a beam of this sun falls upon the random manifold of appearance and concresces it to a unified object of experience.

The objectification of subjective appearance to an object of experience through pure apperception is said to be mediated by "concepts." One will naturally be tempted to think here of *a priori* concepts, of the categories; but this expectation is disappointed. The clearest are the following, much-quoted words: "All knowledge requires a *concept*. . . . But this is, in virtue of its form, something general and serves something as a rule. Thus the concept of *'body'* serves our knowledge of external appearances as a *rule* according to the unity of the manifold which is thought through it. But it can only be a rule of appearances only by representing the *necessary* reproduction of the manifold of given appearances and thereby the synthetic unity in our consciousness. . . . A *transcendental* condition is always at the bottom of all *necessity*. Thus must . . ." The underlined words characterize the peculiar train of thought: appearances become "knowledge of external appearances" as "objects" through the efficacy of a general concept, of the concept "body" whose efficacy participates in the process. But this is, after all, only a general concept of empirical origin [8] and not a category at all. There is not the least discussion of "categories" in all of section II, 3 b, but only of "concepts"; and everywhere in this context only the usual general concepts are understood.

One should note well the quite peculiar presentation: it is the ordinary general concepts which, together with transcendental apperception, bring it about that mere perceptions might become "objects" for us. These general concepts are "rules" which not only

8. Kant's other example—that of a triangle—is characteristic, even though of another kind, since Kant considers mathematical concepts to be *a priori*. But here what is at stake is that a concept which has absolutely nothing to do with a category, the concept of a triangle, serves transcendental apperception as a "rule of combination" in order synthetically to combine the manifold of three straight lines into an object according to that rule.

make appearances necessarily reproducible but also determine an object of their intuition; that is, the concept of something in which they necessarily hang together. General concepts owe this combinatorial and objectifying unitary force to the unity of apperception which is effective in them and alone makes them possible: "The numerical unity of this apperception is thus at the foundation of all *a priori* concepts, just as the manifold of space and time is the foundation of the intuitions of sensibility." Thus all concepts stand under transcendental apperception—a doctrine which Kant otherwise nowhere repeats in this form and which is also quite conspicuous. The archaic impression that this form makes is practically confirmed by the posthumous works, as we shall see in the third part. We have here an intermediary stage in Kant's development, which he did not retain in this form.

A few phrases could, to be sure, lead us to find—at least indirectly—the categories in them. They are not, indeed, expressly discussed. Thus it is said: "This transcendental unity of apperception makes out of all possible appearances . . . a connection of all these representations according to laws." Only out of the sentences which immediately follow does it emerge with certainty that these "laws" are identical with those general concepts or "rules which they [the appearances] not only make reproducible but also determine an object of their intuition." In the same paragraph (the penultimate) it is then said that transcendental apperception "subjects all synthesis of apprehension (which is empirical) to a transcendental unity and first makes possible their connection according to *a priori* rules." Here one could interpret "*a priori* rules" as categories. But it is questionable whether the phrase "*a priori* rules" is grammatically correct at all—whether Kant does not rather want to say that apperception makes possible the connection of apprehended appearances *a priori* according to rules, that is, according to the ordinary general concepts which have already been discussed. One could also give this interpretation to the similar phrase in the last paragraph, where it is said that "all appearances, insofar as objects are to be given through them, must stand under rules *a priori* of the synthetic unity of them [of appearances]." But if one will not allow that interpretation here, one is not therefore obliged to find in this phrase a definite reference to the categories. Whenever Kant spoke

of the efficacy of transcendental apperception, to which he ascribes
the positing of objects under the mediation of general concepts, he
naturally had to assume also that transcendental apperception as an
a priori function had to have its *a priori* conditions of function ("*a
priori* rules of the synthetic unity of the same"); but at the time
he did not by any means need to understand of which kind these
"*a priori* rules" are—in which definite way they show themselves—
and that they needed to be cited in greater detail at all. At most one
can look upon these passages as the buds out of which the categories
later developed, but not as the categories themselves. How little
Kant was at that time clear about the matter is shown above all by
his finding "necessity" and thus transcendentality in general concepts themselves and especially in the example of them, in the
concept of "body." There is evidence for this above all in the passage in the second paragraph of II, 3 b, where it is said that the
relation of all knowledge to its object "carries with it something of
necessity, which is against the view that our knowledge is determined at random or arbitrarily but rather *a priori* in a definite
way. . . ." A similar formulation is found in the third paragraph:
"such a function of synthesis according to a rule. . . , which makes
the reproduction of the manifold *a priori* necessary. . . ." And then
the concept of "body" is introduced as an example which produces
such an objectivity. But this is an *a posteriori* concept. This shows
with how little definiteness Kant knows at this time how to separate the *a priori* from the *a posteriori*. How indefinitely he will later
have understood those "*a priori* rules"! It is natural that the categories had to grow out of these. But to grasp those "*a priori* rules"
as categories in this context would be artificial. There are the rudiments of them but not the categories themselves.

Thus those formulations give in their indefiniteness evidence for
the view that we are dealing here with an earlier stage of the doctrine. A decisive proof of the rather early composition of the entire
passage lies in the following passage (in the third-to-the-last paragraph): "That it [transcendental apperception] deserves this name
is already evident in the fact that the purest objective unity, namely,
that of *a priori* concepts (space and time), is possible only through
the relation of intuitions to them." Here it is quite concisely said
that space and time are *the a priori* concepts; that is, the only *a
priori* concepts which interested him at that time, that Kant at that

time still had not yet considered *a priori* concepts [9] other than space and time, at least for the world of sensuous phenomena, which is the only thing of concern in this context.

Thus we have, then, the following result: in the section II, 3 b there is not yet a discussion about categories; [10] their cooperation is not necessary in order to force the manifold into unity. The ordinary general concepts perform this service now: they play the mediating role. They are the organs through which transcendental apperception produces that unity of the manifold and introduces objective unity into the separated manifold. Objective unity is the counterpart, the reflection, the effect of the unity of the subject. But that this unity of the subject manifests itself in categorial functions of unity—about this there is not yet any discussion. *In this way Kant solves the problem of objectivity with respect to sensuous representations still without reference to the categories.*

How did Kant come to bring together this theory of the object from the early period of his criticism with that which he later calls the "synthesis of recognition in the concept"? The answer to this obvious question is the task that we shall attempt to solve below.

II. *The Level of the Categories Without the Productive Imagination*

We encounter a reference to the categories—in opposition to II, 3 b—in II, 4; here the insight is clearly present that only the categorial functions of unity can make that unified connection of the sensuous manifold into "objects" that we call "experience"; and this latter concept now appears much more prominently than in II, 3 b. This insight hardly came immediately after the draft of II, 3 b. We have even less reason to assume that because, among the other sections, there is one draft present to which we must ascribe very great age—I ¶13. From which signs must we infer to the early composition of this section? Primarily from two: first, from the circumstance that the pure concepts still appear applicable to the transcendent world; secondly, from the circumstance that "the categories of the understanding do not at all represent to us the conditions under which objects are given in intuition." The latter,

9. The designation of space and time as "*a priori* concepts" is, on the other hand, quite harmless. Cf. my *Kommentar zur Kr. d. r. V.* II, 155. Kant appears here not to have thought of "intellectual representations" at all.

10. This has not escaped Adickes (p. 667) either; but he draws another consequence out of this; namely, the section lost its natural conclusion.

however, we found similarly stated in II, 3 b: Kant probably had the insight there that the "object" of sensuous representations owes its origin to the unity of the ego; but the insight was still lacking that the categories are the functions of unity of this ego and thus are the medium necessary to the origin of that object.

The section I ¶13 is evidence for the view that Kant originally did not bring the problem of the object of sensuous representations into connection with the problem of the validity of intellectual categories and that he originally treated both problems quite independently of each other. Here in I ¶13 the problem of the categories is introduced quite independently: wherein does the right of their application lie? And, more specifically, as was mentioned, the right of their *unlimited* application. In this manner the letter to Herz of February 21, 1772, introduces the problem of the categories; there, too, there is still no discussion of a limited application of the categories. But the question with regard to these "intellectual representations" is not quite general: "What is the source of the agreement that they are said to have with objects?"—particularly since these concepts are just as independent of objects as objects are of them. This is the second way in which the problem of the relation of the representations to the object is introduced in that letter. The first problem—which Kant at that time still regarded lightly— referred to "sensuous representations"; the second problem refers to "intellectual representations." We encounter this latter problem also in I ¶13. This section probably dates from approximately the same time as II, 3 b. Indeed, one may assume that II, 3 b is the earlier passage: Kant discovers that the first problem—that of the "object" of sensuous representations—is not quite so simple as he had first thought; and he makes the fundamental discovery that the "object" of sensuous representations is nothing other than a counterpart of the unity of the subject, of apperception. Only now is he in a position fruitfully to take the second problem in hand; and we have before us in ¶13 the transition to the answer of the second problem—that of the "object" of intellectual representations. This passage gives for the first time an exposition of the problem as Kant conceived it at that time still before the solution: for, after the solution, he would have made the exposition different.

Kant probably arrived only gradually at that great new decisive insight: the same principle that explains the factual relation of

sensuous representations to their object—the synthesis of the manifold through the ego—is also capable of explaining the lawful relation of intellectual representations to objects. Intellectual representations function as the necessary means in the synthesis by the ego
of the manifold into "objects"; and these "objects" in whose origin
they have functioned are just for that reason legitimate and, indeed,
the only legitimate "objects" to which the categories necessarily
refer. Now there must have also come the insight that apperception,
whose effect is the representation of the "object" and which is
identical with the pure understanding, whose concepts are the categories. At the moment at which these two streams flowed together,
the basic conception of the Transcendental Deduction was born—
not earlier and not later.

We have the expression of this discovery in I ¶14 (without the
conclusion, which dates from a later period) and in "II, Introduction a," which essentially belongs together with it. The discovery is
especially clear and distinct in the former; the concepts *a priori* are
the "sole conditions of the *a priori* possibility of experience." Therefore I ¶14 goes far beyond the letter to Herz of 1772, to which
I ¶14 is otherwise externally quite similar—but only externally:
probably what is common to both is the enumeration of two cases;
but the presentation is quite different. (1) Empirical representation:
it arises through the affection of the subject by the object (cf. letter
to Herz) = the object makes the representation possible (the
Critique). But while in the letter no difficulty is found in saying
that such a representation "refers to an object," in the *Critique* it is
cautiously said only that this relation of the representation to the
object applies, in the case of empirical representations, only "with
respect to that in them which belongs to sensation"—but this is the
natural causal relation to the affecting object. But the other relation
—the relation to the transcendental object—is not thereby explained.[11] This arises only through the categorial functions of unity

11. By "transcendental object," only "object" in Kant's sense is to be under
stood, which we cognitively add to the manifold or think into the manifold. The
real affecting (transcendent) object (thing in itself) is to be definitely distinguished from this immanent object which we add. In the letter to Herz, Kant
had not yet separated the two and believed that he could solve the problem of
the relation of sensuous representations to their object through a reference to
affection. That this cannot be done, that the "transcendental object" in the above-
determined sense is to be distinguished from the affecting object—in this consists
the progress of the first level over the letter of Hertz of 1772.

and their artful synthetic activity. And this coincides with the second case, the problem of *a priori* concepts. (2) *A priori* concepts are possible and have objective validity when and in so far as they are the conditions "of knowing something as an object." And thus the problem is solved which was broached for the first time in the letter of 1772. The presentation I ¶14 must therefore be rather later than this letter.

Only now will the presentation II, 4 have followed.[12] The section begins anew and independently and makes the impression of a discussion which is completely independent of what has gone immediately before. Here for the first time the idea is pressed home that the categories effect unity of experience and thus objectivity of intuitions. One should especially notice the sentence: "The conditions *a priori* of a possible experience in general are at the same time the conditions of the possibility of objects of experience." Here the confluence of those two streams is clearly indicated. Why do intellectual representations refer to objects? Because they alone make experience possible. Why do sensuous representations refer to objects? Because these "objects of experience" are combined only through *a priori* synthesis; and this *a priori* synthesis is accomplished only by means of the categories. The latter are the *a priori* functions of combination through which the raw material of sensuous representations is crystallized into objects. Now there is no more discussion of the "transcendental object," which is really always the same =X in all our knowledge. Rather the "relation of knowledge to objects," the possibility "to think objects to appearances at all," is ascribed now to the newly introduced intermediary of the various categories. Now the favorite category of causality is introduced also. But the productive imagination is still lacking. The "extreme faculty of all our knowledge" is solely transcendental apperception, the ground of a "transcendental affinity of appearances of which the empirical affinity is simply a consequence."

---

12. Adickes [p. 683 (666)] is also inclined to regard this passage (on Adickes' view=II. Deduction) as chronologically late. In this sense Kant rightfully gives it the title of a "Preliminary Explanation . . ."

III. *Level of the Productive Imagination (Without the Threefold Synthesis)*

Temporally the presentation III b is to be placed at this point. For only in this presentation is the productive imagination introduced and, moreover, in a form which proves that this is a new discovery that has just been made and which still impresses one as odd. This presentation also begins anew, as if nothing which was mentioned in II, 3 b were ascribed to apprehension and the reproduction of empirical imagination; and the productive imagination—the newly discovered intermediary—is set over against this, and to it the affinity which was mentioned already in II, 4 is traced back. But affinity is again introduced anew, as if it had never been mentioned up to that time—proof that the individual presentations arose independently of one another and were only later loosely connected.

III a, in which the presentation which III b had given from below is repeated from above, dates apparently from the same period as III b. Here the main emphasis lies on the categories—the achievement of II, 4—and on the imagination—the achievement of III b; and the connection of both is brought out.

III d may have been attached to the presentation in III a; [13] III b is, as we saw, probably earlier; and III c is, as we shall see, probably later. In III d the first small paragraph ("The order and regularity . . .") attaches to III a in so far as there is present in III d a discussion of the original, subjective sources of knowledge of our understanding in just the sense of III a and III b. And this expressly included pure imagination. To be sure, of this there is no express mention in the entire passage III d. On the basis of this criterion alone, one could be tempted to remove the second part of this passage from this third level (that of the transcendental imagination) and place it in the second level (that of the categories). And it is, moreover, not impossible that a draft from the second level is at the basis of this passage. Even so, that criterion alone is

13. The short summary of the three subjective "original sources" of knowledge—sensibility, imagination, and apperception—given in the short passage "I Conclusion" is to be placed in the same period as III b and III a. Kant later inserted this table there at the conclusion of I and before the beginning of the second section—a completely inappropriate place, right in the middle of a discussion that belongs to the second level.

not decisive in this case because the entire passage here is a concluding passage in which only the main result had to be stated with
the exclusion of the intermediary element. But the main result is
this: that the lawfulness of nature has been originally introduced
into it by the understanding itself; and for this reason the categories,
the concepts of the understanding, claim and find a legitimate application to the nature which is given to sensibility. This main result is the sole concern here and, in this sense, it is rightly said in
the last paragraph: "We did not have to accomplish more in the
Transcendental Deduction of the Categories than to make intelligible this relation of the understanding to sensibility and, by means
of them, to all objects of experience, and thereby the objective
validity of its pure *a priori* concepts. . . ." That the main result was
only attainable through the proof of the mediating role of the pure
imagination could probably have been mentioned; it was, however,
not at all necessary. Indeed, it is probably a special refinement of
the presentation that the pure imagination is no longer mentioned:
while the pure imagination here recedes into the background again,
Kant wants to point out by this that its introduction has only a
hypothetical character and belongs only to that "subjective" deduction whose problematic character he has expressly emphasized in
the preface.

The situation is somewhat different in the "Summary Presentation" (=S). This does not merely emphasize the main result—
validity of the categories for objects of experience. Rather, it intends to give a summary of the entire previous development and
its main ground. In this sense, and for this reason, this section discusses the "synthesis of pure imagination" again through which
"the unity of all representations"—*qua* phenomena—is constituted
"in relation to original apperception." Pure imagination could not
dominate things in themselves, but it can do this with mere
appearances.

The three paragraphs that we have designated as III c will probably have followed only at this point. To be sure, they also distinguish between sensibility, imagination, and apperception. But
imagination receives a somewhat different position. Previously (in
III b, III a, and S) it was an auxiliary function of the pure understanding. But now it is an independent intermediary that even
stands closer to sensibility. What is new in these pages is also the

introduction of a "recognition" as a separate and new stage in the sequence of apprehension, association, and reproduction. And the new stage, which is planted on these three, has a rather unclear place. On the one hand, it is placed with the "empirical elements"; on the other hand, it is supposed to "contain" the *a priori* concepts. This "recognition" is therefore a very dubious achievement. Its unclear position characterizes it as a symptom of transition to the following fourth level.

In a way that is just as unsatisfactory, the same "recognition" appears then in "III Introduction," in a comprehensive presentation which probably followed temporally. But independently of this "recognition," the presentations III c and "III Introduction" belong to the following group: III b, III a, S, "I Conclusion," with which they have the principal common feature of the threefold division of sensibility, imagination, and apperception. This clear threefold division sharply distinguishes this third level from the second, in which the pure imagination is still lacking, and from the fourth, in which the pure imagination dissolves into the unclear threefold synthesis.

That threefold division is presented best and most perspicuously in the two small sections, "I Conclusion" and "III Introduction," to which we have already given the name of first and third table of the subjective sources of knowledge.[14] Both tables coincide in the essential points. The following table consists, therefore, of a combination of both presentations.

First (and Third) Table

1. The synopsis of the manifold—through *a priori* sense; that is, pure intuition
2. The synthesis of the manifold—through pure, transcendental imagination
3. The unity of this synthesis—through pure, transcendental apperception

This table enables us to assume that the section L (¶10) must also date from the same period. For in it we encounter the same threefold division (especially in the fifth section): (1) intuition which gives the manifold; (2) synthesis of the manifold through

---

14. Adickes (p. 119) did not observe this formulation and consequently put L (¶10) with III a rather than with II, 1-3 a. Moreover, this peculiar formulation has a precursor in II, 3 b (more about this below).

imagination; (3) unity of this synthesis through the concepts of the understanding. That the understanding directly replaces apperception, which is not mentioned here, is not an essential difference. But an idea occurs in this section which is new and thus characterizes this section as a transitional passage to the following phase. That is the peculiar idea that the manifold given through intuition (=1) is "a manifold of *a priori* sensibility," that is, the *a priori* manifold which is already contained in the pure intuitions of space and time as such without any empirical content. And this manifold must be combined synthetically through the imagination and the understanding. This idea is new. In all the presentations which have been so far considered, the manifold which was given through intuition was always only empirical—understood as the infinite plenitude of sensations or appearances. Only now the idea occurs that the manifold—"whether it be given empirically or *a priori*" —must be synthetically combined. Indeed, the latter, the *a priori,* manifold is in the forefront. That a new line of thought thereby occurs is obvious.[15]

Just this line of thought links the presentation in L (¶10) with the presentation in II, 1-3 a, the last and latest phase. There the same idea occurs in a very conspicuous way, especially in numbers 1 and 2. The transcendental activities of synthesis which are depicted there refer not only to the manifold that is empirically given but also to the manifold that is given *a priori;* and through the synthesis of the latter the *a priori* representations of space and time come about.

This idea, therefore, is common to both presentations L (¶10) and II, 1-3 a. But the presentation in L (¶10) is distinguished essentially from the latter since it still rests on the threefold distinction of sensibility, imagination, and understanding.

IV. *Level of the Threefold Synthesis*

A totally different division of the "subjective sources of knowledge is given by the presentation in II, 1-3 a in addition to "II Introduction b"—a new introduction which is not an organic development of the one that has gone before but rather involves a complete break with the previous one; thus the new introduction must

15. Kant frequently takes up ideas that he introduces earlier only incidentally and discusses them further.

also be temporally removed from the first one. In order to prove this, we need only represent the new outline in a table.[16]

Second Table

A) Synopsis of the manifold through sense
B) Synthesis
   1) Synthesis of apprehension of representations in [inner] intuition
   2) Synthesis of reproduction of representation in imagination
   3) Synthesis of recognition of representations in the concept

"These [last three] give a clue to three subjective sources of knowledge which make . . . even the understanding possible." Naturally these three subjective sources of knowledge do not agree with the three sources of knowledge which were enumerated in the first table. For the "synthesis of apprehension in intuition" (B, 1) cannot be identified with the first element in the first table, which agrees more readily with element A of the second table to which Kant obviously refers here (cf. Adickes, p. 653). Both are a "synopsis of the manifold through sense" and therefore belong not to the Transcendental Analytic but to the Transcendental Aesthetic.[17] The "intuition" discussed here is only the inner intuition of time.[18] Thus we have here not the least similiarity to the first table.

16. Adickes assigned a completely different position to this outline (cf. *op. cit.,* pp. 653ff., 672).

17. One must in neither case put too much into the notion of synopsis. The notion does not really play a role here. For since all combination is an affair of the activity of synthesis, what remains to the synopsis is only external juxtaposition without inner connection. Indeed, even unified "pictures" of objects are a matter of synthesis (cf. III b). In connection with a few suggestions of Kant in the *Reflexionen* and *Lose Blätter,* one can probably say that synopsis must also be present in animals, while synthesis is specifically human. The place of animals in Kant's epistemology is notoriously very problematic. "Kant's Conception of the Animal" would nevertheless—or perhaps just for that reason—be a worthy topic.

18. I expressly call attention here to this important circumstance, which up to now has hardly been noticed. I shall give a detailed analysis elsewhere. Here it is enough to point out the following. The section, "Regarding the Synthesis of Apprehension in Intuition," begins with a "general remark" which says that all appearances belong "to inner sense as modifications of the understanding"; and thus they are "subject to time as that in which they must be ordered as a whole, combined, and brought into relation." This is apprehension in intuition; namely, in inner intuition. Apprehension is directed to "every intuition" as an object.

But B, 2 "the synthesis of reproduction in imagination" does not correspond to imagination, the second element of the first table. Imagination was meant there only as productive, while here the reproductive imagination is enumerated. And now this is even introduced as a transcendental activity.[19] The "recognition in the concept" does not correspond to the third element of the first table, that is, to pure apperception itself, even though recognition may finally lead to apperception—which, however, is nowhere said clearly (cf. "III Introduction," where pure apperception parallels empirical recognition). Thus we stand here before a completely new table and thus before a great riddle. How could Kant have let two completely different tables exist side by side? And for us, who have solved the previous difficulties by the chronological-genetic method, there arises the difficult problem of finding a plausible explanation for this new and very great difficulty by the same method.[20]

We will probably succeed in finding an explanation if we fasten upon the greatest and most conspicuous divergence in both tables: the second table lists apprehension and reproduction [and recognition?] as transcendental activities; but in the presentation out of which the first table grew, they were considered to be solely empirical. This is the case with apprehension and reproduction as early as II, 3 b; with apprehension and association = reproduction in II, 4 and in III b. To this recognition is added in III c, with which "III Introduction" agrees. Now this difference is extraordinarily conspicuous. At that time apprehension, reproduction, and

---

Apprehension itself comes about through the means of inner intuition as the relevant capacity of the subject. This is also the capacity whose absence was noted above and which was cited as an apparent desideratum. The previous presentations of Kant's doctrine have missed this point—and in an especially classical way K. Fischer (4th ed., p. 405). One thing should be noticed: that the section "III Introduction" already contains the rudiments of this doctrine in the remark that "the form of inner intuition, time" lies at the basis of all perceptions as representations.

19. Riehl attempts (*Kantst.* V, 268) to remove this contradiction through a correction of the text and reads, instead of "reproductive," "productive imagination" in this place. I do not believe the context admits this alteration.

20. K. Fischer is a typical and tragic example of the confusion that had to occur in the secondary literature through the conflation of those two tables. In his presentation (4th ed., pp. 404-415), accordingly, a great confusion dominates: at first (pp. 404ff.) the three syntheses are regarded as transcendental; then (pp. 410ff.) they are empirical.

also recognition were empirical occurrences; [21] now suddenly they are represented to us as transcendental. That is indisputable in II, 1-3 a, where especially the "reproductive synthesis" is listed as a "transcendental activity" to which the other two must be regarded as parallel. How did Kant arrive at this gaping divergence from his own earlier discussions?

In order to explain this, one must remember the following. Kant had distinguished—and this was the heart of the Transcendental Deduction—between the origin of the experienced world (W) through the pre-conscious and prior functioning of transcendental imagination and apperception on the one hand, and the subsequent conscious grasping of appearances (W) through empirical-psychological functions of apprehension, reproduction (association) and recognition. The empirical and conscious (analytical) grasping of the empirical world external to us as spatial and lawful appearances is something that comes later, which has been preceded by an original synthetic fashioning and forming of raw sensations into those spatial and lawfully ordered appearances. And this is just the transcendental and pre-conscious synthesis the demonstration of which is the concern of the subjective deduction.[22] Indeed, it is the great discovery of the Transcendental Deduction that the activities of the understanding—in pre-conscious activity, of course—must constitute the substructure of all empirically conscious intuition, and that the understanding does not constitute the fruition of intuition as one had generally assumed until that time. In this consists Kant's peculiar transformation—one would like to say, transvaluation—of all cognitive values that were accepted to that time.

21. More specially, all three were functions of empirical imagination, while now only reproduction is ascribed to imagination.

22. This interpretation of the Transcendental Deduction—one could call it the deeper interpretation—is opposed to the usual—one could call it the superficial interpretation. According to the former, there are two series: (1) the *a priori*, synthetic creation of the external world out of the manifold through transcendental and pre-conscious functions; (2) the empirical analytic interpretation of the external world created in this way through conscious psychological functions. According to the popular interpretation, however, there is only one series (which is, however, complex) where the empirical grasping of the manifold is simultaneously determined through *a priori* functions. According to the first interpretation, on the other hand, the empirical grasping follows upon the transcendental creation of the external world and is pre-determined by this transcendental creation. In Kant himself, of course, both views are represented at the same time; and in this way many unclear points of the Deduction are determined and explained.

This account of the transcendental and pre-conscious creation of the experienced world out of the manifold remained, however, only at a very general level. In the attempt to enlarge this by going more into detail, Kant naturally had to cling to the paradigm of conscious empirical grasping of appearances, in which apprehension and reproduction (through the activity of association) play a principal role. Thus it is hardly surprising that he had to come upon the idea that transcendental apprehension and reproduction precede empirical apprehension and empirical reproduction (going, as it were, an octave lower).[23] And so he did indeed come with a certain consistency to the new presentation. Thus he had to assume that there exists a pure (transcendental) synthesis of apprehension which can be carried out only in inner intuition, just as there is a pure (transcendental) synthesis of reproduction, since reproduction of the apprehended manifold appears necessary for the unconscious creation of the world of experience. He then wanted to add transcendental recognition corresponding to empirical recognition to these two transcendental activities as a third activity.[24] But here he ran out of patience, as we saw, and hurriedly broke off.[25]

This presentation of the sources of knowledge in II, 1-3 a cannot be reconciled at all with the earlier one. Above all, there is the question of which position the productive imagination, which was regarded earlier as so important, can have in this second table. It can have no position at all. *It is completely eliminated; and thus the entire earlier line of thought is given up.* What deep confusion must therefore descend upon the reader is obvious. But this is not the end of the confusion: it worsens.

What is genuinely Kantian is that this entire new presentation is not cleanly carried out but is rather complicated to desperation

23. A rudiment of this is found as early as III b.

24. III c contains an unclear beginning of this. There recognition is assigned to empirical functions but it nonetheless includes the categories.

25. In the analysis of Adickes (*op. cit.,* pp. 656ff., 666ff.), these ideas hardly occur (p. 660). The deep-seated differences in the doctrine of the subjective sources which have just been discussed are not sufficiently appreciated by Adickes (pp. 661, 672, 675-676). Consequently, Adickes did not separate II, 1-3 a, and II, 3 b, but rather carries the line of thought of II, 3 b over to II, 1-3 a, whose peculiarity was thus bound to escape him. Thus he conceives of II, 1-3 a as a unity and, more specifically, as the first deduction with various later insertions through which he seeks to explain those differences (p. 661). Moreover, this first deduction is supposed to lack a natural conclusion (through the doctrine of categories) (cf. pp. 666ff.).

by a further line of thought which is inserted here. In II, 1-3 a the idea is inserted that all the transcendental activities which condition the origin of experience (that is, of empirical appearances) like-wise condition the origin of pure representations (that is, the intui-tive representations of space and time) themselves. This idea was already briefly dealt with on occasion. As early as II, 3 b it was said "that even the purest objective unity, namely, that of the *a priori* concepts (space and time) is possible only through the rela-tion of intuitions to transcendental apperception." The use of the mathematical example of the triangle in III c belongs here too (also in II, 3 b). The idea was also obvious. For we do not have only empirical representations of objects of experience but also the pure *a priori* representations of mathematical space, mathematical time, and of mathematics in general. These representations, too, are grasped by us later through conscious thought. Thus transcendental activities must have cooperated in their origin as well. Thus even the intuitive representations of space and time are, accordingly, only products of a higher synthetic function. But instead of emphasizing this interesting idea purely for itself and devoting a separate section to it (at best through a supplement at the conclusion), Kant mixed this idea into the beginning of II, 1-3 a, where, even without this, there were enough difficulties through the entirely new presentation of transcendental activities. In this way the passage at II, 1-3 a took on such a confused shape.

The short paragraph at the conclusion of II, 2 is the clearest where it is explained that the reproductive imagination also belongs to the transcendental activities but is exercised in a twofold way: (a) in relation to the empirically given manifold; (b) in relation to the manifold that is given *a priori*. The latter refers to what has been explained in the preceding paragraph; namely, that even "the purest and first primary representations of space and time" and the other mathematical representations are possible only through the help of that reproductive imagination. Although this could have been more sharply worked out in the text, it is at least clear. It is also clear that the empirical (conscious) reproduction, treated at the beginning of II, 2, is to be strictly distinguished from transcen-dental reproduction. And this empirical, conscious reproduction is particularly not to be confused with the transcendental (pre-con-scious) reproduction of the empirically given manifold.

The presentation in II, 1 is much less clear. The final short paragraph treats of the activity of apprehension in relation to the non-empirical representations of space and time. Non-empirical representation is called "pure synthesis"—which must create the impression that apprehension exercised in relation to empirical representations (the empirically given manifold) might also be empirical. But that apprehension of empirical material is also a transcendental activity follows not only from the analogy with transcendental reproduction but also from the entire context just as it follows from the program enunciated in "II Introduction b." In the second section this side of transcendental apprehension was probably to be depicted. But according to the wording, one must think that the empirical apprehension is treated there.[26]

With the concept of recognition Kant himself seems to have lost his patience. He does not make any application of it to space and time themselves but only to counting and gives only a very short and vague presentation of the entire matter.

As was already remarked above, the separation of empirical and transcendental recognition should follow here first, in keeping with the analogy of the separation of apprehension and reproduction into an empirical and a transcendental activity for each one. But this was omitted; and the entire *parallelismus membrorum* is thereby destroyed. According to the remarks in the third table concerning "recognition," one must assume that Kant—at least at that time—wanted to give that name only to "the empirical consciousness of the identity of reproductive representations with appearances . . ." and that he regarded "pure apperception" (that is, "the thoroughgoing identity of the self . . .") as the transcendental correlate of that empirical recognition. Apparently nothing would have stood in the way of designating pure apperception here as "transcendental recognition." Then the missing *parallelismus membrorum* would have been at least outwardly established. But, as a matter of

26. This vagueness probably hangs together with the following circumstance, through which the *parallelismus membrorum* goes overboard from another direction: in reproduction Kant distinguishes the empirical and "the transcendental capacity of imagination." Analogically, he should have had to distinguish the empirical and the transcendental capacity of inner intuition in apprehension. For this latter is, as we saw above, the capacity that is relevant here. Such a distinction cannot be made by Kant, however, since the inner intuition in time is only transcendental. Empirical apprehension is probably the affair of the five senses.

fact, this would have come to nothing anyway. The heading, "Concerning the Synthesis of Recognition in the Concept," arouses a quite false idea of the content of what follows. For there the concern is not with the pure empirical synthesis of the recognition of empirical representations in an empirical concept but rather with transcendental apperception and its function. To be sure, this unity of transcendental apperception is regarded as the condition of the construction of empirical concepts and of their empirical unity; but there follows, as was remarked above, no detailed explanation of this mysterious activity; that is, to what extent transcendental apperception is necessary for the construction of empirical concepts. Instead of that, we are suddenly led in a very different direction, into the doctrine of the object, and ascertain the peculiar news that an *empirical* concept is necessary for the cognition of an "object" in the transcendental sense, while we thought that the categories, the *a priori* concepts, were necessary for that. There is, however, something that is even more incongruous. That is the opposition established between transcendental and empirical apperception. The latter should be identical with empirical recognition. But there is nowhere any mention of that here.

All these and other inconveniences are best solved through the assumption that Kant has put together two pages here which date originally from different periods. Here he conceived the notion of the threefold synthesis. He wanted to establish a transcendental apprehension through inner intuition just as he wanted to establish a transcendental reproduction through imagination. He took over from psychology the view that, besides apprehension and reproduction, recognition belongs to empirical knowledge; and he wanted to join to recognition a corresponding transcendental function. But here the parallelism was more difficult to carry out; and then the remembrance of those notes might have come to him in which years before he had jotted down the idea that transcendental apperception can project "objects" into the manifold only by means of empirical "concepts."

The corresponding proof that what is concerned here is a combination (albeit cleverly concealed) of discussions from different lines of thought, lies in the following: that the beginning of the third number is planned on the opposition of an empirical and a transcendental recognition, while the further development of the argument culminates in the opposition of an empirical and a transcendental apperception, during which recognition is not discussed any longer.

Should one still want to conceive of transcendental apperception as transcendental recognition (which Kant himself does not authorize one to do), this transcendental recognition would have nothing more to do with the empirical "concept" at which empirical recognition aims, as the heading indicates.[27]

Thus it appears as if Kant had willy-nilly introduced here and needily fitted in (perhaps with a few changes and insertions) those old discussions about the relation of representations to their "object," which do not, to be sure, exactly coincide with his present doctrine.[28] In haste he ended this difficult chapter with the understandable wish of final completion and perhaps in the hope—present in many authors—that a second edition would give him the opportunity for revision. Thus it may have come about that the earliest and the latest levels are brought together here in the third number under the heading, "Concerning the Synthesis of Recognition in the Concept."

With this not inappropriate geological comparison, we shall close this discussion of the Transcendental Deduction in the first edition. Indeed, there are various levels which we have distinguished according to the structure and time of origin, some owing their existence perhaps to sudden eruptions; other slow drafts, to protracted intellectual work. But the levels do not lie one on the other according to their chronological order: they are "cast out," thrown together; and in part they cross one another. But if the geologist succeeds in distinguishing such levels with approximate certainty and thus determines their genetic order, why should not

27. Another difficult inconvenience is the following: the synthesis of apprehension takes place in inner intuition; the synthesis of reproduction takes place in imagination. But in which capacity does the synthesis of recognition take place? To say "in the concept" disturbs the *parallelismus membrorum;* for "concept" is not a capacity. It would have to take place in consciousness; namely, empirical recognition in empirical consciousness and transcendental recognition in transcendental consciousness. But that was not possible either, because recognition does not have anything to do with transcendental apperception.

28. I have discovered with delight a similar interpretation in B. Erdmann; cf. the words of his cited above on p. 24: "The discussion of the relation of representations to their object enters the line of the argument in a completely unmotivated way, despite the fact that it belongs together with the last elements [with the "synthesis of recognition"].

a similar attempt—even if only as an hypothesis—be permitted here? Whether it has succeeded can only be decided by the reader when he resolves to work through *the individual sections that we have distinguished in the chronological order which we have assumed.*

I. Level of the transcendental object (without the categories) II, 3 b. The unified "object" of sensuous representations is brought forth only through the unity of the subject whose counterpart it is, but still without the cooperation of the categories.
Transition: I, ¶13. The problem of the categories (that is, of intellectual representations).

II. Level of the categories (without the productive imagination) I, ¶14 (without the conclusion); II, Introduction a; II, 4. The categories are now recognized as the conditions of objectivity and thus of experience but without the intervention of the imagination.

III. Level of the productive imagination (without the threefold synthesis) III, b; III, a; I, Conclusion; III, d' S.; III, c; III, Introduction.
The productive imagination is now recognized as a necessary intermediary in order to combine preconsciously the manifold into objects through categorial synthesis, upon which the empirical apprehension and empirical reproduction (in addition to recognition) bring about a conscious empirical grasping of those experiential objects which are transcendentally combined pre-consciously.
Transition: L ¶10

IV. Level of the threefold synthesis II, 1-3 a in addition to II, Introduction b. The conscious-empirical apprehension and reproduction (and recognition) are preceded by the parallel pre-conscious and transcendental functions of the same kind, which are efficacious as early as the unification of the *a priori* manifold in space and time to the objective unities of spatial and temporal intuition.

IS THE TRANSCENDENTAL

DEDUCTION A PATCHWORK?

H. J. Paton

§

"Auch scheinbare Widersprüche lassen sich, wenn man einzelne Stellen, aus ihrem Zusammenhange gerissen, gegeneinander vergleicht, in jeder, vornehmlich als freie Rede fortgehenden Schrift ausklauben, die in den Augen dessen, der sich auf fremde Beurteilung verlässt, ein nachteiliges Licht auf diese werfen, demjenigen aber, der sich der Idee im Ganzen bemächtigt hat, sehr leicht aufzulösen sind." [1]

"In every writing, above all when it proceeds as a free discussion, it is possible to ferret out apparent contradictions by comparing together isolated passages torn from their context. Such apparent contradictions cast a prejudicial light upon it in the eyes of those who depend upon criticism at second hand, but they can be easily solved by any one who has mastered the idea as a whole."

I

In the year 1902 Professor Hans Vaihinger, perhaps the most distinguished of all Kantian scholars, published at Halle a short, but

---

1. *Kritik der reinen Vernunft.* B xliv. (A and B refer throughout to the first and second editions respectively of the *Kritik.* Passages peculiar to the second edition are referred to by *B* in italics.)

very remarkable, pamphlet entitled *Die Transcendentale Deduktion der Kategorien*. In it he adopted and developed a line of criticism which had its origin in previous writers, among whom the most conspicuous was the late Professor Adickes. This line of criticism maintains, on the ground of certain alleged contradictions, that the *Kritik of Pure Reason* in general, and the Transcendental Deduction in particular, is a mosaic, or in plainer language a patchwork, of different arguments composed at different times and representing very different points of view. Doctrines of this type are widely accepted in Germany at the present time, and Professor Kemp Smith in this country has lent the weight of his authority and support even to the details of Vaihinger's hypothesis. What has been propounded as a hypothesis is on the point of hardening into a dogma.

Similar methods of criticism have been applied, and similar conclusions have been reached, in other spheres. Among the works which have been treated in this way are the Old and New Testaments, the poems of Homer, the song of Roland, and the dialogues of Plato. There can be little doubt that these methods have at times been carried too far, especially toward the end of last century. But there can also be little doubt that they have proved their value when guided by discretion and directed to suitable material.

The question whether such methods can be legitimately and successfully applied to the writings of Immanuel Kant is, it seems to me, one of great importance for philosophy. Whether deservedly or not, he has exercised a great influence on the history of thought; and there are many thinkers even today who believe that he has a message for the world. It is doubtful whether such a belief can be retained, if the new doctrines are to be accepted. Our pleasure in the Iliad is not sensibly diminished, when we are informed by critics that the heroes of some foray are clad in armor which is altogether inappropriate; but the *Kritik of Pure Reason* must stand or fall as a philosophic argument, and if it is not such an argument it is nothing. It is idle to assure us that it is still interesting as throwing light on the development of Kant's mind through a series of inconsistent positions. The Transcendental Deduction is the very core and center of Kant's philosophy, and if it turns out to be a medley of incongruities, we have little reason in a busy world for being interested in Kant's mind at all.

It may be thought that such a criticism is exaggerated and such an attitude unduly despondent. After all, a mosaic may have a design. It is therefore necessary to scrutinize more closely the main questions which are at issue.

There are certain things which no reasonable man, however great his admiration for Kant, need deny. The Transcendental Deduction is full of difficulty, obscurity, inconsistency, and, it is not improbable, error. This would in some degree be admitted by Kant himself, and he would plead in defense that the difficulty and novelty of the subject was to some extent an excuse. Furthermore, we have no reason to doubt, and we have definite grounds for believing, that Kant made many notes in preparation for the writing of his greatest work—we are fortunate enough to have samples of his casual jottings published by Erdmann and by Reicke. Again, he no doubt made use of his notes when writing his final version—was there ever a philosopher engaged in a considerable work who has proceeded otherwise? As to inconsistencies in his argument, we need not suppose that it was impossible for Kant to think inconsistently, or to retain in a pioneer work traces of his earlier views; but such inconsistencies may be due partly to the fact that he was making an uncritical use of notes composed at different times. If no more than this were maintained by Vaihinger, no reasonable man could object to his contention; although one might still regard it as a hazardous and unprofitable task to make conjectures about the temporal development of the different parts of Kant's argument.

But very much more than this is maintained—how much more can be seen only when we come to study the detail. Vaihinger's own general statements leave us no room for doubt. The Transcendental Deduction, in spite of its "apparently strict unity," "is dissolved into a series of loose leaves (*lose Blätter*) which may originate in very different times, and which have been brought by Kant himself, in his final version, merely into a loose external connexion, without internal penetration or fusion." [2] More explicitly still—the Transcendental Deduction is "a very loosely composed juxtaposition and intermixture of different and contradictory expositions which belong to different times." [3] Strong as these statements are, they do not

2. *Op. cit.*, p. 24.
3. *Ibid.*, p. 46.

exaggerate the degree of contradiction and disorder, of confusion and inconsequence, which is imputed by Hans Vaihinger to Immanuel Kant.

It is not unilluminating to compare with this what Kant himself says about the Deduction. In the Introduction to the first edition (A xvi) he describes the Transcendental Deduction as more important for critical purposes than any other investigation; and he adds that it has cost him the most pains, which, however, he hopes have not been spent in vain. If we assume that Kant was neither unintelligent nor dishonest, it is hard to reconcile these words with the contentions of his critic.

II

The Transcendental Deduction, it is maintained by Vaihinger, is a series of fragments written at different dates and loosely joined together. The order in which these fragments were originally composed can be conjectured with a reasonable degree of accuracy; and in particular we can determine, as it were, the main geological strata to which the fragments belong. It is not alleged that the existing order as found in the *Kritik* bears any resemblance to the order in which the fragments, or even the main strata, were composed. On the contrary, the wildest convulsion of nature could hardly cause a greater disorder than has been produced by Kant in the quiet of his study.

All this is to be established by the application of "one single and decisive principle of distinction or division." [4] There is to be only one criterion—if that term may be used for the sake of brevity— by which the different fragments and the different strata are to be determined, and dated, with reference to one another. There are differences in Kant's account of "the subjective sources of knowledge," i.e., in his account of the cognitive faculties or powers of the mind; and it is in these differences that we are to find the criterion or mark by which we can distinguish the divisions, and the order, of the different fragments and strata of Kant's thought.

4. *Op. cit.*, p. 27.

The application of this criterion enables us to distinguish four main strata or layers. The four layers are as follows:

I. The layer of the transcendental object, but without the categories.

II. The layer of the categories, but without the productive imagination.

III. The layer of the productive imagination, but without the threefold synthesis.

IV. The layer of the threefold synthesis.

The one decisive criterion is proposed by Vaihinger without any discussion or justification. Its justification is presumably to be found in its results. Yet, since it is only too easy to lose all sense of proportion in a mass of petty detail, it may be well to consider first of all what the worth of such a criterion is likely to be.

To speak quite plainly, I can conceive no criterion less adapted to the purpose for which it is being used. There are certain obvious objections which ought to be raised, and answered, before we proceed to make use of such a criterion at all.

At the outset it should be understood how heavy is the work which our proposed criterion is expected to perform. We are not starting with a series of arguments which, like the Platonic dialogues, are already separated off from one another, and must have been composed at different times, so that it only remains for us to determine the order of their composition. Here all the arguments are given as one argument, and profess to hold all at the same time. Our criterion has, therefore, a triple function to perform: (1) to prove that the argument is composed of fragments belonging to different times; (2) to determine what those fragments are (i.e., where each begins and ends); and (3) to decide what the order of the composition of these fragments was. In dealing with the Platonic dialogues the criterion would have to fulfill only the third, and the most easy, of these three functions.

In view of that fact alone I would submit that Vaihinger's method is inadequate. One criterion is not enough. We have only to recollect the numerous criteria which would be used by a classical scholar (by Professor Lutoslawski, for example) in attempting the relatively easy task of determining the order of the Platonic dialogues, to realize at once that Professor Vaihinger has approached his problem in what I am almost tempted to call a spirit of levity. Seldom indeed can so slight an instrument have been applied to so heavy a task.

There is, however, a much more fatal objection. The proposed criterion is a negative criterion. The argument employed is the most unconvincing of all arguments—the argument from omission or silence. Each of the first three layers is characterized negatively. At first we have the transcendental object *without* the categories. Then we have the categories *without* the productive imagination. And thirdly we have the productive imagination *without* the threefold synthesis. If we remain at present, as we must, in the sphere of generalities, we are compelled to ask ourselves the question whether it would be possible to find a more untrustworthy criterion than this.

The negative type of criterion is a dangerous one to apply in any circumstances. It is unusually dangerous in the present circumstances. What we have before us is, professedly, a long and complicated argument; and the essential characteristic of an argument is that it should move from one stage to another, not that it should continually repeat what it has already said. Such a material contains manifold pitfalls for the unwary. We must endeavor throughout our analysis to keep the idea of the whole well in view, and we must take every step with the greatest caution and the most searching self-criticism. In places Professor Vaihinger recognizes this, but in practice he seems to me to forget it.

So far our criticisms have been of a very general character, but there is another which belongs more closely to the special subject matter of our investigation. In the Preface to the first edition [5] Kant himself informs us that the Transcendental Deduction has two sides. The first side concerns the objective validity of the categories; the second concerns the subjective powers of the mind. The first side is called by Kant the "objective deduction," and the second the "subjective deduction." The objective deduction is essential, the subjective deduction is secondary. The objective deduction is independent of the subjective, and it has demonstrative certainty; the subjective may at least appear to be without this certainty, and to

5. A xvi-xvii.

resemble a hypothesis rather than a demonstrated truth. Such being the case, could anything be more unfortunate than to choose as our criterion variations (and negative variations at that) in the purely subjective or secondary side of the deduction? Yet this is precisely what Professor Vaihinger, without one word of justification, has done.

One would expect that the application of this criterion would make the Transcendental Deduction fall straight away into two parts, the objective side and the subjective side. This is, as a matter of fact, what actually happens. Layers I and II belong to the objective side of the Deduction, and Layers III and IV to the subjective. If there is any exception to this, it is partly due to the fact that Kant has interwoven the two sides of his deduction, and partly to the fact that Professor Vaihinger does not adhere too closely to his own criterion. But the matter is complicated, and must be considered more closely in detail later.

The inadequacy of the criterion can be shown very clearly by applying it to arguments of which we happen, on other evidence, to know the date. There is no mention of productive imagination in the *Prolegomena,* and very little mention of it in the account of the Transcendental Deduction given in the second edition. On Professor Vaihinger's argument the whole of the *Prolegomena,* and the greater part of the version in the second edition, ought to be earlier than Layers III and IV. We happen to know that they are later. Kant was becoming more conscious of the difficulty, perhaps even of the weakness, of his subjective deduction, and he rightly lays more stress on the objective side. But if the criterion gives us such false results when applied to arguments whose date we know, how can we have any confidence in its application to arguments whose date we do not know?

I do not propose to deal in detail with the confirmation of Vaihinger's argument which is alleged to be found in the written jottings published by Erdmann and by Reicke. It is clear that if a false criterion produces certain layers when applied to the Transcendental Deduction itself, the application of the same false criterion to the jottings will result in similar layers, and so will produce an apparent confirmation. If we had independent evidence of the date of these different jottings, the alleged confirmation would take on a very different complexion. We have, however, no such evidence. There is only one relevant passage (a very important one) which can be definitely dated, and its date is 1780, the very year in which the first edition of the *Kritik* was being written. That passage is asserted by Vaihinger to represent a transition stage between Layer III and Layer IV. It proves that at the time of writing the first edition Kant held views similar to some of those expressed in the first edition—and that we may be said to have known already. By itself it does nothing to prove that other parts of the argument in the first edition belong to an earlier or later stratum of thought.

These general considerations, taken by themselves, are not to be considered as offering a refutation of Professor Vaihinger's argument. Nonetheless their total effect is to suggest, and to suggest very strongly, that the lines upon which he is proceeding are highly dubious, and that the chances of his success are from the beginning extremely slight.

III

The full refutation of this geological doctrine would demand two things: firstly, an examination of Professor Vaihinger's pamphlet line by line and argument by argument; and secondly, a detailed exposition of the Deduction itself, such as to show that it is an argument, although not necessarily a sound argument, which might be produced by a creative thinker developing a very novel line of thought. The first task would involve such a mass of detail that the general effect might be lost, and at the best it would appeal only to a few Kantian specialists. The second I hope I may some day attempt elsewhere. Here my endeavor must be a more modest one—I hope to exhibit some good grounds to the teacher or student of philosophy why he need not accept an interpretation of Kant which is a source of difficulty in teaching and a cause of despondency in study. For this purpose it may be sufficient to concentrate on the major difficulties.

We are told that when the four strata or layers are critically examined, Layer I (that of the transcendental object) turns out to be very early indeed, while Layer IV (that of the threefold synthesis) was put in hurriedly at the last moment and repented of at leisure. This leaves us with Layers II and III as constituting presumably the really important part of Kant's thought and the solid core of his argument. Layer II is that of the categories without the productive imagination, and Layer III is that of the productive imagination without the threefold synthesis. The difference between Layer II and Layer III is, in short, precisely the difference between the objective and subjective sides of the Transcendental Deduction.

It is inevitable that we should now have to face some rather difficult details, but I hope to avoid more complication than is absolutely necessary. When we examine Layer II a little more closely, we find that the arguments for its early date and its inconsistency with Layer III become progressively less plausible. There are three main fragments of this layer called by Professor Kemp Smith II (a),[6] II (b)[7] and II (c).[8] To this may be added the fragment I (b),[9] which belongs to Layer II at least as much as to Layer I. Now if we reserve II (c) for later discussion, we find that I (b), II (a) and II (b), form a practically continuous passage from A 84 to A 97. The continuity is broken only by one paragraph (A 94-95), which, since it gives a provisional summary of the faculties of cognition (that is, of the subjective side of the deduction), is attributed to Layer III. The bulk of Layer II is therefore one practically continuous passage.

To see the significance of this we must consider Kant's own divisions of his argument. There is first of all what (following a hint of the second edition [10]) may be called the Metaphysical Deduction, divided into three sections. This is followed by the Transcendental Deduction proper, which is also divided into three sections. Now Layer II (apart from the exception mentioned) coincides with Kant's First Section of the Transcendental Deduction proper, and overlaps slightly into his Second Section. It is in short introductory. It states the problem and outlines the solution. It does not, however, give Kant's elaborate argument, and it does not con-

6. A 92-94.
7. A 95-97.
8. A 110-114.
9. A 84-92.
10. B 159.

cern itself with the machinery of the subjective side; it is, in fact, concerned, as an introduction ought to be, with the objective and essential side of Kant's doctrine. Kant himself points out this clearly (A xvi) in regard to its most important passage (A 92-93), which he asserts to be by itself adequate on the objective side of the deduction. We should, however, expect that in the introduction there would be an allusion also to the subjective side. There is such an allusion (A 94-95); but just because it is such an allusion, it is regarded by Vaihinger as irrelevant to this passage and attributed to Layer III. Nothing to my mind could be more pathetic than the simplicity with which this greatest of Kantian scholars, whenever he comes to any passage dealing with the subjective side of the deduction, solemnly extracts it from its context and attributes it to a different layer of thought.

It may be objected that this introduction of Kant does deal with the subjective side; it mentions sense and understanding and ignores the imagination. Here surely we have a real inconsistency. Such an objection, however, shows a misconception of what must inevitably be found in any introduction dealing with the deduction on its objective side. The problem of the objective deduction is just this—how can the categories of the understanding be valid of the manifold given to sense? When it is explained to us how it is possible to state or describe this problem without mentioning sense or understanding, it will be time enough to take this criticism seriously. It is the subjective side of the deduction alone which investigates the machinery that makes knowledge possible, and which introduces imagination to mediate between sense and understanding. Once this is clearly grasped the alleged inconsistency between Layer II and Layer III disappears. The differences between the layers are merely the differences between an introduction and an argument, with the further complication that the introduction is concerned mainly with the objective side, while the subjective side is interwoven into the whole structure of the argument which constitutes the so-called Layer III.

It is to be remembered, of course, that there are also minor arguments brought forward by Vaihinger in support of his conclusions, and these minor arguments develop a considerable importance in regard to the passage called I (b), which, though I have taken it as belonging to Layer II, is for Vaihinger a transition stage between Layer I and Layer II. Detailed discussion of these minor arguments is here impossible, but we must note that I (*b*), i.e., A 84–92, contains phrases alleged to suggest that the categories might be applied beyond the bounds of sense—an argument which is clearly pre-critical. On this point I must speak dogmatically. Kant is here dealing with the "principles of a transcendental deduction in general," and this passage is in a very special sense introductory. He starts from the dogmatic or rationalist point of view, and explains the need for criticism. Once the dialectical character of the argument is understood, the difficulties disappear, and many of them are (on my view) due to misunderstanding. The passage is pre-critical only in the sense that it states the problem which awaits a critical solution. Kant was not so unintelligent as to include, in his proof that categories apply necessarily and only to the manifold of sense, an argument which asserts the very opposite. The supposition is fantastic as a whole, and in detail I believe I could show that it is unnecessary.

I suggest, then, in regard to the main bulk of Layer II—including the passage I (*b*)—that it is not a separate layer at all but is what it professes to be, a very sound introduction to the Deduction as a whole. The alleged peculiarities of it all arise from the fact that (1) it is an introduction, and (2) it is concerned with the objective, and not with the subjective, side of the Deduction.

Layer III we can dismiss more briefly. It constitutes the main body of the argument to which Layer II is the introduction. Professor Vaihinger, indeed, cuts up this layer also into a series of fragments—seven or eight in all—the order of whose composition he professes to determine. These details need not concern us. It is manifest that if he can be shown to be wrong in his fundamental divisions, his minor ones can be neglected. The remarkable fact (and it is a very remarkable one) is that here again Layer III constitutes a solid block of the argument. It constitutes, in fact, Kant's Third Section of the Transcendental Deduction proper, which, as we shall see later, Kant himself asserts to be the authoritative and systematic exposition of his argument. All that Vaihinger does is to divide it up into a series of fragments and to suggest an order of composition which may be indicated by applying to the successive fragments in the text the letters (*g*), (*b*), (*a*), (*f*), (*d*), (*e*).

It must be observed that two letters are missing—(*c*) and (*b*). Of these III (*b*) comes very early in the text (in A 76-79); it belongs to what I have called the Metaphysical Deduction, and it anticipates the Transcendental Deduction proper. Without it, however, it should be noted, there would be no Metaphysical Deduction at all. The other, III (*c*), also comes early (in A 94–95) and is the short table of the faculties of cognition, which is very properly inserted by Kant into the introduction, otherwise regarded by Vaihinger as belonging to Layer II. The first passage is of fundamental importance both for the Metaphysical, and for the Transcendental, Deduction. Here we need recognize only that, in Vaihinger's view, these passages are akin to the most authoritative and systematic parts of Kant's argument, but the first and more important passage is alleged to show traces of a transition to Layer IV, that is, to the layer of the threefold synthesis.

So far, then, we have no real difficulty, and indeed no layers at all. The so-called Layers II and III (apart from one passage, which we have yet to consider) are, speaking broadly, the introduction and the main body of the argument. The real difficulties all center round the other two layers, i.e., Layers I and IV, the earliest and the latest of all. It is in these layers that there are alleged to be discrepancies (both between themselves, and between them and the rest of the argument) which could not possibly have arisen unless Kant had hurriedly tacked together passages written at different times and dealing with different subjects.

IV

Our main problem, then, concerns only Layers I and IV—the first a very early piece of pre-critical work, and the second a very late and hurried piece of work, subsequently retracted (according to Vaihinger) by Kant himself.

Observe, firstly, the very curious character of this hypothesis. Layer I has been tacked on to Layer IV—it is, in fact, the completion of Layer IV, and the only completion which Layer IV ever received. Yet this completion is necessary, for Layer IV is manifestly incomplete in itself. The hypothesis, then, amounts to this. On the eve of the production of the *Kritik,* Kant hurriedly worked out a new line of thought (Layer IV). Finding himself unable to carry it out successfully, he ran away from the difficulty, and filled out his attempt at an argument by tacking on a discussion which was written many years before, and—most surprising of all—had nothing to do either with the subject of Layer IV or even with the subject of the Transcendental Deduction of the Categories. For in Layer I there are no categories at all, and empirical concepts are alleged to perform the functions which are ascribed elsewhere to the categories.

I venture to suggest that this hypothesis (which I do not think I have exaggerated) verges on the inconceivable. Nothing short of the absolute compulsion of the facts can induce us to accept such a conclusion. And if such a conclusion is true, we must say that Immanuel Kant was either abnormally stupid, or else that he took his thinking in a frivolous spirit. He is not here dealing with a mere side issue but with the pivot and hinge of his whole philosophy.

It is to be observed that this remarkable combination of layers occurs only in what Kant calls the Second Section of the Transcendental Deduction, and it is advisable to consider what Kant himself thought of this Second Section. Of the three sections into which the Transcendental Deduction is divided, the First Section is introductory, while the Third Section is, as he himself asserts, the main body of his argument. What are we to make of the Second Section, which is alleged to display such astonishing incongruities? Why, indeed, is there a Second Section at all?

Let us look at the Second Section as a whole. It begins with an introduction which deals firstly with the objective side of the Deduction and finishes up with a paragraph on the subjective side, referring to the "three subjective sources of knowledge" and "the threefold synthesis" which is about to be discussed. This is succeeded by what Kant calls four "numbers," which are as follows:

1. Concerning the synthesis of apprehension in intuition.
2. Concerning the synthesis of reproduction in imagination.
3. Concerning the synthesis of recognition in the concept.
4. Preliminary explanation of the possibility of the categories as *a priori* cognitions.

On Vaihinger's principles the first part of the introduction is, like other introductory passages, accredited to Layer II. The second part of the introduction and "Numbers" 1, 2, and the beginning of 3 constitute Layer IV, the layer of the threefold synthesis. The remainder of "Number" 3 is alleged to belong to Layer I, the layer of the "transcendental object," which has nothing to do with the categories at all. Finally, "Number" 4, that is, "the preliminary explanation of the possibility of categories," is assigned to Layer II. It is, in fact, II (c), the one part of Layer II which we reserved for subsequent consideration. It is, of course, assigned to Layer II simply because it is a portion of Kant's argument in which he deals exclusively with the objective side of the Deduction. As such, it no longer specially concerns us.

The central question with which we have to deal is, therefore, whether Kant's Second Section can be regarded as a continuous philosophical argument, or whether, as Vaihinger maintains, it is a series of incongruous fragments tacked together in an arbitrary and external manner. If Vaihinger's contention breaks down here, it breaks down altogether. This is the crux of the whole problem.

Now it is obvious that unless there were special difficulties in this crucial section, so acute a critic as Vaihinger would never have been induced to put forward so seemingly fantastic a hypothesis. So much smoke must surely indicate a little fire; and we must admit that there are genuine difficulties in this section, much more serious than the difficulties with which we have hitherto dealt. It is interesting to observe that Kant was himself aware of these difficulties, and that he himself offers an explanation of them. He placed two danger signals [11] very clearly before us—the first of them immediately after the introduction to the Second Section, and the second immediately after the end of the Section Section.

The first danger signal occurs in A 98, and is headed "Preliminary Reminder" (or Admonition). Kant says, "The Deduction of the Categories is bound up with so many difficulties, and compels us to penetrate so deeply into the first grounds of the possibility of our knowledge in general, that (in order to avoid the wide ramifications of a complete theory, and at the same time not to neglect anything in so necessary an investigation), I have found it advisable in the following four 'Numbers' rather to prepare the reader than

11. The warning in A 88, I believe, also refers to the same point.

to instruct him; and to deal systematically with the exposition of the elements of the understanding only in the following section, that is, in the Third Section. For this reason the reader must not allow himself to be put off at first by an obscurity which is inevitable to begin with in a road hitherto quite untrodden, but which will, I hope, be cleared up in favour of complete insight in the aforesaid [Third] Section."

The second danger signal occurs in A 115. The very first words of the Third Section are a reference back to the original warning in the Second Section, so as to make absolutely sure that we should not forget it. The words are these: "What in the preceding section we set forth separately and individually (*abgesondert und einzeln*), we now wish to expound in systematic interconnexion (*vereinigt und im Zusammenhange*)."

These are perfectly clear statements. Kant warns us, both at the beginning and at the end of the Second Section, that we have in it a statement which is preparatory or provisional, which deals in isolation with things which require subsequently to be united, and which has not the authority of the systematic exposition in the Third Section. Kant is perfectly aware of what he is doing, and he is anxious to avoid any possible misunderstandings on the part of the reader. In the Second Section he is preparing the way for his final argument, and he wishes to lead the reader by a series of separate stages which may be incomplete in themselves and must be set in their proper relation to one another in the light of what comes after. I wish to suggest that the difficulties and inconsistencies which are alleged to exist in this section are to be explained as Kant himself has explained them. The fantastic geological hypotheses are partly due to neglect of these plain and insistent warnings. One would imagine that even the most careless reader would sit up and take notice when these warnings were thrust upon him. Yet (and this is the most remarkable fact in Vaihinger's remarkable pamphlet) there is in all his elaborate and microscopic examination of Kant's argument not a single breath of allusion to these two passages which are staring him straight in the face. As far as he is concerned, these two passages simply do not exist.

V

We have now before us two theories in regard to the Second Section—the theory of Vaihinger and the theory of Kant himself. The first is that in the last resort the Second Section is a medley of unrelated and inconsistent fragments. The second is that this section is a provisional exposition of the deduction, admittedly unsystematic and in itself obscure, dealing with interdependent factors in temporary abstraction from one another, but clear enough in the light of the more systematic exposition for which it prepares the way. The question is, which of these two theories is true?

Let us look at this section with unsophisticated eyes. It is composed of an introduction followed by four "Numbers"—to use Kant's own term. The introduction is in no way startling. It opens with a clear statement of the problem at issue—the objective validity of the categories; it explains the nature of the proof required, and indicates the necessity of dealing with the matter on its subjective side; it follows this up with a brief summary of the threefold synthesis and the subjective factors at work in it; and finally adds a warning as to the preparatory or provisional character of the subsequent portions of the section.

In the First "Number" Kant deals with the synthesis of apprehension in intuition. He points out that all our ideas, whether empirical or pure, are on their subjective side modifications of mind, and therefore subject to inner sense and to its form which is time. The manifold which is given to us is always given successively, and therefore for its apprehension synthesis is necessary. The first aspect of this synthesis is the synthesis of apprehension, the awareness of the different elements of the given manifold one after another. This is as necessary to apprehend a pure manifold like time, as it is to apprehend an empirical manifold like a house. Hence we have a pure as well as an empirical synthesis of apprehension, and (although he only makes the point in the next "number") the pure synthesis of apprehension is the condition of the empirical. We must apprehend time to apprehend what is in time.

In the Second "Number" we pass on to the synthesis of reproduction in imagination. If we are to apprehend a manifold given successively in time, we must keep the earlier elements before our mind when we come to the later, and this Kant believes to be due dealing with a pure manifold or an empirical manifold, and once to reproduction in imagination. This, again, is true whether we are more the pure synthesis of reproduction in imagination is the condition of the empirical, and for the same reason as before. This contention is surely sound enough, but Kant adds to it one of much more doubtful validity.

Reproduction of past ideas in imagination takes place by the laws of association, and we have a faculty for associating ideas. But this faculty would never be able to work unless appearances were given to us in a regular order, for association can arise only where there is a regular order in given appearances. Therefore a regular order in given appearances is necessary for experience. By this argument Kant passes—I believe illegitimately—from an empirical regularity to a necessary regularity in appearances. This regularity, because necessary, must, on Kantian principles, be known *a priori,* and must be due to the nature of the knowing mind. It cannot be due to pure intuition, which gives us only the forms of sensibility. It cannot be due to pure understanding, for that gives us only the categories. Therefore it must be due to pure imagination which mediates between sense and understanding. Pure imagination gives us the pure or transcendental synthesis of reproduction, and this pure or transcendental synthesis of reproduction is without further ado presumed to be the source of the necessary regularity of given appearances.

In the Third "Number" we have the synthesis of recognition in the concept. It would be no use reproducing our past ideas (whether empirical or pure), unless we recognized that what is reproduced is the same as what was given before. This manifestly requires a concept, and apart from this the manifold which is successively intuited and subsequently reproduced cannot be gathered together into one idea, nor can it constitute one object. So much is obvious, but Kant takes a further step for which he has already prepared the way in § 10 (the Third Section of the Metaphysical Deduction). He believes that, in order to have one object, the synthesis which constitutes it must be one synthesis, and that therefore there is implied in the knowledge of the unity of the object a knowledge (however vague) of the unity of the synthesis through which it is known. Hence for him the concept of the object is always also a concept of the synthesis which makes the object an object. Furthermore, consciousness of the one object and the one synthesis implies, necessarily, not only consciousness of unity but also unity of consciousness. And this unity of consciousness would seem to be more than mere self-identity; it would appear to be some sort of consciousness of self-identity.

The remainder of this "number" is only an elaboration of these points. Kant has to explain what he means by "concept," what he means by "object," and what he means by "unity of consciousness," and this he proceeds to do.

If we analyze what we mean by an "object" as distinct from mere given and passing appearances, or sensible ideas, we find that it is something in general = X (later called the transcendental object), to which the given ideas correspond or refer. When we consider it more closely we find it involves some sort of necessity or unity in the given ideas. If they all relate to one object they must necessarily agree with one another and so have that unity which constitutes the very concept of an object. Such is surely a fair analysis of what appears to be involved in our experience.

This unity of the object must, on Kantian principles, be due to the nature of the mind, if it is itself necessary and known *a priori*. Kant asserts that the unity which makes the object necessary *is* the formal unity of consciousness in the synthesis of the manifold. We may not be happy with this identification, but for Kant the unity of the object, the unity of the synthesis, and the unity of the consciousness of the synthesis are one and the same. He illustrates this with an object of pure intuition, a triangle, and an object of empirical intuition, a body, in a passage which anticipates his subsequent discussion of the schematism of the categories.

Unity and necessity are therefore involved in any object whatsoever, even in empirical objects known through empirical concepts. Such necessity must always have a transcendental ground in the nature of the mind itself. Kant finds this in the transcendental unity of apperception, the necessary unity of the knowing self, without which all knowledge of any kind of succession and any kind of object is manifestly impossible. He regards this, however, not as a mere abstract self-identity, but as "an original and necessary consciousness of self-identity" which is, at the same time "a conscious-ness of the necessary unity of the synthesis of all appearances in accordance with concepts." The knowing self is manifested only in the synthesis of the given manifold, and consciousness of the unity of the knowing self is necessarily a consciousness of the unity of the synthesis.

There is in all this no direct mention of the categories, although some of the phrases towards the end of this discussion may be, and probably are, allusions to them. The concepts mentioned are par-ticular concepts, those of triangle and of body. Kant is waiting to extract the categories dramatically from the unity of apperception, ✓ and his main business has been to work up to the unity of apper-ception. There is, however, present throughout one truly universal concept—the concept of an object in general. And it must be remembered that we already know the categories to be concepts of objects in general (A 93), as we already know them to be concepts of pure synthesis represented in its universal form—*allgemein vorgestellt*—(A 78). We must always keep in mind this distinction between particular (or general) concepts and universal concepts or categories, and it is unfortunate that Kant does not make sharp differences in his terminology. A particular concept (whether em-pirical or pure) is for Kant a concept of objects of a particular class, that is, of *some* objects, but not of all objects without excep-tion; and it is also, as we have seen, a concept of the particular synthesis necessary to know objects of that particular class. A truly universal concept or category, on the other hand, is a concept of every object *qua* object, and it is also a concept of the pure synthesis which is necessary for knowing all objects *qua* objects. It is this pure concept of the transcendental object which gives objective reality to all our empirical concepts.

Kant introduces the categories explicitly in his Fourth "Num-ber," which is very properly entitled "Preliminary Exposition of the Possibility of the Categories as *a priori* Cognitions." There he as-serts that the orderly interconnection of all sense perceptions can take place only in one experience. The synthetic unity of appear-ances in accordance with empirical concepts would not be necessary, as we have found it to be, unless these empirical concepts them-selves depended upon a transcendental ground of unity. Without this there could be no reference of ideas to objects, and we should have no necessary and universal laws to which all appearances must be subject, if they are to give us knowledge.

Here again we have the necessary unity of experience and the necessary unity of synthesis involved in the cognition of an object. Hence it is clear that the *a priori* conditions of experience are also *a priori* conditions of objects of experience. But thought (or recognition by means of concepts) we have seen to be necessary to experience; and, therefore, since the categories are (as we have seen in the Metaphysical Deduction) the conditions (or forms) of thought in a possible experience, they are the conditions of experience and of its objects. Indeed they are the ultimate concepts by means of which we think objects in general for (or to) appearances; they have objective validity, i.e., they apply necessarily to all objects of experience.

All this rests upon the fact that all possible appearances are in a necessary relation to original apperception. The unity of apperception which is necessary to all experience is and must be manifested in certain universal functions of synthesis. The categories are the concepts in accordance with which such universal functions of synthesis operate. Hence it is through them alone that unity of consciousness and unity of synthesis is possible, and, therefore, it is through them alone that experience and the objects of experience are possible.

The rest of this number merely insists that no deduction is possible except a Transcendental Deduction of this kind: it elaborates the doctrine of Transcendental Affinity (obscurely hinted at in the Second "Number") and insists that the necessity to be found in Nature is due to the fact that Nature must appear to one mind whose necessary unity is manifested in synthesis. All appearances are, therefore, necessarily subject to the *a priori* conditions or laws of synthesis which are the categories.

It is not for us to deny that there are obscurities and difficulties in this argument—Kant himself admits them. His extraction of the categories from the unity of apperception must inevitably appear to us a trifle facile, but this is due to his confidence in the Metaphysical Deduction. We need not maintain that his argument is watertight—that is a matter for discussion. All I assert is that the whole section sounds like an argument, and reads like an argument, and, in fact, is an argument. It is indeed broadly the same argument as is set forth more compactly in the later passage, A 119–126; and so far from confusing the categories with particular or empirical concepts, it passes by means of such concepts to the unity of apperception and from the unity of apperception to the categories.

VI

It remains for us to consider as briefly as may be the reasons for Vaihinger's hypothesis. The most important case is clearly the case of Layer I. It is not inconceivable that Kant should, in a provisional section, have hurriedly developed a doctrine not wholly consistent with his other arguments. What is inconceivable is that he should complete this doctrine, when only half-developed, by a piece of altogether irrelevant and pre-critical thinking.

Professor Vaihinger brings forward some seven or eight arguments in reference to Layer I. If some of these appear to be trifling, it must be remembered that insignificant details may have a cumulative effect.

The first point is that in this layer there is no mention of the (productive) imagination. Why should there be? Kant has a perfect right to separate off different parts of his argument from one another, as he himself asserts he has done in this section. One can not argue from a mere omission, and there is in this "number" no place for imagination, which has been discussed, whether well or ill, in the previous section. Kant is no longer concerned with the subjective machinery of knowledge. He is arguing that the concept of an object in general is necessarily involved in all our knowledge; that it is this pure concept of the understanding which alone gives objective reference to all our empirical concepts and all our sensuous representations; and that this pure concept is impossible apart from the transcendental unity of apperception. We have already been informed that the categories are concepts of an object in general, but Kant has a perfect right to hold back the categories till "Number" 4, whose very title implies that we must not expect to have the categories in the preceding three "numbers." In this respect also, as Kant says, he is dealing with certain aspects of his proof in isolation from one another.

Vaihinger's second point is that we have here the only discussion of the nature of an "object." Elsewhere it is assumed that the concept of an object is already understood. But obviously, in discussing whether categories apply to objects we must ask what an object is. The theory of the object is one of the turning points of Kant's philosophy, as is very clear in the Second Analogy. There might have been certain advantages gained if he had discussed this question earlier, but he had to make certain things clear about synthesis before he could profitably do so, and this he attempts in the Metaphysical Deduction. On the whole, we may say that the object here positively clamors for discussion, and that this is the place both where Kant ought to discuss it, and where, as a matter of fact, he does discuss it.

The third point is trifling. Kant says (A 104), "We have said *above* that appearances are nothing but sensible ideas." This is alleged to be a reference to the Transcendental Aesthetic as immediately preceding. It is, on the contrary, a reference to the statement three pages before (A 101) that "appearances are not things-in-themselves, but the mere play of our ideas." And even if it were a reference to the Transcendental Aesthetic, I cannot see that this would prove anything.

We now come to the most serious argument—that the whole layer is concerned with empirical knowledge, and that it does not ask, as it ought, how the categories can apply to objects, but deals only with the relation between empirical concepts and objects.

Broadly speaking, this contention is true, although Kant touches also upon non-empirical objects, the mathematical triangle and space and time. He is, however, primarily concerned with the empirical, and this is altogether intelligible when we remember that his ultimate aim is to show that the categories of the understanding are valid of the objects given to sense. The difficulty lies not in the fact that Kant is concerned with empirical knowledge but in the fact that empirical concepts derive their objective reference from the pure concept of an object in general, instead of from the pure concepts (in the plural) of objects in general, which pure concepts are the categories. The empirical concept of body is used quite as freely in the Deduction given in the second edition as it is in the Deduction given in the first (*B* 128-129 and *B* 142). And in both editions alike it is through the transcendental unity of apperception that the concept of body receives its objective reference.

Once this is grasped—and to grasp it is merely to see the argument as a whole—the alleged difficulty disappears. It would be surprising if it did not, for unless Layer I really fits into the argument, there is no argument in the Second Section at all; and every commentator is bound to refer habitually to this despised layer, if he is even to pretend that the Transcendental Deduction is any kind of argument. It is both right and proper that empirical and other particular concepts should be discussed in this connection. Every concept, we were told as early as A 68, rests upon a function, i.e., upon the unity of the activity by which different ideas are arranged under a common idea. It is because of this that we can show the unity of apperception to be the necessary condition of every concept, of every judgment, of every experience, and of every object. Kant elaborates in a separate "number" this essential stage of the argument before he passes to the next stage, and shows that the unity of apperception is necessarily manifested in the categories. He gives us a hint of the categories by references to *a priori* rules toward the end of this "number," and he gives us more than a hint of them in his concept of an object in general which is so closely identified with the unity of apperception. It is, however, a merit rather than a defect that he keeps the different stages of his argument separate from one another, and in view of the explicit warning that he has done so, we have no excuse for misunderstanding him.

It may be admitted that this method of exposition gives rise to certain difficulties on a first reading—is there any method of exposition which would not? In particular, it gives rise to the difficulty of Vaihinger that empirical concepts seem to be sources of necessity. But Kant has already analyzed the concept of an object and shown that it involves unity and necessity in any and every object. The particular example of body is precisely what we ought to have in order to show that this necessity is to be found in empirical objects. And Kant is perfectly right in saying that when we call anything a body, we imply that it is one object whose given qualities must agree with one another. As soon as he has made this clear, he proceeds to insist that such necessity must have a transcendental ground, and this transcendental ground is discovered in the unity of apperception and the concept of an object in general. From thence he passes to the categories which are the source of the necessity found in our empirical experience of bodies and of all objects whatsoever. And these categories are nothing other than concepts of objects in general or of objects as such. If this is not an argument, I do not know what is.

The essential aim then of the first three "numbers" (and especially of "Number" 3) is to establish the intimate interconnection of synthesis, concept, and object (whether empirical or pure), and to show that the unity of apperception is the ultimate and necessary condition of all alike. The essential aim of "Number" 4 is to show (provisionally) that the unity of apperception necessarily involves synthesis according to the categories, which Kant thinks is easy in view of the Metaphysical Deduction. Broadly speaking, the same argument is found in the Third Section, especially in (A 120–125), and the same transition from particular concepts to categories is to be found in A 125. But there, as Kant himself suggests, the argument is more compact, if not more systematic, though I doubt whether it would be intelligible apart from the Second Section.

We need only notice one more point which is brought forward by Vaihinger to support his case. In discussing transcendental apperception (A 107) Kant observes that "even the purest objective unity, that, namely, of the concepts a priori (space and time) is possible only through the relation of intuitions to it" [that is, to transcendental apperception]. This, Vaihinger suggests, shows that Kant was interested in no other a priori concepts than space and time, that he did not yet take any other a priori concepts into consideration. So remarkable a conclusion can hardly ever have been grounded on evidence so slight. There was no time in Kant's adult life when he could have failed to recognize a priori concepts other than space and time. If this passage is to be so interpreted, it must indeed have been written early; it must, in fact, have been composed in the cradle. The "purest objective unity" is the unity of an object the manifold of which is given a priori, and this could be nothing other than space and time, just as Kant says. There is no need to attribute to Kant a view incompatible with all we know of his philosophical development.

I submit then that Layer I is an intelligible and necessary part of Kant's whole argument, and that so far from being pre-critical it is an essential element in Critical thought.

VII

It is unnecessary for us to examine Layer IV in the same detail, although some of the points raised by Vaihinger have a bearing also on Layer I. The question of the threefold synthesis is more complicated than the question of the transcendental object, and it is also less important, since Vaihinger's hypothesis is here—although (as I believe) mistaken—not manifestly repugnant to common sense. There is no difficulty in showing that Kant's terminology varies, that his exposition is not symmetrical, and that there are obscurities and inconsistencies in his account of imagination. Imagination is intermediate between sense and understanding, and Kant never made up his mind where it began and where it ended. The simplest explanation of his inconsistencies is not that he tacked together different views written at different times, but that he was thoroughly muddled on the subjective machinery of cognition, and in particular on the subject of imagination. The same kind of confusion for the same reasons is to be found in the new version of the Deduction which he gives us in the second edition.

There is, however, an inconsistency between Layer IV and the other parts of the Deduction which, it must be admitted, can with difficulty be experienced in this way, and this constitutes by far the strongest argument in support of Vaihinger's case. It is this. The transcendental synthesis of imagination is here described as reproductive, while everywhere else it is described as productive. In *B* 152 it is even expressly denied that the reproductive synthesis of imagination contributes anything to the explanation of the possibility of *a priori* knowledge. It is therefore excluded from transcendental philosophy and relegated to psychology. How is this to be explained?

Vaihinger's theory is that Kant devised Layer IV hurriedly just before publishing the *Kritik,* and subsequently retracted it. But to hold this is to hold that Kant first of all made the productive synthesis of imagination transcendental, and then the reproductive, and then went back in the second edition to the productive. A more natural view would surely be (if we accept the hypothesis of composition at different times) that he first of all thought of the transcendental synthesis as reproductive, and later made it productive, leaving, however, the two views side by side in the first edition. By the time he came to the second edition, he was convinced that his first view had been a mistake.

All such conjectures are hazardous, but I confess that this seems to me also the natural logical development of Kant's thought. He believes that the order of given appearances is a necessary order, on the ground that, without this, association, and therefore experience, would be impossible. As necessary, it must be due to mind, and, as we have seen, it must be due to some pure synthesis of imagination, since it cannot be attributed either to pure intuition or to understanding. Kant looks around for such a pure synthesis, and observing the obvious truth that reproduction is necessary for apprehending even pure intuitions, he hurriedly and without argument ascribes the necessary regularity of appearances to a pure synthesis of reproduction.

It is, however, obvious that such a view offers no plausible ground for the necessary regularity of appearances. Indeed, this pure synthesis of reproduction, though it is necessary to apprehend a pure manifold, as for example a period of time, is governed by the ordinary laws of association, and it is in that sense empirical. We simply recall or reproduce what we have recently had before our mind, and it is a mere accident that what we reproduce happens to be pure. There is, however, another pure synthesis of imagination which is much more fundamental and offers us a more plausible ground for the regularity of appearances. We can construct *a priori* intuitions in accordance with our concepts; for example, knowing what a triangle is, we can construct it *a priori* in space. This is the work of productive imagination, and it is necessary for the *a priori* apprehension of space and time. I cannot myself see how such activity can be the source of the necessary regularity of appearances, but it may be put forward as a reason why all objects in space and time must have extensive quantity, and why by analogy they must have other *a priori* characteristics. There is thus far more plausibility in making the productive synthesis of imagination the source of the necessary regularity of appearances, and I cannot conceive that anyone who had put forward this as his explanation could ever go back to the reproductive synthesis.

Another point which I think offers some confirmation of my view is this. There is a considerable resemblance between Kant's threefold synthesis and the account of experience given by Baumgarten in his Metaphysics—I refer to the second edition of the German translation published in 1783, the only copy to which I have access. Kant's acquaintance with, and respect for, this work is well known. It contains many doctrines which are to be found in Kant modified to suit his own purposes. Baumgarten's chapter on the psychology of experience begins with inner and outer sense, and then passes to imagination, which is the source of representations or ideas of my *past* condition or state. Then, after a short section on perspicacity (a faculty which apprehends the agreements and differences of things), we have a section on memory. This begins as follows, "I represent an idea which once again is developed in me as identical with the idea which was developed in me before, that is to say, *I recognize it again,* namely for the idea which I have already had, or *I remember it (recognosco, recordor)."* When we add that Baumgarten has the habit, wherever possible, of dividing a faculty (e.g., perspicacity) into a sensuous and an intellectual faculty, it is hard to believe that we have not here the original germ of Kant's thinking on this matter. At any rate, there would seem to be in the doctrine of the threefold synthesis something which had its roots in the orthodox theories of the time, and as such it might plausibly be regarded as early rather than late.

On this point I do not believe there can be any certainty. One thing does indeed seem to me to be certain—that the Second Section is an argument and not a patchwork, and that it has to be read and understood as a whole. I therefore see no ground for believing that the different parts of the Second Section were written at different times. On the other hand, the treatment of reproductive imagination as a transcendental faculty is so much at variance with Kant's doctrine elsewhere as to suggest that this discussion may have been written at a different time from the Third Section. If such be the case, it is reasonable to ask whether the whole of the Second Section may not have been written at a different time, and if so whether the Second Section is earlier or later than the Third.

For the reasons I have given, it seems to me probable that it is earlier rather than later. Such a view is plausible both in regard to the threefold synthesis and in regard to the transcendental object, although the account of them is in neither case pre-critical. It seems also tolerably clear that the Third Section could have been written by Kant only if he had something like the Second Section already before him. Because of the discussion in the Second Section, he is able, as he says, to avoid "the ramifications of a complete theory" in the Third Section, and much of the Third Section would be unintelligible without reference to the Second Section. Kant says expressly that the Second Section is to prepare rather than to instruct us; and he may well have thought it was fitted to do so, if it represented the road by which he had himself reached his conclusions.

I doubt whether Vaihinger would have suggested that the doctrine of the threefold synthesis was late—Adickes regards it as early—apart from its relation to the one relevant jotting of Kant which can be definitely dated, an interesting discussion written subsequent to January 20, 1780. Yet even this jotting (Reicke, *Lose Blätter*, Fragment B 12, pp. 113-116) is admitted by Vaihinger to resemble Layer III very closely, and the main ground of his argument is "that the characteristic point of view of Layer IV had not yet been worked out." To say this is to beg the question. The question we must ask ourselves is whether the point of view of Layer IV has not yet been worked out or whether it has already been superseded. Vaihinger finds some statements in it which he regards as the origin of the characteristic doctrines of Layer IV. The discussion of these, however, would involve an examination of the whole doctrine of transcendental synthesis (on which I am unable to accept Vaihinger's view), and I can only say that his arguments on this point leave me quite unconvinced.

VIII

Our task is now completed, so far as it can be completed within a limited compass. The onus of proof, it must be remembered, lies on those who support the geological hypothesis, and not on those who accept the *Kritik* as what it, and indeed what every philosophical work, professes to be, namely, a continuous philosophical argument. I have shown in general how inadequate, how inappropriate, and how misleading the proposed criterion, or principle of division is. I have maintained that the alleged difference in the two central layers evaporates into the difference between introduction and argument, and between the objective and subjective sides of the Deduction. As regards the so-called earliest layer, I have attempted to show that it fits naturally into its place in the Second Section, as soon as we grasp the argument as a whole; that the detailed objections to it will not hold water; and that the whole theory is a misconception arising largely from an almost inexcusable neglect of Kant's reiterated warning. The difficulties raised in regard to the fourth and latest layer can, I have suggested, be overcome in the light of the same considerations, but the inconsistency between the account of transcendental imagination as reproductive, and the account of it elsewhere as productive, does, it must be admitted, offer some ground for the suggestion that it represents a different level of thought, and possibly a different date of composition. I suggest, however, that if such a hypothesis is to be entertained, it is far more plausible to suppose that the Second Section as a whole is Kant's first attempt to expound the Transcendental Deduction, and I maintain that it is a continuous argument and not a patchwork. For the understanding of the Deduction, however, such a hypothesis is unnecessary. All that we require to remember is Kant's own statement that the Second Section is to be taken as provisional and not as authoritative.

I am therefore compelled to reject the view that the Transcendental Deduction is a patchwork, and to maintain that, if the different parts of the Deduction were written at different times, Vaihinger's account of the order of their composition is erroneous. His theory as a whole shows the defects of a microscopic, as opposed to a macroscopic, vision; it shows, in short, the very tendencies against which Kant protested in the sentence which I have placed at the beginning of this paper. Kant was unduly optimistic in believing that his apparent contradictions could be easily solved, once we had grasped the idea as a whole; but he was perfectly right in asserting that his argument is a whole, and not a patchwork of unrelated incongruities. The recovery of that belief seems to me vital for the teaching and the study of the *Kritik*. For that reason I have felt obliged to criticize Professor Vaihinger with severity, though not, I hope, without respect. Perhaps it may therefore not be inappropriate if I add—although the greatest of Kantian scholars is in need of no testimonial from me—that in spite of what I regard as his fundamental errors, I have learned more of the Transcendental Deduction from his brief pamphlet than from all the commentaries I have ever seen.

Part II

Kant and the Problem
of Metaphysics

THE THREE articles in this group all ask about Kant's relation to metaphysics. The way in which that relation has been traditionally characterized is that Kant rendered something called dogmatic metaphysics impossible and offered something called a critical metaphysics in its place. But is this in fact a correct account of the relation between Kant's position and the metaphysical tradition? Arthur O. Lovejoy has claimed that it is not. Lovejoy's main contention is that much of what Kant called critical philosophy was already present in dogmatic metaphysics and, consequently, that there is no genuine opposition between dogmatism and criticism in metaphysical method.

Lovejoy's defense of this claim runs as follows. The way in which Kant himself sought to distinguish between dogmatism and criticism was to contrast two ways of dealing with synthetic judgments *a priori:* the dogmatist made such judgments without giving us a way in which they could be verified, while the critical philosopher recognized such judgments for what they were and supplied us with a way of demonstrating them. But, Lovejoy argues, dogmatic metaphysicians were both aware that they were making such judgments and provided a way of defending them. True, the account of truth given by Leibniz and his successors made all true judgments analytic. But the distinction which Kant was later to make between analytic and synthetic judgments was nonetheless recognized by that school. For Leibniz distinguished between virtually identical propositions and identical propositions properly so called. The former kind of proposition can be seen to be true only by analyzing the subject concept into concepts whose opposites are seen not to be compossible. This, according to Lovejoy, is the Leibnizian counterpart of Kant's synthetic judgments. There are, on the other hand, identical propositions—tautologies—which Leibniz was careful to distinguish from propositions that are *virtualiter identicae* and which correspond to Kant's analytic propositions.

Lovejoy's argument comes, then, to this. The distinction that Kant wanted to make between synthetic and analytic judgments was in part that between propositions which tell us something about the world and those which are arbitrary and thus not governed by the way the world is. Lovejoy is arguing that the Leibnizian distinction between virtually identical propositions and identical propositions reproduces this distinction. And the main support of Lovejoy's interpretation is that, for Leibniz, virtually identical propositions are always based upon relations of compossibility between simple concepts which comprise the definition of the subject term of such propositions. Thus a virtually identical proposition is true if we can, upon analysis, arrive at the concepts comprising its subject concept, the denial of which would give us incompossible concepts. Which concepts are compossible and which incompossible is not, so Lovejoy insists, an arbitrary matter. Hence, there are some non-arbitrary propositions which express these relations and which can nonetheless be certified by the Law of Contradiction. This kind of proposition cannot, however, be classified as a Kantian analytic judgment just because the latter is arbitrary and tells us nothing about the way the world is, while the former does give us information about relations of compossibility and incompossibility which are not subject to our legislation. Lovejoy's conclusion is, accordingly, that dogmatic metaphysicians could make the distinction between synthetic and analytic truths and, further, that they could accommodate Kant's classification of synthetic *a priori* propositions; for the truth of Leibniz's virtually identical propositions could be ascertained *a priori* by the Law of Contradiction.

According to Lovejoy, Kant could have criticized this use of the Law of Contradiction in any one of the three following ways. First, Kant might have argued that the law is applicable only to phenomena and not to noumena, concluding that we cannot apply that law to all virtually identical propositions. But this way is not open to Kant; for, as Lovejoy points out, the Law of Contradiction applies to all reality: on Kant's account, there are some propositions certifiable by the Law of Contradiction (like "The soul is a simple substance") which do apply to noumena. Secondly, however, Kant could have held against Leibniz that the Law of Contradiction is valid for both phenomena and noumena but that judgments stating compossibility or lack of compossibility between simple concepts are synthetic. Kant could, that is, have held that such judgments are synthetic because their truth or falsity could not be ascertained by any process of analysis. And the truth or falsity of such judgments would not be ascertainable by analysis simply because the concepts contained in such a judgment would be simple. Lovejoy admits that, if such were the line Kant took, then he would indeed have succeeded in pointing out the inadequacy of dogmatism. But Lovejoy says nothing about whether Kant did in fact take this line.

Kant could, according to Lovejoy, have held that the law of contradiction is valid for both phenomena and noumena, saying only that conclusions about the characteristics of certain kinds of entities are not inferable by means of the law. Thus Kant might hold that certain conclusions concerning God, the soul, and the totality of appearances which dogmatic metaphysicians had sought to derive by means of the law of contradiction do not in fact follow. This way is not, however, open to Kant; for errors in inference are purely formal and do not set apart one way of doing philosophy from another.

Lovejoy's general conclusion, then, is that Kant did not succeed in showing exactly how the distinction he wanted to make between synthetic and analytic judgments was different from the dogmatist's distinction between virtually identical propositions and identical propositions. Consequently, Kant did not make good his case against dogmatic metaphysics when he held that it had no way of justifying synthetic propositions *a priori*. For what corresponds to a synthetic *a priori* judgment in dogmatic metaphysics—the virtually identical proposition—could be certified as true by the application of the Law of Contradiction. And, if this is so, Kant did not succeed in establishing the necessity for another method to justify such judgments.

Lovejoy's paper raises two issues, only one of which is, I think, genuine. The issue which I do not believe to be genuine concerns whether Kant simply concedes to the dogmatists that there are some genuinely analytic propositions, the predicates of which cannot be deduced from the subject concept. Lovejoy thinks Kant does this; and he quotes a passage (p. 123) from Kant's polemic against

Eberhard in which Kant allegedly admits as much. On Lovejoy's reading, Kant is conceding that there are predicates called attributes which are not part of the logical essence of the subject concept of a necessary proposition, but which nonetheless follow necessarily from that concept. And from this Lovejoy concludes that Kant simply concedes that the application of the Law of Contradiction will yield such predicates from an analysis of the subject concept. But Lovejoy has misinterpreted the text. What the passage he adduces in support of his claim in fact says is this: predicates called attributes can be deduced from the predicates contained in the subject concept of analytic propositions; but there are other kinds of predicates—Kant calls them extra-essential marks—which are neither essential predicates nor attributes. And it is this kind of predicate which Kant says is present in a synthetic proposition. Hence Lovejoy's claim that Kant simply concedes the dogmatist's claim is unfounded.

But there is a more serious issue which Lovejoy raises: are the propositions stating the compossibility or incompossibility of simple concepts synthetic or analytic? On Lovejoy's account, Leibniz's virtually identical propositions state such relations; and it is this kind of proposition which allegedly corresponds to Kant's synthetic *a priori* propositions. Now I believe that a virtually identical proposition is the Leibnizian counterpart of Kant's synthetic *a priori* proposition: both propositions tell us something about the structure of the world, and both propositions can be certifiable independently of experience. But Leibniz's virtually identical propositions, unlike Kant's synthetic *a priori* propositions, supposedly can be certified as true by the Law of Contradiction.

Once it has been admitted that the virtually identical proposition is the counterpart of the synthetic *a priori,* are we forced to say that the former has all of the characteristics of the latter? Lovejoy thinks we are. I think we are not. That we are not forced to such a conclusion can be shown by distinguishing between two very different kinds of incompossibility and showing how each differs from Kant's notion of the synthetic *a priori*. First, to say that two simple concepts are compossible can be to say that they are not mutually exclusive—that their combination in a proposition does not generate something of the form p.-p. It is, of course, true that I discover this kind of compossibility by discovering whether the negation of such a combination of concepts produces the contradiction. But do I discover whether a proposition containing these concepts is *true* by applying the law of contradiction? I think not. That, among several different aggregates of compossible concepts, some give us combinations that are found in the world and others do not—this cannot be vouchsafed by the Law of Contradiction. All the Law of Contradiction tells us here is that each concept cannot be other than what it is. And this requirement can be fulfilled by any cluster of compossibles without our knowing that such a cluster tells us what the case is. And we cannot find out whether the cluster tells us what the case is by analyzing concepts; for we are dealing here with simples. And they are not susceptible of analysis. For this reason, then, any proposition stating that certain simple concepts are compossible must be synthetic, since none of the concepts which are related by it is contained in any of the other concepts. And this is, accordingly, an exception to Leibniz's category of virtually identical propositions. It also happens to be the case that such exceptions are examples of what Kant understood by synthetic propositions.

But there is another kind of proposition relating compossibles which is to be distinguished from propositions that tell us merely that a certain cluster of simple concepts does not generate a contradiction. There are propositions which relate compossibles and whose negation generates a contradiction. Let us consider the case of a proposition which states that the combination of two simple concepts does generate a contradiction. How do I know that such propositions are true? One thing is clear: I cannot know that they are true by analyzing any of the concepts involved, for they are *ex hypothesi* simple. And, for this reason, the incompatibility involved in conjoining such concepts cannot be discovered by applying the Law of Contradiction. True, that law can be invoked as a reason why we cannot conjointly assert two incompossible concepts. But it will not enable us to ascertain which concepts are incompatible. We must, therefore, assume another criterion prior to the Law of Contradiction in order to say, with regard to any two simple concepts, that they cannot be combined. But if this is so, then Lovejoy's case against Kant is weakened, for it is just this kind of prior justification which Kant demands but which cannot be supplied by the dogmatic metaphysician.

The essay by Ernst Cassirer, which was written in answer to

Heidegger's *Kant und das Problem der Metaphysik,* asks whether Kant had an implicit ontology. Heidegger had claimed that the *Kritik* contained a theory of being in the sense of a theory of human existence. More specifically, the analysis of human existence which Kant allegedly gave consisted in two principal claims. First, Kant argued that human existence is essentially finite since we are limited in our relation to objects by our capacities to receive them. We can, of course, form a notion of another kind of intellect—an *intellectus archetypus*—which creates the objects it knows; but this merely underscores the fact that our intellect is finite. Secondly, on Heidegger's account, the threefold division in the *Kritik* between sensibility, understanding, and reason is provisional since all three have a common root in the productive imagination, which is the essential mark of the finite human being.

The foregoing claims are, Heidegger argued, the main outlines of the ontology which underlies the *Kritik.* Cassirer responds by denying both that the human intellect is finite and that Kant can be properly interpreted as offering an ontology of human existence at all. Regarding the claim that Kant regards human existence as finite, Cassirer argues that you can just as well choose reason as imagination to characterize human existence. And if you choose reason, then the very fact that we possess conceptions of freedom, a purely intelligible Kingdom of Ends, and the moral law shows that we are not limited, as Heidegger suggests, to whatever the forms of our experience present us. For reason can entertain notions to which no experience can conform. Thus our relation to the moral law is not like our relation to perceptual objects: we are not given the moral law through the faculties which limit our intuition. Nor do we derive any other pure concept from a sensuous manifold; hence it is false to claim, as Heidegger does, that human existence for Kant is finite in that it is limited by forms under which objects are presented to us. That same human existence which Heidegger takes to be finite can entertain concepts the objects of which cannot be given in that way at all.

But Cassirer brings an even more serious objection to Heidegger's thesis that the *Kritik* contains an analysis of human existence. When Kant's doctrine of imagination is cited as giving the principal characteristic of human existence, Heidegger has not correctly interpreted the place of imagination in the *Kritik.* The doctrine of imagination belongs not to Kant's theory of man but rather to his theory of empirical objects; thus, that doctrine refers only to conditions of applying the categories to objects. It does not serve as a way of characterizing the nature of man.

Cassirer's paper raises two issues of especial importance. First, in what sense is Kant in fact offering an analysis of the nature of man? Cassirer thinks that the argument of the first *Kritik* contains no such theory because Kant is presenting a theory of empirical objects. But to say that the human intellect is divided into reason, imagination, and understanding is to tell us something about the constitution of our cognitive faculties. And to make the claim that the productive imagination is the root of understanding and sensibility is to do the same thing. Thus the opposition which Cassirer sees between the theory of man and the theory of objects does not appear to be genuine; for, in asking about the character of empirical objects, Kant is asking not about these objects as they are in themselves but rather about how these objects can be objects for us. And an answer to this question surely involves telling us something about the character of human intellection.

What is perhaps more important, however, is the sense in which claims about human intellection can be construed as ontological. They are certainly not ontological in the way in which claims about God, Freedom, and Immortality are held by Kant to be ontological: none of the claims Kant makes about the division of human cognitive faculties is a claim about a transempirical entity. Thus the issue which the Cassirer-Heidegger dispute suggests—but which Cassirer nowhere brings into sharp focus—is this: what is the status of such propositions as "All human knowledge is divided into sensibility, understanding, and reason" and "The productive imagination is the root of sensibility and understanding"? The truth of such propositions is assumed throughout Kant's analysis of empirical objects. Yet such propositions do not appear to fit into Kant's classification of propositions. They are not analytic because we do not discover their truth by merely analyzing the subject terms of such propositions. But neither are they synthetic *a posteriori;* for they are not propositions which can be falsified by our experience just because they give us the conditions under which we are to have experience of objects. And if we say that they are synthetic *a priori,* they must be very different propositions from those enumerated in the Analytic of Principles of the first *Kritik.* There such propositions refer to transcendental time determinations. But propositions like those concerning the threefold division of human intellection or the productive imagination as the root of sensibility and understanding cannot be verified by reference to transcendental time determinations. Still less can propositions of this kind be synthetic *a priori* in the way in which the supreme principle of morality is said to be synthetic *a priori*. For that principle is certified by reference to the Idea of Freedom, while there is no such Idea which can certify propositions like the one about human intellection or the one about the productive imagination. If propositions about human intellection are synthetic *a priori,* then, they must be of a very different type than the usual examples Kant gives.

Heinz Heimsoeth, like Heidegger, argues that what we have been calling the Critical philosophy rests on a set of purely metaphysical propositions. Unlike Heidegger, however, Heimsoeth finds these propositions in the pre-Critical metaphysics; and Heimsoeth argues further that what appear to be the principal epistemological doctrines of the *Kritik* are really consequences of purely metaphysical doctrines. Let us consider what these doctrines are.

One of the fundamental distinctions of the *Kritik* is that between receptivity and spontaneity: we receive perceptual particulars and interpret them by subsuming them under concepts. This distinction, Heimsoeth argues, is primarily ontological, for what Kant is claiming here is that all finite substances have two sides. They are at once receptive and spontaneous in order to relate to a community of objects. Thus, what we have taken to be an epistemological claim is really a claim about the relation of substances to one another in the real world. And it is only because this latter claim is true or believed by Kant to be true that the former is held to be true.

The distinction between things-in-themselves and appearances is another *prima facie* epistemological distinction which, according to Heimsoeth, follows from a prior ontological claim. That objects are in themselves and are appearances for others follows from a theory of substance according to which every substance relates to other substances in virtue of the expressions of its activity. One substance is acted upon by another by a force or action which is not to be confounded with the substance exerting the force. And this, Heimsoeth argues, yields the Kantian distinction between thing-in-itself and appearance: every substance can relate to others only through its accidents and hence cannot be directly presented to another substance; every object given to us can relate to us only through its accidents but cannot present itself directly to us.

Finally, what is perhaps the most distinctively epistemological claim of the *Kritik*—that space and time are subjective forms under which objects are given to us—is for Heimsoeth a conclusion to which Kant was forced by antecedent metaphysical concerns. Here I single out two such concerns. First, there was the problem of relating the divine presence to space. If God were located spatially, it would follow that He would be present in all places, and this would be incompatible with the simplicity of God. The same conclusion follows from the assumption that God is temporal. Kant's solution is, according to Heimsoeth, to make space and time phenomenal—from which it follows that space and time are not determinations of God but only properties of our human intellection.

A similar problem arises for mind-body interaction. If we say that space is a real determination of things and not merely a subjective form of our apprehension, then we are committed to saying —what is absurd—that minds are localized in space. Wishing to avoid this absurdity, Kant concludes that minds are not in space but that space is merely a form under which the mind apprehends objects of outer sense.

The main issue which the Heimsoeth paper raises is the importance of the dogmatic residue in Kant's mature philosophy. Kant frequently expresses his own position in terms that survive from dogmatic metaphysics. Are we therefore entitled to infer that the position, expressed in this fashion, presupposes certain tacit metaphysical positions? This cannot be decided apart from an examination of individual cases where Kant actually expresses his own views in a language taken over from dogmatic metaphysics. Regarding the three principal survivals that Heimsoeth points out, there are, however, some replies that could be made.

Consider the claim that the distinction between receptivity and spontaneity rests on a prior claim about the relation of substances to one another. In the *Kritik* Kant neither claims nor needs to claim that every finite substance exemplifies this distinction. All he claims is that the distinction operates within our cognitive relation to objects: if we are to know a perceptual object, he holds, we must receive particulars and interpret them in various ways. But this does not presuppose any more general claim about the characteristics of finite substances. And if this is so, then it is not correct to say that making the distinction in question presupposes an ontological claim.

What about the distinction between a thing-in-itself and appearances? Is this a consequence of the more general ontological relation between a substance and its accidents? There is, of course, an analogy between the two: just as a substance is presented through its accidents, so the thing-in-itself is presented through appearances. But this analogy very soon breaks down. If the relation between an appearance and a thing-in-itself is like that between a substance and its accidents, then it would follow that space and time are objective properties of things; for then space and time, since they are appearances, would have to inhere in a substance. And since the self is not a substance for Kant, the only substances in which they could inhere would be objects as they are in themselves. This consequence alone would be enough to cast doubt on whether Kant understood the relation between things-in-themselves to appearances as analogous to that obtaining between a substance and its accidents. But there is a further reason why Kant would have separated the two relations. The relation between a Kantian thing-in-itself and an appearance is that between two modes of presentation of one and the same object. The relation between a substance and an accident is that between an object and one of its properties. Thus the two relations are radically different, from which we may infer that the distinction between a thing-in-itself and appearances is not a deductive consequence of that between a substance and its accidents.

Let us consider, finally, Heimsoeth's view that the subjectivity of space and time are consequences of positions which Kant adopts concerning the divine presence and mind-body interaction. I propose to concede for the sake of argument that the assumption of the subjectivity of space and time does remove both of the difficulties that Heimsoeth mentions. But are we forced to conclude that this is the reason why Kant argues for their subjectivity? I think not. What Heimsoeth shows is, at most, that, assuming the truth of certain propositions about the divine presence and the characteristics of mind, we can derive the conclusion that space and time are subjective forms. But this is not to say that these assumptions are the only premises from which the conclusion can be derived; and still less does it show that Kant himself sought to derive that conclusion solely from these premises.

KANT'S ANTITHESIS OF

DOGMATISM

AND CRITICISM

Arthur O. Lovejoy

§

Kant's distinction between two sharply contrasted types of philosophical method, designated by the names of "dogmatism" and
"criticism" has come to be one of the accepted rubrics in the current
treatment of the history of philosophy. It is commonly supposed to
correspond to actual historical differences that are both definite and
important. For this celebrated antithesis not only sums up in a single
phrase what Kant conceived to be the most important and distinctive feature of his own doctrine; it also, as Kant sets it forth, contains several plain implications as to matters of historical fact which
concern much more than his own doctrine: implications, namely, as
to the real character of the philosophical procedure of his predecessors, especially of Leibniz and Wolff; as to the measure of his
own divergence from them, in his conception of the nature and
scope of the ultimate criteria of truth; and as to the degree of essential novelty and originality that can be claimed for the Kantian system. In particular, the customary assumption of the validity of the
antithesis has brought about that many more or less instructed persons carry about with them, as their one firmly fixed philosophical
idea, the persuasion that between the method of philosophy in
vogue before Kant's day, and that in vogue since, there is a great
gulf fixed. I propose here to show that the antithesis in question is

seriously misleading, and to point out certain misrepresentations of historic facts, certain exaggerations and certain ambiguities in Kant's way of presenting it, and certain errors in those ideas about the criteria of truth employed in metaphysical reasoning, upon which the antithesis is based. Behind this simple and popular and apparently convincing scheme for classifying historic tendencies lies a very considerable, though not uncharacteristic, confusion in Kant's thinking. He was able to make so sharp the antithesis between his own and earlier systems only because he had been guilty of three rather singular oversights. In the first place, he had failed to hold clearly in mind what the doctrine of philosophical method held by his immediate predecessors had actually been. In the second place, he had failed to consider duly and define clearly the relation of his own doctrine to a familiar principle which has been the main and the generally accepted instrument of metaphysical reasoning, as well before his day as after it. And in the third place, he had forgotten —and most of his expositors have ever since overlooked—the fact that, of the special arguments in which he worked out his own "critical" method, the most important and ostensibly the most "critical"—namely, the argument about causality embodied in the Second Analogy of Experience—was merely an elaboration of an argument already employed by Kant's "dogmatic" predecessor, Wolff, from whom he seems unconsciously to have borrowed it.[1] These considerations will, I hope, throw an appreciable, and, if that be conceivable, a somewhat new illumination upon the limitations of Kant's thought and upon its historical connections. Now that the world, and especially the Germanic part of it, has ceased celebrating—not without a certain measure of unphilosophical *Schwärmerei*—the centenary of the worthy Koenigsberger's death, nothing, I take it, could be more fitting than that students of the history of thought should undertake a new inquest into the real originality, and the real value, of this central idea of the thinker who is credited, above all, with giving to philosophy a new and definitive method. The outcome of the inquiry will, I think, tend somewhat to qualify the conventional high estimate of Kant's importance, so far as the methodological question is concerned. Prof. William James has, in a public address, laid

---

1. This third point cannot be dealt with within the limits of this paper. The proof of it is offered in an article by the present writer in the *Archiv für Geschichte der Philosophie*.

hands on our father Parmenides with some boldness: "I believe," he says, "that Kant bequeaths to us not one single conception which is both indispensable to philosophy and which philosophy either did not possess before him, or was not destined inevitably to acquire after him, through the growth of men's reflection upon the hypotheses by which science interprets nature. The true line of philosophic progress lies, in short, not so much *through* Kant as *round* him, to the point where we now stand. Philosophy can perfectly well outflank him, and build herself up into an adequate fulness by prolonging more directly the older English lines." This is rather more than I care here to maintain; it is not so much from Kant's positive contentions as from his negations and his unfair reflections upon his precursors, that this paper will offer reasons for dissenting. Yet it is true, I think, that our present somewhat minute inquiry will make it evident that the tendency of Kant's influence has been to obscure or disguise the proper and the historic method of metaphysical reasoning, and to lead to the assumption of a breach of continuity in the secular working out of philosophical problems, where none really exists.

What Kant means by his antithesis is, of course, sufficiently clear. The distinction between dogmatism and criticism is represented as radical; and it has a perfectly definite technical character. A dogmatist, in the special sense, is a philosopher who deliberately goes about making synthetic judgments *a priori,* without first pausing to ask himself whether, or how, such judgments are logically possible. That is the definition of the creature; and of the motive which leads him to be such as he is, Kant gives a plain account in various passages of the *Transcendental Dialectic* and of the *Prolegomena.* The weakness in human nature which causes men to construct dogmatic systems of philosophy is the passion for completeness in the conception of things and in the explanation of their conditions, the disposition "to find for every conditioned an unconditioned and so to complete the unity of knowledge." The speculative metaphysician, in short, is the man who suffers from an uncontrolled craving for the absolute and ultimate. The reader of Kant cannot fail to derive the impression that the philosophical ambitions of earlier thinkers, and especially of the school in which Kant himself had been brought up, had been characterized by a general ignoring of limits, by a naïve assumption of the adequacy of the powers of human reason, and by a careless neglect to define the criteria of truth with either proper narrowness or proper explicitness. Kant's whole picture of the motives and the achievement of all constructive pre-Kantian metaphysicians is the picture of the motives and the achievement of an Icarus.

Now this picture is entirely in keeping with the view about metaphysics commonly held by the man in the street, and even by many natural scientists and some philosophers; but to anyone who will take the trouble to understand the inner springs of the historical movement of metaphysical reflection, it must seem an unintelligent caricature. The primary and exigent philosophic passion, as the history of philosophy displays it, is not the passion for completeness in the conception of the world of experience and of the conditions of it, but the passion for consistency and coherency in that conception. The greater philosophers have been distinguished not by a more insatiable lust for the synthesis of abstruse ideas but by a superior talent for the analysis of the common ideas used in all thinking. Philosophy begins, no doubt, in the case of a Thales or any similar pioneer, with a demand for completeness and ultimateness of explanation of given facts; but—if I may repeat what I have already remarked elsewhere—philosophy once begun is kept going and endlessly changing by the continual fresh discovery of latent inconsistencies in the accepted interpretations of experience. Every man is more or less disturbed at any intimations of the presence of such inconsistencies in his body of apparently settled opinions; and the philosopher, as he is usually exemplified in history, is merely the man who is peculiarly alert to this situation, and peculiarly—and, perhaps, unnecessarily—uncomfortable at finding himself in it. Often enough, no doubt, it has been some religious or practical need that has set him to looking for the contradictions in the current opinions; but in so far as his revision of those opinions has been philosophical, the motive that shaped it has been the demand for consistency in the explication of the conceptual necessities implicit in the facts of experience. We are not called upon here, however, to review the whole history of metaphysics; and it is therefore not possible to point out in detail how, at nearly all the great steps of philosophical transition, the method, both of metaphysical criticism and of metaphysical construction, has consisted in some special application of the two logical maxims involved in the principle of

contradiction, in its broader meaning: *that which, after the complet-*
est analysis of the ideas involved, implies the coinherence, in a
single subject, of concepts that the mind is incapable of combining
in thought, cannot be real, and *that proposition of which the oppo-*
site is, in the sense just specified, inconceivable or self-contradictory,
must be true.

It suffices for our present purpose to recall the manifest fact that
Kant's more immediate "dogmatic" predecessors, Leibniz, Wolff,
and Baumgarten, so far from constructing their metaphysical edi-
fices without first examining the foundations, had been entirely
explicit in naming the criterion of *a priori* knowledge, through the
use of which metaphysics was to be possible; [2] and had limited that
criterion to the single principle of contradiction—or, to give it a
name that better covers their full meaning, the principle of the
compossibility of concepts. There had, moreover, during the period
just before the appearance of the critical philosophy, been taking
place a progressive clearing up of the significance and scope of this
principle, and an especially determined effort to elucidate the whole
question of the nature of *a priori* judgments. Since this was the case
it will be of use to inquire, first, just what Leibniz and Wolff meant
by the principle of contradiction, especially in its relation to the
question of "the possibility of synthetic judgments *a priori*"; and,
second, to ascertain precisely what Kant's own views were about the
validity and the reach of that principle. We shall find the results of
such an inquiry somewhat surprising.

The principle of sufficient reason is still sometimes represented as
holding in the Leibnitian system an independent place, virtually
coordinate with the principle of contradiction. But in reality Leibniz
fully recognized that this principle can apodictically establish no
conclusions *a priori;* and Wolff either treated it as a special case of
the principle of contradiction, or else attempted to justify it by a
peculiar mode of argument, of which Kant would have been obliged to recognize the legitimacy on strictly "critical" grounds. With
the exception, then, of this last-mentioned argument, which cannot

---

2. In his criticism of Kant, Eberhard declared that "die Leibnitzische Philosophie ebensowohl eine Vernunftkritik enthälte, wie die Kantische; denn sie
gründe ihren Dogmatismus auf eine genaue Zergliederung der Erkenntnissver-
mögen." Upon this Kant remarked that, if such was the case then, indeed, "there
is no dogmatism in that philosophy, in the sense in which our Kritik always
employs the word" (*Reply to Eberhard,* 1te Abschn).

be dealt with here, Leibniz and Wolff rested the whole possibility of demonstrative proof or disproof in metaphysics upon the principle of contradiction, and professed to have no metempirical theoretical knowledge save such as could be gained through the use of that principle. Wolff takes pains to point out that even the Cartesian *cogito ergo sum* is nothing more than a special case of the sort of logical necessity which the principle establishes.

What, then, did these philosophers understand by the *Grund des Widerspruches?*

We must remember, to begin with, that Leibniz—a fact of which both Mr. Bertrand Russell and M. Couturat have made much, in their recent expositions of his doctrine—liked to call all judgments analytical, contingent ones no less than necessary; this because of the familiar truth of formal logic that the connotation of the predicate of a proposition is always embraced within the connotation of the subject. As M. Couturat points out, the whole metaphysics of Leibniz follows from the logical principle: "Dans toute vérité, universelle ou singulière, nécessaire ou contingente, le prédicat est contenu dans le sujet." But while Leibniz thus makes all judgments analytical in a sense, it is also true that he fully recognizes a distinction corresponding to Kant's distinction between analytic and synthetic judgments. Some predicates are contained in their subjects essentially and inextricably, so that, lacking those predicates, the subject would cease to be itself, would become an inconceivability; in other words, the concept, as a whole, is made up of a complex of attributes, some one or more of which are inconceivable without the others. In other cases, the inclusion of the given predicate with the several other predicates that make up the essence (or definition) of the subject is purely accidental; the several attributes do not coinhere of necessity. In the latter cases, the connection of predicate with subject can only be known *a posteriori;* the former class constitute the field where *a priori* reasoning is legitimate, and where necessary and eternal truths are to be looked for. It is, of course, true that Leibniz called propositions of this class identical propositions, their distinguishing mark being that their opposites involved self-contradiction. But by identity Leibniz did not really intend to mean mere tautology, and by contradiction he does not always signify merely verbal contradiction. It was, indeed, difficult for him to make out how he could mean anything else; but he was, nonetheless, firmly persuaded that the *Grund des Widerspruches* is no empty and sterile maxim but the fruitful source of important insights; and he especially (if not always very successfully) exerted himself to prove its positive utility. Thus he remarks (Gerhardt vii., p. 299) that though there may seem to be nothing but a *coccysmus inutilis* in identical propositions, yet *levi mutatione utilia inde axiomata nascuntur*. This, to be sure, is a somewhat *naïf* way of putting it, and the examples which follow are hardly convincing; but it all shows Leibniz's unwillingness to take his principle in its strict and narrow sense. There are, moreover, he maintains, two distinct kinds of judgment included within its range of application: (1) identical judgments, of which the opposite is formally self-contradictory, e.g., A is A; (2) judgments *virtualiter identicae,* of which the opposite can be seen to involve contradiction only *per terminorum intellectum et resolutionem*— that is, only by an examination of the whole implicit connotation of the terms involved, showing that the two notions are "incompossible." It is chiefly these latter, or "virtually identical," judgments which constitute the substance of our demonstrative knowledge, and especially of metaphysics. Demonstration consists in just the process of conceptual analysis whereby the implied content or meaning of two concepts is thus brought out with such definiteness as to make clear to the mind the impossibility of thinking them together, and therefore the necessity of thinking each of them and the opposite of the other together. "Virtually identical" judgments, to be sure, always bring us back *ad indenticas formales sive expressas,* that is, to propositions involving two "simple" concepts, the necessary coinherence of which, in the given proposition, is manifest because the opposite of that proposition involves an explicit and literal contradiction: "Manifestum est omnes propositiones necessarias . . . ad primas veritates revocari possunt, ita ut appareat oppositum implicare contradictionem et cum identica aliqua sive prima veritate pugnare" (Gerhardt vii., p. 300).

There is still, it is true, in all this a singular inconsistency, or failure in clear thinking, on the part of Leibniz, which Mr. Bertrand Russell has already noted (*Philosophy of Leibniz,* p. 18). If the *primae veritates* are literally "identical" propositions—A is A, B is not non-B—and if other necessary propositions are demonstrable only in so far as they are reducible (by the process of definition of the concepts involved) to such *primae veritates,* then nothing but identical propositions can be really demonstrable at all—the principle of contradiction can never help us to prove anything more than that a thing is itself and is not anything not-itself. And again, to note another aspect of Leibniz's confusion—if all demonstration consists in definition, and if definition is the analysis of complex concepts into truly simple ones—then, once more, between these simple concepts there can be no relations except those of identity and (mere) difference, and therefore no possibility of demonstrating any synthetic truths. For it is not clear how a genuinely simple concept can contain within itself the necessity for the coinherence with itself of other and distinct concepts, or even any special or preferential repugnancies towards any particular other concepts. If the fundamental concepts were really simple in their connotative content, they would be a sort of logical atoms, or windowless monads, capable, perhaps, of entering casually and contingently into any kind of intellectual combination, but not necessitated by their own nature to enter into (or to refuse) any. And so we could discover no really instructive logical relations between distinct ideas, could find in a given subject no necessary coinherence with any predicate except its own simple and unanalyzable self. And so, once more, no truly synthetic judgments *a priori* would be possible anywhere, even in mathematics; and metaphysics, possessing no means of demonstration except the Principle of Contradiction, would indeed be condemned to perpetual sterility.

We must, then, recognize this blunder in Leibniz's treatment of the Principle of Contradiction. By describing the judgments based upon that principle as "identical"—by regarding the relation between subject and predicate in such judgments as purely analytical, and then further treating both concepts as ultimately "simple" notions—he undeniably destroys by implication the possibility of constructive metaphysics; and by his confused thinking upon the point he is, unquestionably, largely responsible for Kant's aberrations in the matter of the distinction between synthetical and analytical judgments. But on the other hand, one must repeat that Leibniz intended no such result. He fully meant his Principle of Contradiction to be a positive and constructive principle; and if he habitually employs the sort of language that I have quoted, implying that there are no necessary relations between any two distinct simple concepts except that of bare non-identity, it is also true that there is an essential and frequently reiterated point in the Leibnitian system which implies exactly the contrary. This is to be seen in Leibniz's doctrine of definition. Definition consists in forming a complex idea by the conjunction, in a single meaning, of several simple ideas —or of less complex ideas which are ultimately resolvable into simple ones. The contrary process, as we have already seen, is analysis—the taking apart of the complex which definition puts together, and so the eventual discovery of the simple conceptual elements of which it is composed. Leibniz, now, on the one hand, always insists that the analysis of a definition must bring us to such simple and indefinable concepts; but on the other hand, he constantly insists that definition is not an arbitrary process but is always (when legitimately performed) limited from the outset by the requirement that the notions united shall be "compossible," compatible with one another.[3] But these two contentions taken together are equivalent to the assertion that there may subsist, even between ultimately simple and indefinable concepts, relations of incompatibility. For if there were no such relations of ultimate incompatibility, definitions *would* be arbitrary, and any conjunction of *positive* simple concepts into a single notion would be possible and legitimate. In such a case, though you would not be entitled to say that a triangle is a non-triangle, there would be nothing to prevent your saying that a triangle is a parallelogram. For if someone urged that a triangle is definable as a three-sided figure while a parallelogram has four sides, and that three-sidedness and four-sidedness are incompatible, one would have to ask: how, unless "simple" concepts have relations of fixed incompatibility *inter se,* can I know that what has three sides cannot have four sides? It could not be merely because the two concepts *are* two, i.e., merely distinct; for three-sidedness and whiteness are also distinct, yet no objection arises when I define a figure as a white triangle. If there are incompatibilities anywhere in definitions, they must inhere in the original elements, the primary concepts, of which the definition is made up; and if there were, contrariwise, no such original incompatibilities—self-evident,

3. Gerhardt iii., p. 443: "Les définitions ne sont point arbitraires, et on ne peut point former les idées comme l'on veut. Car il faut que ces idées qu'on prétend former soyent véritables, c'est-à-dire, possibles, et que les ingrédiens qu'on y met soyent compatibles entre eux." So frequently elsewhere.

not capable of being demonstrated by further definition, and not to be confused with mere non-identity—everything under heaven in the way of a definition would be permissible. In asserting, then, that definitions are not arbitrary, Leibniz plainly points to the affirmation of ultimate repugnancies to coinherence between distinct and positive concepts; and thus to the affirmation that *synthetic* relations of incompossibility, on the one hand, of necessary coexistence, on the other—are to be found, in some cases, between the ultimate and irreducible ideas upon which our thinking finally depends.[4]

As regards Leibniz, then, we must sum up the case thus: He sought to give definiteness and self-evidence to the method to be used in philosophical construction, by reducing the grounds of all *a priori* reasoning to a single principle. But in his treatment of this principle he fell into a twofold and inconsistent doctrine. On the one hand, in the pursuit of extreme rigor and simplicity in the definition of his ultimate criterion of truth, he tended to reduce it to the useless and trivial principle of the mere self-identity of concepts. But on the other hand, in another part of his imperfectly concatenated system, he plainly implied that there exist synthetic relations of compatibility and incompatibility between several distinct concepts, and that by the elucidation of these relations, important and significant truths *a priori* may be discovered. And in the form of this open choice between unharmonizable alternatives, Leibniz left the problem of metaphysical method to his successors.

What has rarely been remarked is that those successors—the immediate predecessors of Kant—took up the problem and gave a reasonably clear answer to it; that to the fundamental Leibnitian principle they gave an enlarged but an explicitly defined meaning, corresponding to the second and sounder of the alternatives suggested by Leibniz; that between this enlarged meaning and the narrower one from which Leibnitz had not fully distinguished it, they drew an unequivocal distinction, corresponding to Kant's distinction betwen synthetic and analytic judgments; that they thus answered in advance Kant's question: "How are synthetic judgments *a priori* possible?"—and answered it in a sense to which Kant could not consistently have made objection.

It was, of course, Wolff who accomplished this advance upon the position of Leibniz; Baumgarten and Kant's contemporary and

4. This point has already been clearly set forth by Mr. Russell (*Philosophy of Leibniz, loc. cit.*).

critic, Eberhard, did little more than rearrange or expand Wolff's ideas. What Wolff did was, in the first place, distinctly to abandon the theory that the only thing that you can logically discover *a priori* about any concept is that it must always mean whatever it happens to mean. On the contrary, he remarks in an instructive passage of the *Horae Subsecivae* (1730, vol. i, p. 154), we ought to recognize that there are such things as *notiones foecundae*—"pregnant concepts"—of which the peculiarity is that they contain *determinationes rei, per quas cetera quae rei conveniunt, colligi possunt;* in other words, they are such that *ex iis, quae in iisdem continentur, certa ratiocinandi lege colliguntur alia quae in iisdem non continentur.* It is because it is a fact of psychology that there are such pregnant notions, that we are able to frame a number of propositions *quarum praedicatis positis, ponuntur alia ejusdem rei praedicata.* Here, then, we find Wolff asserting that some ideas contain within themselves—inseparable from, yet not expressed in, their formally defined essence—necessary implications as to their relations of co-predicability or incompatibility with other ideas; and that meanings are thus organically interconnected.

Now in the technical logical and metaphysical treatises of Wolff and his school, the theory here implied as to the grounds of the legitimacy of synthetic judgments *a priori* is set forth with great fulness and definiteness—and copious iteration. In summarizing the doctrine I shall quote in part from the *Acroasis Logica* of Baumgarten, which, while following Wolff's expressions without significant deviation, is sometimes more concise and compact. Logic, says Baumgarten, taken in the strictest sense, is precisely the science which shows how knowledge *a priori* is to be had (*scientia cognoscendi a priori*). Now "whatever is known *a priori* is known *ex internis veritatis characteribus*"; by this is meant, in modern language, that the presence of *a priori* knowledge is to be verified essentially by a *psychological* fact, namely, the actual inability of the mind to divorce certain predicates from one another. There are two kinds of universal judgment, and only two, which are characterized by this inward compulsiveness or necessity. Whereas in all other judgments predication is justified only *a posteriori,* since the subject is, as such, found to be thinkable as a single coherent notion without the implication of the given predicate—in these two cases predication is necessary, and therefore valid universally and *a priori,* for the reason that the denial of the predicate carries with it for the mind the disappearance of the subject as a consistently definable and thinkable notion.[5] These two sorts of judgment *a priori* are distinguished from one another with respect to the manner in which the inseparability of predicate from subject is grounded. The first class is that of identical propositions, in which the predicate is merely the whole (*essentia*) or a part (*essentiale*) of the attributes included in the definition of the subject. Such propositions are, evidently enough, axiomatic, that is to say, necessary yet indemonstrable truths; but they are purely tautological and add nothing to our knowledge. The second class of axioms is the one which is made possible by the existence of *notiones foecundae,* and yields us, therefore, pregnant and instructive truths. Its logical character consists in this, that the predicate in such propositions is a "property" (*attributum, Eigenschaft*) of the subject. Whereas in the merely identical proposition, or definition, the several predicates are merely *put* together by the mind to make the chosen meaning, and do not co-determine the presence of one another, two "properties," on the other hand, *stick* together as inseparable *"joint-determinations"* of any subject into the definition of which either of them is introduced—even though the framer of the definition may have meant to admit only one of them into his proposed meaning.[6] The test of a "property," once more, lies in the subjective necessity of thinking the predicates together; no other test can be either had or imagined.[7]

Wolff, then, on the basis of this distinction between judgments

5. "Notæ entis sunt vel necessariæ et immutabiles, quibus sublatis tolleretur ens; vel contingentes et mutabiles, quæ possunt adesse et abesse salvo ente. Ad priores essentia, essentialia et attributa pertinent." From *Acroasis Logica* in Toellner's edition (1773), § 171. The preceding citations are from other sections of the same.

6. Wolff, *Philosophia rationalis sive Logica,* 1728, §§ 64, 65: "Ea quæ constanter enti cuidam insunt, quorum tamen unum per alterum non determinatur essentialia appello. . . . Ea quæ constanter insunt, sed per essentialia simul determinantur, attributa dico."

7. Wolff puts it thus in his German logical treatise: "Wenn nun zwei Gedanken so beschaffen sind, dass der andere notwendig statt findet, wenn man den ersten heget, oder dass ich mir das andere notwendig gedenken muss, wenn ich von einem Dinge das erste gedenke, indem nämlich durch das erstere das andere *mit determiniret* wird; so stimmen die Gedanken mit einander überein. Kann ich aber das andere von einem Dinge unmöglich gedenken, wenn ich mir das erste von ihm gedenke: so streiten meine Gedanken wider einander, oder einer widerspricht dem andern" (*Vernünftige Gedanken von den Kräften des menschlichen Verstandes,* 6te Aufl., 1731).

a priori per essentialia and judgments *per attributa,* adds to the enumeration of the axioms (underlying mathematics and metaphysics) that are purely identical, another class, not clearly recognized by Leibniz of a "pregnant" or synthetical character. "Si definitum sumitur ut subjectum, et de eo praedictatur quidpiam, quod notis ad definitionem spectantibus, in ejus notione animo praesente, indivulso nexu cohaeret: propositio axioma est" (*Philosophia rationalis sive logica,* § 273).

In view of all this we may well ask, as Eberhard asked, to Kant's great irritation, shortly after the promulgation of the critical philosophy: how can one say that the so-called "dogmatists" neglected to undertake a preliminary *Vernunftkritik,* or neglected to distinguish betwen analytic and synthetic judgments *a priori,* or neglected to show the logical justification of judgments of the latter sort? And if one accepts the principle upon which this last-mentioned justification rests, how is one entitled to reproach those who professed to found their metaphysics upon no other principle, for uncritical dogmatists?

These questions bring us to the essential issue upon the settlement of which must depend one's estimate of Kant's genuine originality and historic importance as an epistemologist. Metaphysical methodology had culminated just before his time in an explicit limitation of all *a priori* philosophizing within the range where the testing of propositions by the principle of contradiction,[8] in an enlarged sense, is possible, and in an equally explicit indication of just what that enlarged sense was to mean. It is therefore impossible for anyone to judge Kant intelligently, or to know where he stands historically, who has not determined the precise attitude which Kant took toward this Wolffian theory of knowledge. There are three possible positions which Kant might have assumed, in order to maintain, in some fashion, his charge of "dogmatism" against his forerunners; and it is essential to determine which of the three he adopted—or whether he wavered between two or more of them. He might, in the

8. I refer both forms of the *a priori* judgment, in the Wolffian classification, to the principle of contradiction, although the phraseology of different members of the school appears to be inconsistent upon this point. Eberhard, for example, prefers to label judgments *a priori per attributa* as examples of the "principle of sufficient reason." The question, however, is merely one of nomenclature; and Wolff himself certainly appears to me to intend the subsumption of both forms of *a priori* reasoning under the principle of contradiction.

first place, have held that the principle of contradiction, even in its narrowest Leibnitian sense, is not applicable to reality as such but only to the phenomena of experience; in this case the contrast between the "dogmatic" systems and the Kantian criticism would undeniably be radical. Kant might, again, have held that the principle is valid *a priori* for all Being, noumenal as well as phenomenal, but only in so far as it is purely analytical; that judgments based, not upon formal tautology or formal contradiction, but upon relations of coinherence or incompatibility between distinct and positive ideas are (as Wolff's language had suggested) synthetical; and that as synthetical, such judgments can have no *a priori* validity for *either* phenomena or noumena. In this case, also, he would have presented a fairly definite and significant, though somewhat paradoxical, antagonism to the method of Wolff and his school. Or, finally, Kant might have held that the principle is, in its fullest sense, valid *a priori;* that a judgment based upon the discovery of implicit incompatibilities between the subject and predicate of the contrary proposition, no less than one based upon explicit and verbal inconsistencies between them, is legitimate, and applicable to reality *überhaupt;* but that certain of the special conclusions concerning God, the soul, etc., which his predecessors had sought to justify by appealing to the principle, are not really inferrible by means of it. In this last case Kant could not properly have charged his predecessors with a radical error of method; he could fairly have charged them only with errors of formal logic, in the application of a valid method to certain special problems. And he could not in consistency have maintained that an *a priori* science of metaphysics is impossible; for he would virtually have admitted that metaphysical conclusions are possible wherever the principle of contradiction can be carried—wherever incompatibilities or necessary implications between ultimate concepts can be made out. Such are the issues, in the interpretation and criticism of Kant, which depend upon our answer to the question: which of these three positions did he actually assume?

Laas has already raised the inquiry whether Kant regarded the principle of contradiction in general as a valid criterion of the nature of reality *an sich;* and he has justly insisted that the point is one of capital importance.[9] "Upon a philosopher," Laas observes,

---

9. *Kant's Analogien der Erfahrung,* p. 33.

"who places between our world of time and space and the world of
reality as such a chasm so wide and deep that for the latter the most
conflicting possibilities remain open, it is decidedly incumbent to
give a definite answer to such questions as these: Is the formula (of
the impossibility of the self-contradictory) valid 'only in relation to
a sensuous perception'? Is its extension to things in themselves in-
admissible? Does it apply only to phenomenal existence? For who
would venture to declare that there are other forms of being besides those known to us, and then deduce from the mere concept of
Being the conclusion that all Being must be free from self-contradiction?" Important these questions certainly are; but there can be
no doubt about Kant's answer to them. His declaration on the subject is precisely the declaration of which Laas speaks. In both the
earlier and the later period of his thinking, Kant adheres consistently to the view that an object in which self-contradictory predicates are said to be united is not truly an object of thought at all,
but a mere *nihil negativum irrepraesentabile.* In his earliest philosophical writing, the *Dilucidatio Nova,* Kant, in criticizing the
customary Wolffian way of formulating the principle of contradiction, expresses only the more clearly his recognition of the importance of that principle in metaphysics. Under the name of a single
formula, he maintains, philosophers have really been making use
of two distinct principles, namely, *impossibile est idem esse ac non
esse* and *cujuscumque oppositum est falsum, illud est verum.* These
two are not, Kant thought, reducible to one another; but they are
equally and independently valid. As an instrument of philosophical
proof the latter is the more important. In the essay on the *Idea of
Negative Magnitude* Kant declares that the self-contradictory is
gar nichts; and in the paper on "The Only Possible Ground for a
Demonstration of the Existence of God" he writes: "All that is self-
contradictory is inherently impossible. . . . This logical repugnancy
I call the formal character of inconceivability (*Undenklichkeit*) or
impossibility." Similar expressions are abundant in the writings of
the so-called critical period; e.g., from the *Reply to Eberhard:*
"whatever does not agree with this principle (of contradiction) is
obviously nothing at all; for it is not even an idea (*Gedanke*)";
and from the *Progress of Metaphysics:* "anything of which the idea
is unthinkable, i.e., anything of which the concept contradicts itself, is an impossibility." The passage in the *Kr. d. r. V.* (first ed.,

p. 150) should be familiar: "Whatever the object of our knowledge may be, and whatever the relation between our knowledge and its object, it must always be subject to that universal, though merely negative, condition of all our judgments, that they do not contradict themselves. . . . The Principle of Contradiction is a general though negative criterion of all truth. . . . No cognition can run counter to that principle without destroying itself."

Kant's general recognition of the *a priori* validity and importance of the principle of contradiction as an absolute criterion of the nature of reality is thus unmistakable. Did he, however, accept the principle in one of those modified and restricted senses which I have indicated as open to him?

The answer must be that Kant's attempts, in the writings of the critical period, to tell what he takes the principle of contradiction to mean, are characterized not only by a curious vagueness and confusion of ideas but also by a persistent ignoring of just that distinction between the two kinds of judgment *a priori* which Wolff and Baumgarten had made so essential. One point, indeed, is clear: Kant always speaks of judgments resulting from the principle of contradiction as purely "analytical." This, however, does not settle much more than a question of nomenclature; the usage of Wolff's own disciples was not well settled upon this point. The important thing is not so much to determine whether the relation of predicate to subject in judgments *per attributa* can best be called analytical or synthetical—there are intelligible reasons for calling it either— but whether such judgments are legitimate at all, and what their logical nature is. And here Kant writes as if he had read nothing in German philosophy since Leibniz—and only a part of Leibniz.

For, in the largest class of passages on the subject, Kant goes on as if nobody had ever suggested the possibility of finding in judgments *per impossibilitatem contrarii* anything more than the *coccysmus inutilis* which even Leibniz had declared that they were not. In "analytical judgments," we are told, the connection of predicate with subject *durch Identität gedacht wird;* and hence "our knowledge is in no way extended by them," their only service being "to put the concepts that I already possess into better order, and to make them more intelligible to myself" (*Kr. d. r. V.*, first ed., pp. 7, 8). In the *Prolegomena* Kant goes so far as to say that the notion which serves as the predicate of such a judgment is actually always expressly present to the mind when the subject is thought; the judgment "expresses nothing in the predicate but what has already been *wirklich gedacht* (though not *ausdrücklich gesagt*) in the subject." Leibniz, in his narrowest definitions, would have avoided such language; for he at least placed judgments *virtualiter identicae* side by side with the purely tautological ones. And occasionally Kant himself remembers that concepts sometimes implicitly involve more than one happens, at any given moment, consciously to think in them. He then adds that the predicate of an analytical judgment may be contained in the subject "in a confused manner," or "without full consciousness." What this vague qualification precisely means Kant does not further explain. It apparently refers not to the implicit interconnection of "properties" in the connotation of an idea, but merely to the fact that people sometimes forget just what some of the *essentialia* are that they are accustomed to signify by a term. The qualification cannot, therefore, be construed as equivalent to the admission of the distinctness and the legitimacy of *a priori* judgments *per attributa*.

So far, then, and considering only Kant's principal writings, we must say not that Kant rejects the position of the "dogmatists" but that he neglects to face or to oppose it at all. With a degree of obtuseness rare in history, he entirely failed to apprehend the distinction that had been the principal result of the previous half-century of reflection upon the criteria of truth in mathematics and metaphysics—the distinction, namely, between *a priori* judgments *per essentialia* and *a priori* judgments *per attributa*—even though this distinction contained an answer to just the question which he himself declared to be the fundamental one in all philosophy. His attacks upon his predecessors implied that, having no criterion of truth *a priori* save the principle of contradiction in its narrowest analytical sense, they proceeded nonetheless (in their ignorance of Hume) to construct an *a priori* system of metaphysics. But since the criterion which they used was quite other, and since their reasons for accepting it had been carefully explained, Kant cannot be said to have brought any pertinent criticism to bear upon their position at all. The longer treatises nowhere make it certain that, if Kant had grasped the Wolffian distinction, he would not have accepted the Wolffian method.

Fortunately, however, Kant was reminded of this distinction by one of his contemporary critics; and in his reply to that criticism we find him at last brought to face the real issue. Eberhard's *Philosophisches Magazin,* during the brief period of its issue (1789-1790), was devoted chiefly to proving that Kant had not rendered Leibniz and Wolff obsolete, and that he even did not depart so widely from their doctrines as he appeared to suppose. It was in the execution of this task that Eberhard pointed out those obvious facts to which the present paper has again called attention. Long before Kant's *Kritik,* Eberhard insisted, a distinction equivalent to that between analytical and synthetical judgments had been familiar in the Wolffian school. "Analytical judgments are those whose predicates express the essence, or a part of the essence, of the subject (*das Wesen, oder einige von den wesentlichen Stücke, des Subjekts*); those of which the predicates express qualities that do not belong to the essence are synthetic." Now synthetic judgments are valid *a priori* when (and only when) "their predicates are 'properties' (*attributa*) of the subject, that is, determinations which do not belong to the essence of the subject, yet have their sufficient ground in that essence." When, now, this and much more of a similar sort had been publicly pointed out, it was manifestly incumbent upon Kant to define plainly his position with respect to the central epistemological doctrine of the Wolffians, which he had previously ignored.

Plain and unequivocal his answer [10] is not; yet in the end it amounts to an abandonment of his case against the "dogmatists." Here was Kant's opportunity, if he really wished to set his theory of *a priori* knowledge in sharp contrast with that of the older school, to say, in so many words: "I deny that the principle of contradiction is susceptible of the extension which Wolff has given to it; I do not recognize the existence of any such necessary relations of coinherence between distinct concepts, going beyond the purely formal necessity that a concept shall be identical with itself." But so far from doing anything of the sort, Kant readily accepts Eberhard's (that is, Wolff's and Baumgarten's) distinction between *essentialia* and *attributa,* and acknowledges that the latter are no less neces-

10. *Ueber eine neue Entdeckung, nach der alle Kritik der reinen Vernunft entbehrlich werden soll* (1790). To any who wish to understand Kant's relation to earlier logic and metaphysics, and so to determine his place in the history of those sciences, this *Reply to Eberhard* is one of the most important of his writings —for reasons that are made apparent in the text. It is, however, full of flounderings and self-contradictions.

sarily, though they are less directly, connected with their subjects, than are the former. In repeating and making his own Eberhard's classification of the ways in which predicates may be related to subjects *a priori,* Kant even proposes an emendation of the technical phraseology, which has the effect of bringing out all the more clearly the principle that, in *attributa,* we have predicates which do not belong to the definition of a concept, and yet cannot be negated of it without destroying its logical possibility. The passage runs as follows: "A predicate which is ascribed to any subject by an *a priori* judgment is thereby declared necessarily to belong to that subject, or to be inseparable from it. Such predicates are said to belong to the essence, or the inner possibility, of the concept (*ad internam possibilitatem pertinentia*). Consequently all propositions that profess *a priori* validity must have predicates of this character. All other predicates (those, namely, which are separable from the concept without destroying it) are called extra-essential marks of the subject (*ausserwesentliche Merkmale, extraessentialia*). Now predicates of the first sort may belong to the essence in two ways, either as constitutive elements of it (*Bestandstücke, constitutiva*), or as consequences of the essence that have in it their sufficient ground (*ut rationata*). The former are called essential elements (*wesentliche Stücke, essentialia*), and, as such, *contain no predicate that could be deduced from any other predicate contained in the same concept;* and in their totality *they make up the logical essence. The latter are called properties (Eigenschaften, attributa).*" Kant, then, here grants that there may be predicates, technically to be named *attributa rationata,* which form no part of the *essentialia* of a concept, as it is defined, but yet are indispensable to the *interna possibilitas* of it. This is merely another way of saying—which is the substance of the Wolffian theory—that not only tautological judgments but also judgments *per attributa,* are legitimate sources of *a priori* knowledge. And the whole realm of metaphysics, according to Wolff and (in his real intention) according to Leibniz, lay within the limits of this last-mentioned class of judgments, the possibility, validity, and potential fruitfulness of which Kant now admits.[11]

11. Paulsen has summarized this rather important part of the *Reply to Eberhard* in a footnote in his volume on Kant in the *Klassiker der Philosophie* (translation of Creighton and Lefevre, p. 143). Since the book is widely read, it is perhaps worth while to point out that here, as in several other instances, Paulsen goes

Kant, however, neither fully grasps nor long remembers the significance and bearings of his own admissions; and he attempts, furthermore, to save the originality of his doctrine by insisting upon two additional points in regard to these "judgments in which the predicates are inseparably connected with the subject, though not a part of its logical essence." To these two points the whole distinction between the "dogmatic" and the "critical" method now reduces itself.

(1) In the first place, Kant contends, Eberhard was wrong in regarding all judgments *per attributa* as synthetical. They may, he urges, be analytical; the distinction between "analytic" and "synthetic" runs, so to say, crosswise through them. Eberhard had supposed that any *a priori* judgment of which the predicate is an *attributum*—expressing, in Kant's words, something necessarily belonging to the subject, "yet only as a *rationatum* of the essence, not the essence itself nor any part of it"—is *ipso facto* shown to be synthetical in character. But in reality, Kant declares, "this shows nothing more than that the predicate (mediately, it is true, yet still as a consequence of the principle of contradiction) is drawn out from (*hergeleitet aus*) the concept of the subject; so that the proposition, notwithstanding the fact that it expresses an *attributum,* may still be analytic, and therefore lacks the distinguishing mark of a synthetical proposition." In thus arguing that some judgments of this sort are analytical, and are authorized by nothing less than the principle of contradiction, Kant commits himself to a still more thoroughgoing admission. He succeeds, indeed, in establishing a point of verbal opposition to Eberhard; but he at the same time gives up all grounds of real opposition to the substance of the Wolffian theory of *a priori* knowledge. For it now turns out that

somewhat seriously astray in his exposition. For he represents Kant as classifying predicables of the sort called *attributa* or *rationata,* among the *"extraessentialia,* which can be separated from the concept without affecting its nature." But Kant plainly and repeatedly classifies *attributa* as one of the two kinds of predicates that are *ad internam possibilitatem pertinentia,* inseparable from the concept (*vom Begriffe unabtrennlich*) and capable of being deduced from the essence of the concept as a necessary consequence thereof. Paulsen's error, however, is doubtless chiefly due to a characteristic awkwardness in Kant's own use of these technical terms. As Kant employs it, the term *essentialia* is not, as one would expect, the antonym to *extra-essentialia* and the equivalent of *ad essentiam pertinentia;* but is merely a species under the latter genus, the other species consisting of *attributa.*

judgments in which, by virtue of some necessary connection between the concepts, predicates (as Kant elsewhere puts it) are "developed out of" (*entwickelt aus*) the subject may be analytical, and
have the sanction of "the highest principle of all analytical judg
ments." But there is, as we have seen, nothing that Kant asserts
more emphatically and more unequivocally than that all analytical
judgments, involving the principle of contradiction, are valid *a
priori* of all possible reality, and in need of no further justification
or explanation. Kant, in short, for once abandons (though only to
resume it on the next page) his usual language about analytical
propositions and includes within their range some judgments *per
attributa,* which include distinctly more than need be *wirklich
gedacht* in the original conception of their subject. As for the mere
question of phraseology, we need not further discuss whether Kant
or Eberhard is right. Eberhard had sensibly remarked—what Kant
could never be brought to recognize—that "the controversy as to
whether a proposition is analytical or synthetical is a controversy
of no importance for the determination of the logical truth of the
proposition." [12] What is important is the determination of the question whether or not there really subsists between two given concepts,
not defined as identical in essence, such a relation that, if the first
is negated of the second, the latter becomes unthinkable within the
terms of its *own* essence. When this is admitted—and Kant now
admits that such a relation is possible—the rest is merely a dispute
as to the sort of metaphor which may most felicitously express this
logical fact.

(2) Thus far Kant has committed himself to the admissions (*a*)
that some propositions in which the predicates are *attributa rationata* of the subject, are analytical; (*b*) that all analytical propositions
are true *a priori* of reality in general. He further urges, however,
that some propositions containing *attributa* as predicates are synthetical; and he insists that none of his precursors had shown—as he had
done—how, in this case, such propositions can be known to be valid.
Here Kant evidently has in mind the theorems of mathematics.
These, he was sure, could only be called synthetical propositions;
and if synthetical, they required some justification other than what
Baumgarten would have called "the internal marks of truth," their
actual coinherence in the mind. This justification Kant believed that

12. *Philosophisches Magazin,* 1789, p. 331.

he alone had discovered, in his celebrated doctrine of the *a priori* percepts. The reason why synthetical judgments are possible *a priori* is that they are mediated through a *reine Anschauung*. Here is where Kant finally endeavors to come to a really significant issue with his critic; and it is desirable to hear his own words, which, in part, are not susceptible of adequate translation: "Wenn gesagt wird, dass ich sie über die gegebenen Begriffe hinaus, auch ohne Erfahrung, vermehren, d. i. *a priori* synthetisch urteilen könne, und man setzte hinzu, dass hierzu notwendig etwas mehr erfordert werde, als diese Begriffe zu haben, es gehöre noch ein Grund dazu, um mehr, als ich in jenen schon denke, mit Wahrheit hinzutun . . . so will ich wissen, was denn das für Grund sei, der mich, ausser dem, was meinem Begriffe wesentlich eigen ist und was ich schon wusste, mit mehrerem und zwar notwendig als Attribut zu einem Dinge Gehörigen, aber doch nicht im Begriffe desselben Enthaltenen bekannt macht." [13] In so far as they are synthetic, then, we must look farther for a "ground of the possibility" of these judgments containing *attributa* as predicates. But, now, "anyone may see that, in what I have already set forth as the summary result of the whole analytical part of the Kritik of the Understanding, I have therein explained, with all needful explicitness, the principle of synthetic judgments in general, namely: that they are not possible except under the condition of a perception underlying their subject—one which, when they are *a posteriori* judgments, is empirical, and when they are synthetic judgments *a priori* is a pure *a priori* percept. . . . Compare now with this the pretended principle which is presented in Eberhard's account of the nature of synthetic judgments *a priori:* 'They are judgments which affirm of the subject one of its *attributa* —that is to say, a predicate which necessarily but only derivatively (*nur als Folge*) belongs to the subject.' . . . Now one is justified in asking whether the ground for the affirmation of the predicate is to be sought for in the subject, according to the principle of contradiction—in which case the judgment would still be merely analytical; or whether the predicate is incapable of being deduced from the concept of the subject by the principle of contradiction—in which case the *attributum* is purely synthetic. Thus neither the name 'attributum' nor the principle of sufficient reason serves to distinguish

---

13. Kant appears to have forgotten that, a few pages earlier, he had explained to us how predicates not contained in the essence may, by the principle of contradiction, be "developed out" of a concept analytically.

synthetical from analytical propositions; if the former are to be affirmed *a priori,* one could say no more of them (according to this phraseology) than that their predicate is somehow or other grounded in the essence of the concept of the subject—and is therefore a 'property'—but not simply in consequence of the principle of contradiction. But how, as a synthetic property, this predicate comes to be bound up with the concept of the subject—when it cannot be *drawn out* of the subject by analysis—cannot be explained by the concept of a 'property,' so that Herr Eberhard's account of the matter is wholly barren. But the *Kritik* clearly sets forth this ground of the possibility of such propositions, showing that it can be nothing but the pure percept underlying the concept of the subject. Only in such a pure percept is it possible to connect a synthetic predicate with a concept *a priori.*"

Thus the theory of the *reine Anschauung* constitutes the last trench into which Kant retires to defend his antithesis of dogmatism and criticism. About this theory three things may be said, of which only the two last are indispensable to our present inquiry. First, the whole idea of a "pure" percept, which we are under no conditions to be allowed to think as a concept, and which gets some peculiar demonstrative efficacy from its perceptual character—is a logical chimera that belongs with the other hybrid monsters of antiquity. But this is unimportant. Second, and what is more to the point, the theory, though it were true, is, by Kant's own showing, not essential to the proof of the logical validity of the *a priori* judgments in question; and it is therefore irrelevant to the issue. Wolff and Baumgarten had, in effect, declared that, when you have analyzed your concepts to the uttermost and still find that two of them, not defined as possessing the same essence, coinhere *indivulso nexu,* you have reached the ultimate point of verification; beyond this *de facto* psychological necessity, this "internal mark of truth," it is both needless and impossible to go.[14] Now even if it be a fact that a *reine Anschauung* "underlies" our mathematical judgments,

14. This must not be understood as implying that there is anything in common between the Wolffian theory of knowledge and the uncritical affirmation of anything of which one has "clear and distinct ideas" or a strong "emotion of conviction." The prior analysis of concepts is presupposed, the careful framing of definitions, the clear discrimination of the several sorts of predicables, and the testing of *attributa* by the attempt to think the given definition with the given *attributum* negated But the Wolffian logicians had rightly maintained that the touchstone in this final test can be nothing but the ultimate and inexplicable mental fact that the proposed negation is actually unthinkable.

a knowledge of this fact is not necessary in order to establish the truth of those propositions *a priori* (in so far as they *are* true *a priori*); nor does ignorance of the fact subtract anything from the evidence of their truth. The fact would be an interesting piece of psychological information; but the truth of the propositions, as propositions *a priori,* would still require to be tested by inquiring whether, when the meaning of the concepts involved, *as concepts,* is fully understood, the contraries of the propositions prove to be inconceivable. All of which is admirably illustrated by Kant's own procedure when, in the *Kritik,* he undertakes to prove that Space and Time *are* pure percepts underlying the concepts of mathematics. He does it by showing that in mathematical judgments the predicates are "necessarily and universally" connected with the subjects *a priori* and yet are not discoverable by a mere analysis of the definitions of the subjects. Geometry, for example, "is a science which determines the properties of Space synthetically and yet *a priori.* What, then, must the idea of Space be, in order that such a knowledge of it should be possible? It must, primarily, be a perception; for out of a mere concept no propositions can be drawn which go beyond the concept itself [15]—as do the propositions of geometry. But this perception must be found in us *a priori,* and hence, must be a pure, non-empirical preception. For geometrical propositions are all apodictic, that is, they involve the consciousness of their own necessity; and such propositions cannot be empirical" (second ed., p. 41). Evidently, however, since the supposed fact that Space is a *reine Anschauung* is inferred from the fact that geometrical theorems are necessary *a priori,* the necessity and apriority of those theorems cannot in turn depend upon a proof that Space is a *reine Anschaunng.* Kant here, in a word, not only accepts the logical method of the "dogmatists" but even uses it to establish that principle which, so far as mathematical reasonings are concerned, is in the same sentence supposed to show the illegitimacy of their logical method. His own language exhibits better than any commentary how irrelevant is the doctrine of the pure percepts to the epistemological questions concerning the criteria of *a priori* knowledge, which are the only questions at issue between himself and the Wolffians. And now, in the third place, the theory that judgments

15. Note again that this is inconsistent with the admissions which Kant makes in the *Reply to Eberhard.*

a priori presuppose a pure percept, refers only to mathematical judgments; and it therefore does not affect Kant's admission, already noted, that there may be valid *a priori* judgments of which the predicates are (like those in mathematics) *attributa rationata,* but which—being sufficiently explained by the principle of contradiction—do not require the mediation of any such pure percept.

Only one point more needs to be touched upon. It may be urged, in Kant's behalf, that he at least is distinguished from his predecessors—and is more "critical" than they—in that he limits the scope even of our valid *a priori* judgments to "objects of possible experience," and professes no knowledge of the transcendent. Upon this much might be said, if space permitted; but I must limit myself to two remarks. One is that, in Kant's own eyes, it is not upon this consideration that his distinction of "criticism" from "dogmatism" turns, but upon the question how, even within the narrower range, non-identical judgments may be justified *a priori.* The other remark is that Kant himself, as we have already seen, affirmed that no reality whatever "can possess the formal character of *Undenklichkeit,"* that is, can correspond to a logically "impossible" and self-contradictory concept. And inasmuch as he at first fails to deny, and in the end somewhat confusedly admits, that other predicates besides those contained in the definition of a concept may be involved in its *interna possibilitas,* and that other propositions besides tautological ones may be tested by the criterion of the inconceivability of their opposites—it must be said that, even on this point, Kant did not successfully differentiate his position from that of Leibniz and of Wolff.

And thus the whole distinction between "criticism" and "dogmatism"—in so far as it is intended to correspond to an historical contrast between Kant and his German predecessors—falls to the ground. The "dogmatists" were not, in Kant's sense, dogmatic; Kant, in his principal writings, did not refute or even attack their real doctrine of the grounds of the legitimacy of non-identical propositions *a priori;* when eventually compelled by Eberhard to define his attitude to that doctrine, he accepted—though evidently without quite knowing what he was about—the essential principle of it; and he was himself unable to formulate any different doctrine of the grounds of the validity of such propositions—since the theory of the *reine Anschauung,* even in the restricted field where it applies, expressly presupposes the *a priori* legitimacy of synthetic judgments in mathematics, and so cannot be regarded as the logical ground of their legitimacy. Finally, by his inability to deny the general applicability to all reality of the principle of contradiction, in its wider as well as in its more literal use, Kant undermined in advance his professedly negative and agnostic position with respect to the possibility of metaphysics as a theoretical science.

KANT AND THE PROBLEM

OF METAPHYSICS

REMARKS ON MARTIN HEIDEGGER'S
INTERPRETATION OF KANT [1]

Ernst Cassirer

§

In February 1772 Kant reported in a letter to Markus Herz that his investigations of the form and the principles of the sensuous and the intelligible worlds had taken a new and decisive turn—a turn through which he thought he had in his possession now, after long searching and wavering, "the key to all of metaphysics, which was up to that time concealed to itself." He now conceived the problem of the "transcendental object" as the core of metaphysics. The question, "What is the ground of the relation to the object of that in us which is called representation?" now became the central point of philosophy. It created the new intellectual orientation out of which the plan of the *Critique of Pure Reason* grew and in regard to which it was carried out. This new orientation constitutes the content and the basic meaning of Kant's "Copernican Revolution." Now it was no longer a matter of adding a further system of metaphysics to those already on hand—to find, that is, a new answer to questions which had long existed. The transformation and reformation go deeper: they do not pertain to the answers of metaphysics but rather to its own basic conception and its basic problem. Its path had to change because its goal had moved to another

---

1. *Kant und das Problem der Metaphysik,* Bonn, 1929.

position—because the "object" which it wants to know and to which it accords had shifted. And this shift means something different and something more radical than that the object had only changed its position, as it were, in the otherwise firm intellectual atmosphere. Rather, it was a matter of the constitution and structure of this intellectual atmosphere as such. The shift contained a new view, not only of what is known and what is knowable, but of the nature, task, and basic function of knowledge itself.

But here, where we are standing at the threshold of the *Critique of Pure Reason,* the battle of interpretations breaks out. Nothing is more problematic and more controversial than the decision that Kant made at this point. As early as Kant's own lifetime the interpretations of his doctrine stood sharply opposed to one another. To the older generation it appeared as the destruction and devastation of metaphysics: Mendelssohn was expressing a widespread attitude when he complained about Kant as the "destroyer of everything." But there are others, those who are younger scholars, who want to see in the *Critique of Pure Reason* nothing else than a preliminary exercise or "propaedeutic." They enthusiastically greet there the dawn of a metaphysics that is to come. Since that time the judgment about Kant's own position toward metaphysics has continually wavered. Was Kant the critic of reason, the logician and methodologist of scientific knowledge? Or was the *Critique* for him only the point of departure of a set of problems that are directed quite differently? Did he bury metaphysics or only arouse it to a new life? In their answer to these questions, minds and epochs differ from one another. Whoever took up the study of Kantian philosophy approximately a generation ago could, to be sure, get the impression that the question had finally been settled—as if a generally recognized and philologically final conviction—if not of the content of Kant's doctrine then at least of its form—had been formed regarding its logical and methodological character. For all prominent representatives of Neo-Kantianism were agreed about at least one point: that the emphasis of Kant's system is to be sought in its epistemology, that the "fact of science" and its "possibility" constituted the beginning and the goal of Kant's problem. In this formulation of the question and in it alone were the scientific character and eminence of Kant's doctrine founded. This interpretation (for example, in Aloys Riehl's inaugural address at Freiburg,

"Concerning Scientific and Non-Scientific Philosophy"—1883) was expressed in programmatic sharpness and pregnance. Riehl takes as his point of departure that the task of a philosophy that lays claim to the name of a strict science can consist in nothing else than in the grounding of a general doctrine of principles. Only here does philosophy find the field that is peculiar to it and the calling that is appropriate to it. Only the science of knowledge gives it a genuine inner certainty. Only it can free philosophy from fumbling around in mere opinions and give it a firm hold, a lasting foundation. Riehl did not conceal from himself the fact that a large area of questions which had traditionally been customarily assigned to philosophy was thereby excluded from this area. But he looked upon this exclusion as a sacrifice that we must make if we want to preserve the purely scientific character of philosophy. One thing appeared to him as the error which the modern period had taken over from Greek philosophy: that philosophy can and should be more than mere science—that it should include, at the same time, a way of looking at the world and develop it in systematic form. "The relations of general scientific attitudes to man, especially their relation to the demands of his spirit, make out of those attitudes a way of looking at the world." This relation, this application to man, is, according to Riehl, unavoidable; but it does not constitute an object of strictly scientific construction of concepts. And, accordingly, it also lies outside the area of philosophy. "Ways of looking at the world are . . . no affair merely of the understanding. They address the entire man, all aspects of his being. The spirit, not the understanding, is their genuine originator. They are, therefore, predominantly subjective and not a task of science. Ways of looking at the world do not belong . . . to science but to belief. . . . In so far as the requirement of a system of knowledge is justified, it is fulfilled, if only approximately, by science itself. In so far as the way of looking at the world can be objectively founded, this grounding likewise devolves upon science. Its subjective part exceeds the bounds of mere science. *Philosophy as a system and a way of looking at the world is thus not a science.*" [2]

I intentionally place these sentences of Riehl at the beginning of the discussion. For they mark the opposition—with a sharpness

2. A. Riehl, *Über wissenschaftliche und nichtwissenschaftliche Philosophie.* (*Philosophische Studien.* Leipzig, 1925, p. 232f.)

and clarity that can hardly be excelled—that obtains between Heidegger's interpretation of the central task of metaphysics and the mode of thought and philosophical persuasion of the "criticism" that is positivistically directed and oriented. Heidegger fights nothing so forcefully and passionately as this mode of thought—than the assumption that Kant's essential goal consisted in grounding metaphysics on epistemology. Heidegger attacks the assumption that Kant wanted even in part to give such an epistemology. This assumption is supposed to be "finally defeated" through Heidegger's interpretation. (221)[3] The intention of the *Critique of Pure Reason,* according to him, remains fundamentally misunderstood if one interprets this work as a "theory of experience" or even as a theory of the positive sciences. (16) This path could never lead to the discovery of the metaphysical problem. For the sense of this problem cannot be approached from mere logic; nor can it be fitted into a "logic of pure knowledge." Metaphysics is essentially a doctrine of being—ontology. All questions about being, however, lead finally to the one question about man. Thus the problem of metaphysics transforms itself into this one radical question. The question about human existence must precede all questions about existence in general. Questions about human existence constitute the object of the genuine, of fundamental ontology. "Fundamental ontology is that ontological analytic of finite human existence that is to prepare the foundation for the metaphysics which belongs to the nature of man. Fundamental ontology is the metaphysics of human existence which is necessarily required for making metaphysics possible. It remains fundamentally different from all anthropology—even philosophical anthropology. To explicate the idea of a fundamental ontology means to show the characterized ontological analytic of existence as a necessary requirement and thus to make clear in what way, in what limitation, and under which assumptions it asks the concrete question: *what is man?"* (1) This question and no other, according to Heidegger, aroused and inwardly moved Kant, determining the direction of all of his metaphysical investigations. When he plunges into the analysis of the human "faculty of knowledge," he never loses himself in this analysis. It is not for him an end in itself but rather a mere means:

3. The numbers without further specifications always refer in what follows to the page numbers of Heidegger's book on Kant.

insight into the essence of man, into the mode and the sense of his "existence," is supposed to be derived from the insight into the form of human knowledge. "The question which is necessary for the foundation of metaphysics, what man is, is taken over by the metaphysics of existence." Kant's own, properly understood result lies in the uncovering of this connection of problems—of the connection "between the question of the possibility of *ontological synthesis* and the uncovering of the *finitude* in man, that is, in the demand of a reflection concerning how a metaphysics of existence is to realize itself concretely." (221f.)

It would be idle and pointless to dispute with Heidegger about this first and basic statement of his problem or to dispute with him about the choice of his point of departure. If any kind of form of philosophical discussion is to be possible or in any sense fruitful, the critic must decide to place himself on the ground which Heidegger has chosen. Whether he can remain on this ground is a question that is to be decided only through the discussion itself. But he must move to that ground so that criticism does not degenerate into mere polemic and in a constant talking at cross purposes. A polemical discussion of that sort, as I should like to emphasize from the very outset, is quite foreign to me. And I do not feel moved to it, although Heidegger has obviously in no way done justice to the historical service of Neo-Kantianism, and especially to the fundamental interpretation that Hermann Cohen has given in his books on Kant. On this score, however, I should not like to quarrel with him. For here we are not concerned with historical justice but solely with material and systematic correctness. And when Heidegger demands of us that we thoroughly "re-learn" Kant, it is just a Kantian who will least of all withdraw from and set himself against this demand. "I am not of the opinion of a prominent man," Kant himself once said, "who recommends that one no longer doubt that of which one has already convinced himself. That does not work in pure philosophy. One must . . . consider propositions in all sorts of applications . . . attempt to assume the opposite and thus to delay until the truth breaks in from all sides." [4] Thus no one should repose in the dogmatic certainty of possession of Kant's philosophy. Rather, one should seize every opportunity to acquire this knowledge anew. Heidegger's book con-

4. *Reflexionen Kants zur Kritik. d.r. Vernunft,* ed. by Benno Edmann, Nr. 5.

cerns an attempt at such a new acquisition of Kant's fundamental position. And the following considerations are to concern this attempt and exclusively this attempt. The mere opposition of "standpoints" seems, indeed, to be one of the favorite forms of philosophical discussion. But it has always seemed to me to be one of the most unrefreshing and unfruitful. That rule must be applied here which Kant himself established and which he declared to be binding on himself. "In judging the writings of others, one must choose the method of participation in the general cause of human reason and search out that which pertains to the whole from the attempt. If one finds it worthy of examination, one should offer the author, or rather his best representative, a helping hand and treat the errors as secondary." [5] I should like to place the following discussion under this maxim. I should not like to have it understood as a defense of or an attack on any kind of philosophical "standpoint" but would rather ask that the reader consider and judge it in the spirit of the "method of participation in the general cause of human reason."

I. THE FINITUDE OF HUMAN KNOWLEDGE AND THE PROBLEM OF THE "TRANSCENDENTAL IMAGINATION"

Heidegger designated the problem of the finitude of human knowledge as the central theme of Kant's criticism of reason. In the determination of this finitude and in the constant consciousness of it lies, according to him, the decisive mark in virtue of which Kant's doctrine is distinguished from all Pre-Critical, dogmatic systems. Kant does not begin with a theory about the general essence of things; rather, he begins with the question concerning the essence of man. And he finds the answer to this question in bringing to light the specific finitude of man: *"The foundation of metaphysics is grounded in the question concerning the finitude in man and, in such a way, that this finitude can only now become a problem.* The foundation of metaphysics is a 'breaking up' (analysis) of our (finite) knowledge into its elements." (208) It must remain the primary task of metaphysics, not merely to describe and "explain" being as such, but rather to show the essential connection that ob-

5. *Kants Reflexionen,* Nr. 46.

tains between being and the finitude in man. (212) That is the
character and the specific peculiarity of human reason: that its most
intimate interest is directed not to the absolute or "things in themselves" but to finitude itself. It is thus concerned not to extinguish
this finitude but rather to become certain of it in order to remain
in it. (207) But, seen in a purely methodological way, what does
this finitude mean, and how does it express itself in the manner
and character of knowledge? Kant also gave the clear and univocal
answer. This answer manifests itself in the fact that all human
knowledge is dependent upon intuition and that all intuition is
"receptive," that it consists in a primary "acceptance." While
human understanding knows "objects" and places them before
itself, such an understanding is not the creator of these objects.
This understanding does not permit them to emerge in their being
but rather contents itself with their "representation" and "presentation." Thus it is not an archetypal but rather an ectypal understanding—*intellectus ectypus,* not *intellectus archetypus.* Kant
everywhere places the strongest emphasis on this opposition. He
succeeds in setting forth the essence of finite human knowledge
sharply and clearly only by explicating this essence through a contrast with the idea of infinite divine knowledge. Divine knowledge
is *intuitus originarius.* It does not have any kind of objects as mere
"objects," as something before or beyond it. It is rather to be conceived as the source of being, as that which brings the being into
its existence and assists in its origin (*origo*). As opposed to this,
human understanding—as derivative—never permits being to arise
in this sense. Human understanding directs itself to a being that is
already present and is somehow given. The means of "giving" is
intuition—to give an object, Kant explains, means nothing else
than to relate it to intuition, either real or possible. In this consists
the original and essential dependence of all derivative knowledge.
"Finite intuition cannot . . . receive unless that what is to be received presents itself. Finite intuition must essentially be affected
by what is intuitable in it." (21, 23)

If we remain with this as the point of departure of Kant's doctrine, all following doctrines must, according to Heidegger, be related to it and interpreted from it. It is thus unmistakable that
Kant does not remain with the mere "receptivity of intuition" but
rather that he places a pure "spontaneity of the understanding" at

its side. Indeed, in the course of his Deduction, he develops this spontaneity more sharply and emphasizes it increasingly. But this emphasis must be understood and directed in such a way that it does not contradict the original approach of the Kantian problem. The emphasis can always be understood as only a certain characterization of the finitude of knowledge, not as its denial and destruction. That "ascent" of knowledge that appears to take place when we go from sensibility to understanding and from understanding to reason can never mean that we are lifted by its means at all beyond the sphere of finitude or that we can ever leave our finitude behind us. The original connection with intuition can never be removed. The dependence that is conditioned by it cannot be removed. The chain of finitude is not to be broken. All thought as such—even the purely logical use of the understanding—carries the stamp of finitude. Indeed, this is its seal. For all thought needs, as discursive thought, a detour, a view of something general through which and from which the plural particular becomes conceptually representable. "This discursive character which belongs to the essence of the understanding is the sharpest index of its finitude." (26) And it is, finally, no different with reason—with the entire sphere of the knowledge of ideas. Human reason is finite, not only from without, but even in a certain sense from within: finitude encompasses it not merely like a limitation that is accidentally set which is met by reason in its activity. Rather, reason is posited in just this activity itself. All of reason's inquiry and questioning are grounded in finitude: "it [reason] asks these questions because it is finite, and finite in such a way that reason is concerned with this finitude in its being as reason." (207f.) However high reason appears to lift itself beyond experience, it can never simply transcend experience. For transcendence as such is also *a priori* sensuous. And human pure reason is necessarily a pure sensuous reason. (164)

What emerges from all of this is that the entire analytic cleavage that Kant carries out, the threefold division of knowledge into sensibility, understanding, and reason, has a merely provisional character. It does not lead us into the center of Kant's problem but is rather only a means and vehicle of the mode of presentation. There really do not exist for Kant three different faculties of knowledge which are sharply separated from one another. Rather, they are all originally unified in a fundamental faculty. Heidegger seeks

to show that the transcendental faculty of imagination is this original unifying faculty and is thus the source out of which intuition
and concept, understanding and reason, arise. Transcendental imagination is not merely something that combines and mediates in a
supplementary manner. Rather, it is the constitutive center of the
entire *Critique of Pure Reason*. The doctrine of the pure faculty of
imagination and its schematism constitutes the decisive stage in
Kant's laying of the foundations of metaphysics: the chapter on
schematism "leads into the core of the entire problem of the *Critique of Pure Reason* with unparalleled certainty." (107) Both pure
intuition and pure thought must, if they are to be understood in
their peculiar function, be traced back to transcendental imagination
and determined and illuminated in terms of it. (130) Transcendental Aesthetic and Transcendental Logic, when taken by themselves, are basically unintelligible: both have only a preparatory
character and they can really be read only from the perspective of
transcendental schematism. (cf. 137) The proof of this basic relationship constitutes the main task and the core of Heidegger's
analysis.

And it must be at once emphasized and recognized that he has
carried out this part of his task with extraordinary power and with
the greatest sharpness and clarity. It has always seemed to me to be
the strangest sign of a complete misunderstanding of Kant's fundamental intention that one constantly encounters the conception in
the Kant literature that Kant artificially constructs the doctrine of
schematism—that he introduced the faculty of transcendental imagination for merely external reasons of symmetry and architectonics.
Perhaps this charge will finally be recognized in its absurdity when
one enters into Heidegger's detailed presentation, which works out
every individual feature of the chapter on schematism. On this
point I myself can only emphasize complete agreement with Heidegger's interpretation. For the doctrine of the productive imagination seems to me—although from a completely different systematic
standpoint—to be a simply indispensable and an infinitely fruitful
motive of Kant's doctrine as well as of the entire critical
philosophy.[6]

One thing must, to be sure, be emphasized immediately which

6. For further information see the third volume of *Die Philosophie der sym-
bolischen Formen*, Part II.

must not be forgotten, if we want to understand and interpret the doctrine of the finitude of knowledge in Kant's own spirit. This doctrine, too, must be seen under the double point of view which Kant establishes for all investigations in the field of transcendental philosophy and which he retains throughout. In such investigations we must always direct our view to two different goals. We must separate sensuous and intelligible worlds, experience and Idea, phenomena and noumena from one another and keep both areas carefully separate from each other. Kant's characterization of the finitude of knowledge receives its full sense only under this two-fold aspect. Heidegger sees the essential element of this finitude in the fact that human understanding does not create its objects but rather receives them—that it does not bring them forth in their existence but that it must content itself with forming a picture of this existence and holding this before itself in anticipation. But transcendental philosophy as such does not pertain to this relation, does not pertain to the absolute existence of objects and the absolute ground of their being. It does not deal with objects and their origin but rather the mode of knowledge of objects in general, in so far as this is possible *a priori*. The representation of a divine understanding, of an *intuitus originarius,* can be used as a correlative concept for the determination of this mode of knowledge and for its specific differentiation and delimitation. But in this case the representation does not designate a special intelligible object but is rather an understanding that is "itself a problem. For we cannot in the least represent to ourselves the possibility of an understanding which should know its object, not discursively through categories, but intuitively in a non-sensible intuition." (*Critique of Pure Reason,* B 311) Such a problem is not a material boundary which our knowledge comes upon. It is a limiting concept which is constructed by our knowledge itself and which our knowledge holds before itself in order to limit the presumption of sensibility. The idea of a divine, creative understanding which creates the objects that it knows is in this sense admissible. But, on the other hand, the divine understanding cannot be driven beyond its negative use. (*ibid.*) At the same time, however, knowledge cannot by any means be designated as receptive or merely finite in so far as it does not reach to exaggerated heights but rather moves in the peculiar area which is assigned to it. Here, in the area of experience and its phenomena, it possesses a thoroughly creative character. Although it cannot create an absolute existence or derive such an existence from its concepts, knowledge is the foundation of that order and lawfulness of appearances that we intend when we speak of nature as empirical. In this sense the understanding always remains the originator of nature—not as a thing in itself but of the existence of things in so far as it is determined according to general laws. Thus the limitation of the understanding shows most strongly its indestructible spontaneity—its genuine and not merely derived creative power. When the understanding refers to intuition, it does not make itself absolutely dependent upon intuition nor does it subordinate itself to intuition. Rather, it is just this relation that includes in itself the positive force of every formation and determination of intuition. It is the synthesis of the understanding that lends definiteness to sensibility and that makes it possible for sensibility to relate to an object. The objectivity that we ascribe to knowledge is, therefore, always an achievement of spontaneity, not of receptivity. Heidegger insists that, according to Kant, all thought has "merely an ancillary position with respect to intuition." He holds that intuition constitutes the genuine essence of knowledge in the reciprocity of the relation between intuition and thought and thus possesses the real weight. But even if one wanted to concede this interpretation of the merely ancillary position of thought, there would still be a distinction to be made. With respect to the well-known saying that philosophy is the handmaiden of theology, Kant once said that one could concede this in any case; but one must then always ask the question whether philosophy is the maiden that carries the train of the lady or rather the maiden who precedes her with a torch. And he saw the relation between intuition and thought completely in the latter sense. The service that the understanding does for intuition takes nothing away from the freedom and spontaneity of the understanding. The understanding is service *for,* not *under,* intuition. Understanding aims at intuition, but understanding does not simply make itself subservient to intuition. The matter is rather as follows: the being of intuition as definite (and what would an existence be like which was completely undetermined?) depends upon the function of the understanding. This applies to time, which is for Heidegger the absolutely ultimate foundation of being, just as much as it applies to space. We cannot imagine time "save in so far as we attend, in the drawing of a straight line (which has to serve as the outer figurative representation of time), merely to the act of the synthesis of the manifold whereby we successively determine inner sense, and in so doing attend to the succession of this determination in inner sense. Motion, as an act of the subject (not as a determination of an object), and therefore the synthesis of the manifold in space, first produces the concept of succession— if we abstract from this manifold and attend solely to the act through which we determine inner sense according to its form. The understanding does not, therefore, find in inner sense such a combination of the manifold, but produces it, in that it affects that sense." (*Critique of Pure Reason,* B 154f.) This formulation belongs to the second edition of the *Critique.* But even the first— as early as the introduction of the concept of synthesis—stated unambiguously that, without it, we could have *a priori* representations neither of space nor of time, "since these can be produced only through the synthesis of the manifold which the sensibility offers up in its receptivity." (A 99) Analogously, the *Prolegomena* says that, although the pure sensuous intuition of space is the foundation and substratum of all geometrical knowledge, every statement about a definite geometrical object always goes back to the pure function of thought; "what forms space into a circular shape, the figure of a cone, of a ball is the understanding in so far as it contains the ground of the unity of their construction." (*Prol.* para. 38) All construction includes necessarily an element of spontaneity; in construction an object does not present itself as something to be accepted; in construction we are not simply affected by an object (cf. Heidegger, p. 23). Rather, in construction we make something objective out of its original elements, out of the "conditions of its possibility."

And the problem here is further aggravated as soon as we move from the Transcendental Analytic to the Transcendental Dialectic— as soon as we make the transition from the pure concepts of the understanding to the concepts of reason. The latter never refer immediately to intuition but rather pertain to the use of the understanding itself, to which they intend to give the greatest systematic unity. The fulfillment of this requirement, however, places us in front of a new and decisive fundamental concept: the Idea of the Unconditioned. If the understanding comprehends within itself the entirety of the conditions of possible experience, reason never remains satisfied in the area of these conditions but rather inquires beyond them. Indeed, this function of inquiring beyond is its peculiar and essential function. The function does not direct itself toward sensibility in order, by means of it, to determine and grasp a concrete, empirical object. Rather, the task of reason reaches beyond the entire sphere of this kind of objectivity, of constituting things. In the case of reason, therefore, we stand for the first time on the ground of transcendence. In this sense Kant can say that the unconditioned is "the common title of all concepts of reason." (*Critique of Pure Reason*, B 380) and now it is shown that the characterization of the understanding as finite power of knowledge pertains to only one element of its use. For now the opposite determination appears over against this characterization in an apparent dialectical opposition. The understanding can be called "finite" in so far as it never grasps absolute objects, let alone creates these objects out of itself. The understanding is, however, infinite in so far as the absolute totality in the synthesis of conditions belongs to its peculiar and essential task. In virtue of this requirement that reason places before the understanding, the latter is for the first time completely aware of its own nature and boundlessness. If it appears to be bound by its relation to the transcendental imagination of sensibility and thus to finitude, the understanding participates in the infinite through the no-less-necessary relation to the pure ideas of reason. For the latter can be symbolically represented. But they cannot be captured and exhibited in a mere schema or monogram of the imagination. "No corresponding schema of sensibility can be given" of a principle of pure reason, so that such a principle cannot have an object *in concreto*." (*Critique*, B 692) "For how can experience ever be given that should be adequate to an Idea? The peculiarity of the latter consists in the fact that no experience can ever agree with it." (B 649) With this the barrier of mere receptivity is finally broken. When F. H. Jacobi attempted to deduce the concept of reason [*Vernunft*] linguistically from that of perception [*Vernehmen*], and when he saw in reason an essentially receptive function, the entire opposition of Jacobi's "philosophy of belief" to critical idealism comes to light. For Kant, reason is never a merely receptive but rather an autonomous and active force: reason places us before the imperative of the unconditioned. In this fundamental conviction Kant stands with Plato. "Plato remarked quite rightly that our power of knowing feels a much higher need than merely that of spelling out appearances according to synthetic unity in order to read them as experience. Our reason naturally moves to cognitions that go much too far for any kind of object which experience can give to be able to agree with them. These cognitions nonetheless have their reality and are in no way merely mental aberrations." Instead of criticizing Plato for this, one should have wondered at the philosophical leap which drove him from the reproductive observation of the physical world order to the architectonic combination of this world order according to ends (that is, according to Ideas): "an effort that deserves respect and imitation." (B 371, 375) With this the circle of mere temporal limitation, of merely temporal existence and consciousness, is broken. To be sure, there is no doubt for Kant that all purely theoretical knowledge is and remains in some sense temporally bound. Reason strives, considered theoretically, to free "the concept of the understanding from the unavoidable limitations of a possible experience" and thus to extend it beyond the boundaries of the empirical. But reason in this function does not give up the relation to the empirical. For the goal of reason is not simply to transcend the understanding but to give its cognitions systematic unity and completeness. (cf. B 435ff.) Here reason directs itself primarily toward the totality of experience and thus to the entirety of existence under temporal conditions. But, according to Kant, this relation changes as soon as we consider reason, not simply as theoretical but as practical. With the unconditioned of the Idea of Freedom the step into the purely intelligible (the supersensuous and the supertemporal) is finally ventured. In the *Critique* (B 430) Kant had already observed: "Should it be granted that we may in due course discover, not in experience but in certain laws of the pure employment of reason—laws which are not merely logical rules, but which while holding *a priori* also concern our existence—ground for regarding ourselves as legislating completely *a priori* in regard to our own existence, and as determining this existence, there would thereby be revealed a spontaneity through which our reality would be determinable, independently of the conditions of empirical intuition. And we should also become aware that in the consciousness of our existence there is contained a something *a priori,* which can serve to determine our existence—the complete determination of which is possible only in sensible terms—as being related, in respect of a certain inner faculty, to a non-sensible intelligible world."

The *Critique of Practical Reason* begins with this idea and gives it a systematic determination and execution. The second *Critique* shows that the Idea of Freedom does not contain the intuition of a supersensuous substance but the certainty of the supersensuous determination of rational being. The synthetic principle of causality, in virtue of which we simply "spell out appearances in order to be able to read them as experience" is not adequate for this determination. We must venture a step into a new area in order to understand this determination even in its obvious sense. Thus it is the unconditioned character of the moral law that permanently lifts us beyond the circle of merely phenomenal existence and places us in the middle and crucial point of a completely different order. The separation of the *mundus intelligibilis* from the *mundus sensibilis* means for Kant ultimately nothing else than the exhibition of two completely different modes of orientation and judgment. This separation means that all human existence and all human activities are to be measured by two completely different modes of orientation and judgment. This separation means that all human existence and all human activities are to be measured by two completely different standards and are to be considered from two standpoints that are in principle opposed to each other. The concept of the intelligible world is only the standpoint that reason sees itself forced to take beyond appearances in order to think of itself as practical—what would not be possible if the influences of the sensibility were determinative for man but which is absolutely necessary if man is to think of himself as intelligence, as a free personality in a kingdom of ends.[7] Here, in the domain of morality, there is in point of fact the miracle of a kind of creative knowledge. For here the ego is basically only what it makes itself. And the moral law itself has, to be sure, the form of an imperative and, in virtue of that, stands over against us. But this kind of opposition is not the same as in the case of the theoretical object. For here mere dependence or heteronomy does not dominate. Rather only the law which the free personality gives to itself has force. Thus in the Kingdom of Ends

7. *Grundlegung zur Metaphysik der Sitten,* Section III (Cassirer edition, IV, 318).

every will that belongs to it is ruler and subject at the same time. Heidegger attempts, to be sure, to demonstrate an essential dependence and finitude for practical reason as well. And he relies for this on Kant's doctrine of the "incentives of pure practical reason." While Kant shows that the ego can appropriate the moral law in no other way than in the feeling of respect, restriction and finitude again arise in this foundation on a feeling. With this arises the connection with the "primordial constitution of the transcendental imagination." (152) But here we must sharply distinguish between the sphere of specifically ethical and that of psychological problems. The content of the moral law is, according to Kant, in no way grounded in the feeling of respect. The meaning of the moral law is not constituted through respect. This feeling designates solely the way in which the law which is in itself unconditioned is represented in the empirical, finite consciousness. It does not belong to the foundation of Kantian ethics but rather to its application. As Cohen has formulated this relation so sharply and pregnantly, it is not supposed to give an answer to the question of what the moral law is but under which concept it "appears on the horizon of man." [8] The noumenal sense of the Idea of Freedom, however, remains sharply separated as before from this manner of its appearance, its occurrence and self-representation in the area of psychical phenomena. Seen from a phenomenological point of view, a difference must be recognized that cannot be effaced. As regards the Idea of Freedom and the practical reason that goes with it, Kant expressly insists that it, as something that is purely intelligible, is not bound to merely temporal conditions. It is rather the pure view into the timeless—the horizon of transtemporality. The concept of causality as natural necessity concerns only the existence of things in so far as they are determinable in time. Hence it concerns them as appearances in opposition to their causality as things in themselves. "But the same subject that is conscious of itself also as a thing in itself considers its existence *in so far as it does not stand under temporal conditions*. It considers itself only in so far as it is determinable through laws that it gives itself through reason; and in this kind of existence there is nothing that precedes its determination of will." [9] Here we remain entirely in ourselves and,

8. Hermann Cohen, *Kants Begründung der Ethik,* Berlin, 1877, p. 274.
9. *Krit. d. prakt. Vernunft* (Cassirer edition, V, 107).

at the same time, are in principle lifted beyond ourselves. We stand in the middle of our being as personality, as pure rational being; but we do not consider ourselves under the conditions of our phenomenal, our empirical and temporal existence. "Only the concept of freedom allows us to find the unconditioned and the intelligible to the conditioned and sensuous without permitting us to go outside ourselves. For it is our reason itself that knows itself through the highest and unconditioned practical law; and the being that is conscious of this law (our own person) knows itself as belonging to the purely intelligible world, and, moreover, with a determination of the way in which it can be active as such." [10]

Nowhere else than in this passage was Kant more careful to prevent the sense of his transcendental problem from being mislocated in psychology. Nowhere else was he more careful to prevent the discussion from being pushed off into the merely anthropological. He constantly emphasizes that every analysis that proceeds merely from the nature of man must miss the point of the transcendental Idea of Freedom and thereby the foundation of ethics. The concern prompted the statement of Kant that has been so frequently misunderstood and misinterpreted—that one can arrive at a pure conception of the moral law only when one sees to it that it is valid, not only for men but rather "for all rational beings in general." Kant truthfully did not think here of "the dear angels," as Schopenhauer derisively accused him of doing. Rather, Kant speaks here as a critic and a methodologist whose primary concern is not to let the boundaries of the sciences run together and who accordingly wants to separate the tasks of ethics sharply and fundamentally from those of anthropology. This line of demarcation is given to him through the opposition of appearance and thing in itself, of time and freedom. And here lies the essential objection that I have to make against Heidegger's interpretation of Kant. While Heidegger tries to relate and indeed to trace back all faculties of knowledge to transcendental imagination, the only thing left to him is the one frame of reference; namely, the framework of temporal existence. The distinction between phenomenon and noumenon is effaced: for all existence belongs now to the dimension of time and thus to finitude. But this removes one of the foundation stones on which Kant's entire position rests and without which that posi-

10. *Ibid.*, V, 115.

tion must collapse. Nowhere does Kant contend for such a monism of imagination. Rather, he insists upon a decided and radical dualism, the dualism of the sensuous and intelligible world. For *his* problem is not the problem of being and time but rather the problem of "is" and "ought," of experience and Idea.

Heidegger certainly had a right to dispute this dualism from the standpoint of his fundamental ontology. But he should not have denied such a dualism. To be sure, Heidegger will reply to this objection that his interpretation quite intentionally did not remain with what Kant really said. Rather, Heidegger wanted to make visible the problem concerning Kant. Heidegger wanted to restore and repeat the philosophical activity out of which this problem flowed. (204) But it seems to me that Heidegger has made an unjustified use of a maxim of explanation which is in itself justified. Heidegger emphasizes that "if an interpretation merely repeats what Kant expressly said, then it is, from the very outset, not an interpretation, since the task is set an interpretation of making visible what Kant has shown in his foundation which goes beyond express formulation. But Kant was no longer able to say this, just as in all philosophical knowledge what is said expressly must not become decisive but rather what the philosophy presents as unsaid through what is said. . . . In order to force the words to say that which they want to say, every interpretation must necessarily use force. Such force, however, cannot be rampant arbitrariness. The power of an illuminating idea must drive and lead the interpretation." (192ff.) That such an Idea must be dominant in every philosophical presentation I do not intend to dispute in any way. I myself have never interpreted the history of philosophy in any different sense. But does not interpretation become arbitrary when it forces the author to say something that he left unsaid only because he did not want to think it? And the concept of a reason that is a "purely receptive spontaneity," a "purely sensuous reason" (147, 164), could not in fact be conceived by Kant in the sense that Heidegger gives to it. This concept becomes intelligible only in terms of the fundamental assumptions of Heidegger's problem— in terms of his analysis of *Being and Time*.[11] But in Kant's doctrine

---

11. Here a critical discussion of Heidegger's *Being and Time* is naturally quite foreign to me. It must be postponed until another opportunity. In what follows I am concerned solely with Heidegger's interpretation of Kant, not with the justification of his own doctrine.

it remains a stranger and an intruder. For Kant, such a "sensuous reason" would be a wooden iron: For reason is for him just the capacity of the supersensuous and the supertemporal. In this point I must, therefore decidedly dispute the justification, the *quid juris,* of the force that Heidegger places on Kant. Here Heidegger no longer speaks as commentator but as usurper, who penetrates, as it were, by force of arms into the Kantian system in order to subdue it and make it serviceable for his problem. A *restitutio in integram* must be demanded in the face of this usurpation. I am the last one who would like to dispute or diminish the systematic significance and importance of the chapter on schematism. I share with Heidegger the conviction that this chapter is not confusedly constructed but is rather incomparably transparent. I believe that it leads "with an unparalleled sureness into the core of the entire problem of the *Critique of Pure Reason.*" (106f.) Schematism and the doctrine of the transcendental imagination stand in the middle of Kant's analysis but not in the focal point of Kant's system. This system is completed only in the transcendental dialectic and, further, in the *Critique of Practical Reason* and in the *Critique of Judgment.* It is here, not in the schematism, that one comes to Kant's real fundamental ontology. The theme "Kant and Metaphysics" cannot, therefore, be treated exclusively under the aspect of the chapter on schematism but only under the aspect of the Kantian doctrine of freedom and his theory of the beautiful. The *Critique of Practical Reason* and the *Critique of Aesthetic Judgment* surely belong to Kant's theory of man. But they develop this theory in such a way that they place man under the Idea of humanity from the very outset and consider him from the standpoint of this idea. The "intelligible substratum of humanity" and not the existence of man is the goal essential to it. Schematism stands at the beginning of Kant's metaphysics and constitutes, as it were, the entrance to it. But it's real content is developed only on the other side of that entrance. That content determines the "land of truth" as empirical truth; it belongs to the theory of phenomenal reality and constitutes an integral constituent of it. But it leaves room for a being of another sort, for noumenal being, not of things but of intelligences. It leaves room for a kingdom of freely acting and absolutely independent personalities.

And here we stand at a point where a peculiar paradox in Heidegger's way of formulating the problem comes to light. What

Heidegger regards as the dominant idea of his interpretation of Kant is doubtless the effort to overcome that Neo-Kantianism that sought to found the entire Kantian system in his critique of knowledge and finally to let it disappear into mere epistemology. Heidegger opposes this with the thesis of the primarily metaphysical character of Kant's problem. For him, Kant's doctrine is not a theory of experience but is primarily and originally ontology. It is the discovery and revelation of the essence of man. But is Kant's theory of schematism and transcendental imagination the appropriate place for the proof of this thesis? I do not believe that it is. For this theory is not a constituent of Kant's metaphysics but is rather a genuine and necessary constituent of his theory of experience. It does not treat the existence of man immediately and primarily but rather the constitution, the character, and the conditions of empirical objectivity. The schematization that is demanded of the pure concepts of the understanding pertains to this task. And to this task pertains that connection in virtue of which these concepts are forced to restrict themselves by transcendental time determinations to the order of phenomena in time and not to direct themselves immediately to things in themselves. Through this requirement the categories are restricted; but they are realized only through such a requirement in that a definite empirical employment —a relation to an object—is assured them. Only through the connection with the schemata of the transcendental imagination do the concepts of the understanding succeed "in subordinating appearances to general rules of synthesis and thus to make them amenable to thoroughgoing connection in experience." (B 185) Schematism for Kant belongs, accordingly, essentially to his phenomenology of the object but not—or only indirectly—to the phenomenology of the subject. The entire problem of the temporality of the subject, of the interpretation of human existence in relation to temporality, of being-to-death, as Heidegger developed it in *Being and Time*— all of this is not only in fact but in principle foreign to Kant. In order to assure oneself of that, one need only glance at that chapter of the *Critique* in which Kant's doctrine of schematism is really completely and systematically grounded. The discussion and execution of the Kantian doctrine of schematism is to be found only in the section concerning the synthetic principles—a section which Heidegger nowhere consults and considers in his interpretation.

That the concepts of substantiality, of causality, etc. obtain their significance, their objective meaning, only through their relation to temporal intuition—this is proved by the fact that the peculiar function of both concepts consists in nothing other than bringing the temporal determination among intuitions to firm and universally valid rules. These latter are unavoidable because it would not be possible without them—without *a priori* temporal determinations according to rules—to distinguish the merely subjective play of our representation from the objective order of occurrence. The peculiar deduction of the schemata lies here. They are the means of supplying our intuitions with an object. As conditions of the possibility of experience, they are, at the same time, conditions of the possibility of objects of experience. One can count these explanations of Kant as metaphysics if one takes this concept in its fullest sense. But then they belong to the Metaphysical First Principles of Natural Science. And they receive further explanation and elucidation in this work of Kant. Thus the doctrine of schematism and determinative judgment is an indispensable element of that theory of knowledge that Heidegger has audaciously enough denied to the *Critique of Pure Reason* and which he has tried to eliminate from it. (16) Here, too, Heidegger has given Kant's entire analysis a totally different direction despite the care and exactness Heidegger shows in details. Heidegger has attempted to transfer Kant's analysis from the foundation of the objective deduction purely and exclusively to that of the subjective deduction. But he could do this only while he remained with the introduction of the concept of the transcendental schema without developing the concept in the totality of its systematic effects and consequences.

II. KANT'S "DRAWING AWAY" FROM UNCOVERING THE FINITUDE OF KNOWLEDGE

But an objection against the preceding observations may perhaps have been aroused in a person who has followed Heidegger's analyses attentively. Do these observations do justice to Heidegger's fundamental intention? Did this intention consist at all in giving an exposition of the totality of Kant's system, or does Heidegger quite consciously only take up an individual element in that system

that appears to him of fundamental significance? Has he not himself shown that Kant by no means completely grasped and appreciated this significance, although he was the first to point it out? May
we infer anything unfavorable to the disposition of Heidegger's
question from the circumstance that Kant's system doubtless contains doctrines that do not fit into Heidegger's interpretation and,
indeed, seem directly to contradict that interpretation? That this
start found in Kant no completion and no pure execution is very
sharply emphasized by Heidegger. What he wants to show is that
Kant, after he had succeeded in uncovering the common root of
understanding and sensibility in transcendental imagination, drew
back from his own discovery. "In the second edition of the *Critique
of Pure Reason,* the transcendental imagination, just as it came to
light in the moment of the first draft, is forced out and reinter-
preted in favor of the understanding." (153) Transcendental imagination was for Kant the "disturbing unknown" that drove him to
a completely new version of the Transcendental Deduction. Kant
recognized the problem of finitude in man and saw it sharply. But
nevertheless he showed that he was not entirely up to this problem:
he dug away the foundation that he had previously laid. (209)
This fact, *"that Kant draws away from the foundation that he himself had laid in the discovery of the subjectivity of the subject,"*
appears to Heidegger as what is philosophically essential, as the
real activity of the entire *Critique.* (205) Heidegger did, to be sure,
enter his analysis with this thesis as something which is similar to
an hypothesis. And hypotheses are, as Kant remarks, strictly speaking forbidden merchandise in the area of transcendental philosophy. They are, as Kant adds in the section about "The Discipline
of Reason in Respect of Hypothesis," admissible "not in dogmatic
but rather in polemical employment." They are "permitted in the
field of pure reason only as a weapon, not so that a right can be
grounded on them but only for the defense of that field." (B
804f.) Should Heidegger's hypothesis not also be such a weapon?
Do we not perhaps stand with it, instead of on the foundation of
the analysis of Kantian ideas, in the middle of the polemic against
these ideas? It is well known that Schopenhauer raised the objection against Kant that he obscured his own basic conviction in the
second edition of the *Critique,* that he had distorted his work out
of fear of human beings. Heidegger has carefully protected him-

self against such a misleading interpretation, such foolish and crude psychological remarks. But even Heidegger introduces a subjective and psychological explanation where an objective and systematic explanation would have been expected and demanded. And this latter explanation has been set out with sufficient clarity by Kant himself. What forced him to the revision of the first edition of the *Critique of Pure Reason* was the Garve-Feder review. It was the effort to separate his transcendental idealism sharply from psychological idealism. Guided by this concern, he had to transfer the emphasis of the Transcendental Analytic more than previously was the case from the side of the subjective to the objective deduction. He had to show that the main question of the *Critique* consisted in showing how and under what conditions the object of experience is possible, not how the power to think is itself possible. But was it not just this sentence that Kant had most forcefully emphasized in the preface to the first edition of the *Critique?* (A XI) And did did he not retain the core of his doctrine of transcendental imagination even in the second edition and permit it to remain in its decisive systematic intermediary position? Did he not also do this with the chapter on schematism? In all this I am unable to recognize any kind of "drawing away" from the position which he had achieved. Indeed, the abandonment of a metaphysics of the Absolute had for some time concealed no terrors. He had forsworn such a metaphysics for the first time not in the *Critique of Pure Reason* but (in 1766) in the *Dreams of a Spiritseer.* From that time he did not seek to compete with the "spatial masterbuilders of the intellectual world." And this abandonment did not mean for him a painful renunciation. Rather, his abandonment was conceived in complete quiet, joy, and in a sure and self-conscious power of thought. He did not want to lift himself into the clouds, the secrets of the other world, on the light butterfly wings of metaphysics. Rather, he entrusted himself to the power of self-knowledge. "When science has completed its circle, it naturally arrives at the point of modest mistrust and says indignantly about itself: how many things there are that I do not understand! But reason, matured through experience, which becomes wisdom, speaks joyfully in the mouth of Socrates in the midst of the wares of the fair: how many things there are that I do not need!" [12] In the *Critique of*

---

12. *Träume eines Geistersehers, Sämtliche Werke* (Cassirer, III, 485f.).

Pure Reason Kant remained true to this attitude. Finitude as such, the insight that a transcendent perspective is not given us, does not fill him with fear. "If by the complaints—*that we have no insight whatsoever into the inner nature of things*—it be meant that we cannot conceive by pure understanding what the things which appear to us may be in themselves, they are entirely illegitimate and unreasonable. For what is demanded is that we should be able to know things, and therefore to intuit them, without senses, and therefore that we should have a faculty of knowledge altogether different from the human, and this not only in degree but as regards intuition likewise in kind—in other words, that we should be not men but beings of whom we are unable to say whether they are even possible, much less how they are constituted." (B 333) Kant was thoroughly acquainted with the *theoretical* problem of this kind of finitude. And even in a *practical* regard he did not feel himself limited by this insight. For in his ethics there was, to be sure, an absolute of the Idea, an absolute of requirement. But he no longer needed a view of the transcendent in the sense of dogmatic metaphysics in order to perceive this absolute and to stand assuredly in it. "Does not the heart of man," so had the *Dreams of a Spiritseer* asked, "contain ethical prescriptions immediately; and must one not place machines in another world in order for man to move according to his determination?" (*Sämtliche Werke*, II, 389) The "other world" that Kant needed and that he never gave up was not another nature of things but rather a Kingdom of Ends: not the existence of absolute substances but an order and constitution of freely acting personalities. This requirement, however, he found completely reconcilable with the results of the *Critique* and especially with his doctrine of transcendental imagination. For the Kingdom of Ends cannot be subordinated to the laws of this imagination. It cannot be schematized without losing its peculiar character in the attempt of such a schematism without losing its being as something purely intelligible.[13] The moral law is distinguished from physical law in that it does not begin from the place which man occupies in the outer world of sensibility. Rather, it begins from its invisible self, its personality, and represents man in a world "which has true infinity but which is only noticeable by the understanding." (*Critique of Practical*

13. Cf. my work, *Kants Leben und Lehre,* 3rd edition, pp. 273ff.

Reason, Cassirer ed., V, 174) I do not see that Kant ever wavered in one of these determinations: in the limitation of the empirical employment of the categories to the schemata of imagination and in his assertion of the supersensible in that other practical regard. Nor do I see that he ever sensed any kind of antagonism between them. Here there is for him no chasm into which he did not dare to gaze. Rather, there rules, according to him, a complete correspondence, a thoroughgoing correlation. The chasm opens only when one takes as a point of departure and a standard Heidegger's concept of finitude, which is quite differently conceived and justified in a completely different way. All in all, the notion of a fearful Kant that shrank back from the ultimate consequences of his own thought seems to me at this place to be required by nothing and to be completely unfounded. Rather, it seems to me to be one of the essential and specific peculiarities of Kant's mode of thought that it does not stop short of a conclusion out of merely subjective reasons but rather permits the matter at hand and its own necessity to speak.

And here we see ourselves ultimately led to a point at which merely logical discussion and mere analysis of concepts no longer suffice in order to reach a decision. This is a point at which the total attitude by which every philosophy is inspired and determined takes on essential significance. Heidegger's fundamental ontology, that is grounded in the interpretation of care as the being of the existent and that sees a primary revelation of the existent in the fundamental mode of fear must put all Kant's concepts from the very beginning—however much Heidegger attempted to do justice to their purely logical sense—into a changed atmosphere and thus, as it were, cover them up. Kant was and remained—in the most noble and beautiful sense of this word—a thinker of the Enlightenment. He strove for illumination even where he thought about the deepest and most hidden grounds of being. Goethe once said to Schopenhauer that, when he read a page of Kant, he felt as if he were entering a bright room. From the very outset Heidegger's philosophy obeys, as it were, a different principle of style. For Kant, metaphysics is the doctrine of "the first principles of human knowledge." And the concept of principle is understood here in the straightforward and harmless sense that metaphysics is to exhibit and make the first principles of this knowledge intelligible.

On the other hand, for Heidegger transcendence is the proper "region of the question about the essence of the principle." The principle arises out of finite freedom. As a principle of this kind, however, freedom is the chasm of existence. "It is not as if individual free attitude were groundless. Rather, freedom in its essence as transcendence places existence as capability in possibilities that open up before its finite choice, that is, in its fate." "The opening of this ground in grounding transcendence is . . . the primary movement that freedom accomplishes with us." [14] Such sentences, through which, according to Heidegger, the idea of logic cancels itself out "in the whirlpool of a primordial questioning," are explicable in terms of the world of Kierkegaard; but in Kant's intellectual world they have no place. For Kant it was not fear that revealed the Nothing to him and which opened the area of metaphysics to him and drove him into it.[15] He had discovered a basic form of idealism that, on the one hand, directed man to the fruitful bathos of experience and held him fast in this chasm in order to assure him, on the other hand, of participation in the Idea and thus in the infinite. That was Kant's metaphysics—his way of dispelling the fear of Nothingness. . . .

Here I am at the conclusion of my observations about Heidegger's book. And I am concerned to emphasize a point once more in order expressly to guard against a misunderstanding. I emphasize once again that nothing has been more foreign to me in these observations than some kind of personal polemic. The value of Heidegger's book should in no way be denied or diminished. Like all the writings of Heidegger, his book on Kant carries the stamp of a genuinely philosophical attitude and genuinely philosophical work. He proceeds to his work with true inner enthusiasm. He does not stop anywhere with the interpretation of words and sentences but places us everywhere in the vital center of the problems and grasps these problems in their real power and genuine originality. And one will be able to say nothing better in praise of Heidegger's book than that it shows itself quite equal to the problem that it develops before us. It remains at the apex of the task it sets itself. But personal praise or blame are not useful and

14. Heidegger, *Vom Wesen des Grundes, Festschrift für Husserl*, pp. 80ff., 109f.

15. Heidegger, *Was ist Metaphysik?*, Bonn, 1929, p. 17.

adequate measures for judging a philosophical accomplishment. Here only the subject itself should speak. And one cannot do justice to an author in a better way than to seek to hear only the voice of the subject. It would be a false and bad subjectivity that would not inspire us to such an objectivity and pledge us to it. In this spirit I should like to have the preceding remarks considered and judged. I believe that we have to thank Heidegger for again setting before us the true philosophical activity that takes place in Kant's foundation of philosophy. We have to thank Heidegger for letting this activity manifest itself in its entire inner power and force. But he has not, it seems to me, encompassed the entire scope of the problem of transcendental idealism. He has only pointed up a—to be sure—important and essential phase of the entire movement and clarified it in its significance. He has not seen this movement as a whole and has not uncovered it in its inner lawfulness. Measured in terms of the entire scope of Kant's thought, what Heidegger takes up and what he develops before us are ultimately only a partial aspect. On one point I do not intend to contradict Heidegger: that such a limitation and finitude are perhaps the fate of every kind of philosophical thought and interpretation in the history of philosophy and that none of us can delude himself that he has escaped his fate. The ever-renewed reflection upon finitude is perhaps not, as Heidegger thinks, the core of metaphysics. But it is in any case inescapable and necessary as a maxim of philosophical activity. Here what is important is not the mutual interplay and the mediating compromise of standpoints: "There remains rather only the working out of the problem of finitude as such that reveals itself in its essence only when it is made accessible through a start that is guided constantly by the originally comprehended basic question of metaphysics. And this start can never be claimed as the only possible one." (Heidegger, p. 227) In my conversations with Heidegger in Davos, I have already emphasized that I do not nurture the wish and hope of converting him to my standpoint. But what should be sought in every philosophical discussion and what must be attainable in some sense is this: that we can learn to see the oppositions correctly and that we attempt to understand them just in this opposition.

METAPHYSICAL MOTIVES

IN THE DEVELOPMENT OF

CRITICAL IDEALISM

Heinz Heimsoeth

§

The time is probably gone when Kant could be used as the precursor of a purely "epistemological" and scientific way of philosophizing against every kind of metaphysical position. One can no longer believe that Kant's "critical" attitude can be taken as a model for one's own avoidance of all metaphysical problems. Kant's battle against dogmatism applied to a certain type of metaphysics and metaphysical method with which certain dangers of mistaking and distorting fundamental intellectual realities seemed to him to be essentially connected. His own *Critique* was intended to be the preparation for his own practical-dogmatic metaphysics, in whose center just these realities were to stand. Just how much continuity this new metaphysics of the later Kant preserves with the metaphysical convictions of his pre-Critical thought will be shown in another context.[1] The following lines—as opposed to that more extensive task—are intended only to direct attention to the extent to which even the specifically critical part of Kantian epistemology —the Critical limitation of knowledge (especially the separation of

1. In *Kants metaphysischer Weltbegriff,* a book by the author which is to appear shortly, Kant's metaphysical principles, which can only be touched upon in the present essay, are treated more exhaustively there. For most of the questions discussed here, that more detailed treatment of Kant's metaphysics must be referred to.

spatial-temporal experience as knowledge of mere appearance from being as it is in itself)—is determined by certain fundamental metaphysical convictions and in general by a metaphysical formulation of the question. In this more special matter a closer connection of the Critical with the pre-Critical Kant will emerge than is commonly assumed.

I

First of all, the earliest and continuously influential reasons for the formation of the concept of the thing in itself and the limitation of our objective knowledge to appearances are not epistemological in all introspective, reflexive, phenomenological, or even in a psychological sense of the word (and least of all in a scientific sense) but are rather results of a definite metaphysics of knowledge; that is, of a consideration of knowledge as a definite ontological relation between real substances. One thing is too little emphasized: that even the justification of transcendental idealism given in the *Critique of Pure Reason* is metaphysical in character. As opposed to the later idealistic lines of thought which proceed from consciousness and then aim to show that the assumption of a thing in itself transcending consciousness is spurious, Kant sees no difficulty in the transition from being to consciousness—especially in the influence of existing substances or existing intelligences that thereby directly experience properties of those outer substances. For him the riddle lies solely in the synthetic *a priori* elements of our knowledge of reality and especially in our claim to know laws of nature. But the Copernican Revolution of his epistemology is intended to give an explanation of this which has definite advantages over other explanations of traditional metaphysics (especially over the "Preformation System" with its parallelism of ontological laws and corresponding innate *a priori* elements in subjects). Probably no explanation is necessary that "epistemology" in this explanatory sense includes metaphysical positions new to and prior to the "critical-transcendental" (as, for example, phenomenological information). Moreover, it can be shown that the Kantian solution of the problem (the Copernican Revolution) takes its rise from metaphysical considerations.

The present discussion does not concern this, however, but rather the metaphysical origin of the dualism between receptivity and spontaneity that is so important in Kant's epistemology and the resultant separation of all receptively determined knowledge from the thing in itself. For Kant this opposition does not arise out of a primary analysis of a phenomenological character, which would determine the essential correlation of intentional act and fulfilling intuition. That this is not so can be shown simply by the fact that this duality is for Kant by no means an essential part of every kind of knowledge. It does not apply to the knowledge of the logician (and, on a proper interpretation of Kant, not even to that of the mathematician), nor to transcendental knowledge (for example, knowledge of the categories), and not at all to the knowledge of the faculty of knowing itself—only Kant did not, to be sure, specifically talk about this. Rather, that duality is valid only for the knowledge of objective reality. Kant acknowledges only sensuous intuition as human knowledge—intuition of that which is given by real affection and its *a priori* forms, but not eidetic intuition (for example, neither of these forms themselves nor of the kind of thinking present in formal and transcendental logic and dialectic). Thus that distinction, as he intends it, cannot be gained from the plain essence of knowledge.

The first source of the duality of receptivity and spontaneity and, with it, the opposition of appearance and thing in itself is to be found in the ancient metaphysical and epistemological dichotomy, transmitted by Augustine and the Augustinianism of all centuries, between finite and infinite subjects in relation to the world of physical reality. Intellectual intuition for the pre-Critical Kant is not, as it may seem later, an artificially constructed contrast to an essential dualism of sensibility and understanding, intuition and concept. Rather, intellectual intuition means for him the primary representation of knowledge as a purely spontaneous intellectual seeing. Corresponding to its position in the total history of metaphysics, Kant's concept of knowledge does not proceed from the world of things within which mirroring subjects find themselves among other substances (out of such an approach arises the metaphysical and epistemological principle of explanation of Platonic anamnesis). Rather it arises from the original reality of an absolute intellectual spontaneity in comparison with which all thinghood is only secondary. It is a conviction of Kant's, which endures to his last period, that complete and immediate knowledge is present only where the subject posits the object of knowledge. Knowledge—insight—is always primarily knowledge *a priori*, and that always means in this context: a purely spontaneous activity and formation of ideal convictions from which the real which constitutes itself in this seeing actually arises as archetype or originally constitutive. That is Kant's original concept of rational knowledge. From the Ideas, the ideal intuition of totality, the seeing of totality, it penetrates by limitation to the individual, the concrete, and the real, which is posited. Knowledge *a priori* is prior to the object. It grasps the object in and through the very possibility of the object. Knowledge and reason are purely spontaneous. That which knows grasps what it makes.[2]

The problem of knowledge begins—at least for the pre-Critical Kant—only with the question of the *finite* subject. Only the divine spiritual being stands to the world in this relation of production, as in a relation of one-sided dependence of the real upon visionary spontaneity. But every finite substance and thus every finite subject stands in a relation of mutual dependence with other substances. Beginning with dynamic substances, whose result is matter, through the organic principle of life, up to the cognitive and volitional human being—yes, even to possible purely intellectual substances— all finite substances must have a receptive side in addition to the spontaneity that essentially characterizes them as substances distinct

2. The consequence of this concept of knowledge in the theory of the *a priori* and spontaneity in the *Critiques,* with the limitation of our *a priori* knowledge to what we make or put into the given, and with the privileged position of moral and metaphysical knowledge (above all, theoretical knowledge), is not hard to gauge from this point. Cf., e.g., passages like these: Reflex. Nr. 929; R.-V. 96. To the fundamental metaphysical convictions of Kant, which also determine the transcendental idealism of the *Critiques,* belongs the following (which is strictly opposed to the real Plato: that he can conceive the *a priori* (ideas, essences, essential necessities) only in spontaneous acts of subjectivity but never as something objective, as an ideal sphere which existed in itself. The critical idealism of Kant rests on the metaphysical idealism of a Platonism that has been transformed by Augustinianism.

The quotation numbers refer to the Academy edition; "Kr." refers to the Kehrbach edition of the *Critique of Pure Reason;* "M.-V." and "R.-V." are the Pölitz editions of Kant's lectures on metaphysics (1821) and Kant's lectures on the philosophy of religion (1817); "M.-H." is the transcript of Kant's lectures on metaphysics which is found in the university library of Königsberg; "Reflex." refers to B. Erdmann, *Reflexionen Kants zur kritischen Philosophie, II,* 1885.

from the primordial divine substance. Thus there is, aside from outwardly directed inner activity, a capacity of reception and endurance. Only in this way can one finite substance have knowledge of another which it does not posit but which exists next to it. Knowledge that finite substances have of one another is only possible because of mutual direct influence, a metaphysical *influxus realis*. Kant's lasting conviction is that this is not replaceable by a simple ideal or indirect correlation in the manner of a pre-established harmony or Occasionalism. Moreover, this does not itself bring with it an insuperable difficulty in the effect of objects on subjects. All knowledge that finite subjects have of other finite realities must have an element of genuine endurance, receptivity, and affection by something else in addition to the essential part of intellectual spontaneity.

Here we are given the problem of all finite knowledge. It is, as knowledge, necessarily spontaneous. But it must make contact with its object only by receptivity. It follows from this that no finite knowledge is knowledge of the thing as it is in itself, in its inner essence. From the beginning, Kant distinguishes in all substances (and not only in substances with inner and outer sense) an "inner" and an "outer"—their being in themselves as distinct from their externalization in influencing other substances. All substances are for him essentially expressions of force. Neither physical nor mental forces are the substance itself in its essence or principle but are only the activities of substance, its relation to accidents, "the relation of the ultimate subject of reality to the existence" of this substance. In the system of reciprocal causality (and that is generally characteristic of reality, precisely in the cognitive relation of finite subjects to things or to one another) every individual substance exhibits so to speak only its exterior side, which consists of accidents and expressions of force. Consequently no finite subject, dependent as it is on a presentation or reception of the effects of the force of other substances, can know what these substances are in themselves, their ground or principle—the substantial core or "the substantial," as Kant calls it. "No being except the creator can perceive the substance of another thing." "Substantiality is the thing in itself and is unknown." [3] One single possibility for knowledge of the thing in itself by a finite subject is conceivable: through a mystical participation of the latter in the pure spontaneity of the

3. M.-V. 97; Reflex. Nr. 704.

divine, existence-giving Ideas, the mystical intuition of Plato and Malebranche, as Kant says without clearly distinguishing the fundamental difference between the two thinkers (throughout his life he saw Plato only through the eyes of Augustine). For Kant, this way out is blocked, at least for knowledge as it really is in the world. He holds open the possibility of a mode of knowing peculiar to spiritual Beings as well as to the human soul freed from the body after death.[4] But this is empty and for us it is a possibility that cannot be thought out in more detail. Thus we always grasp other substances only as they are for us, their relation and effect on us, the thing *quoad causalitatem*. "We know every thing of the world only as a cause or only the causality of the effect—that is, only the effect and thus not the thing itself and the determinations through which it brings about the effect." [5] "We conceive substances through the accidents and not through the substantial; for the substantial is intuitive" (that is, it is directly accessible only to intellectual intuition, which is not dependent upon expression and self-presentation of substances, but which rather posits them with all their powers of expression). However many essential components the finite subject might recognize in other real substances, the real essence of things remains inscrutable to us.

We can only infer to the inner principle of the thing which makes itself known to us through affection. We think it into what is given of the expressions of power and accidents.[6] Our (finite) intellect is not an archetype but only an ectype. "Intellectual intuition in the case of man is a nonentity. Indeed, I venture to say that no created being [7] can know intellectual objects except that being which is the cause of things. This being knows objects as

---

4. Cf. M.-V. 255f.; R.-V. 97f; Reflex. Nr. 929 (conclusion); cf. also Nr. 236-238; Kr. 330-331 [A 392-395]. I derive the most characteristic expressions of Kant frequently from the lectures on metaphysics and philosophy of religion. The question of dating, which is still unanswered, can be omitted for our present interest. The main concern here is to pursue connections of thought which are presented in the pre-Critical works in their continuous influence at all times on Kant's thought. The corresponding formulations of the critical works are especially cited.

5. Reflex. Nr. 1171.

6. M.-V. 39; M.-H. 84-85, 124; Reflex. 1042.

7. The "noumena" of the *Critique;* in general, both expressions are ambiguous in that, on the one hand, things in themselves in general and, on the other, those things in themselves are meant of which there can be no sensuous appearance—"purely intellectual beings" not only in the sense of pure intelligible things but of intelligences, of subjects of the understanding.

they are, but we [know them] only as they affect us." [8] The opposition between thing in itself and appearance is thus fundamentally
affirmed. The discursive character of our knowing and that of all
finite knowing is thereby established. Since the finite subject grasps
other substances only through their modes of expression or accidents, finite knowing is always a knowing through "properties" or
"marks" and ultimately through general marks or concepts.[9] Our
knowledge of reality shows itself to be essentially discursive, not
because of its own inner finitude but rather because of its external
limitation—its dependence upon other things.

These epistemological formulations of the question apply to the
cognitive relation of every finite, dependent being to other substances outside it, especially to other corporeal things and to non-
spatial centers of force which, according to the view that Kant early
developed, are at the foundation of corporeal things as "elements of
matter." Similarly, the corresponding formulations of the *Critique
of Pure Reason* refer primarily to corporeal, "outer" appearances
and their being in themselves. The situation seems to be different
for the self-knowledge of the finite subject. Many statements from
the seventies (and perhaps even later) emphasize that there is
here—where outer influence and relation disappear and the object
itself appears to be given immediately to the subject—a genuine
knowledge of substantiality without restriction to "predicates." Just
as in the *Dreams of a Spiritseer* the soul is said to have representations of itself as a spirit by immediate intuition, so also the lectures
on metaphysics speak of the "immediate intuition of oneself
through the absolute unity of the ego" as "the sole case in which
we can immediately intuit substance." While the outer senses give
only impressions I can recognize the object which lies at the basis of
the impressions only in the special case of inner intuition. "The
intellect intuits its own substantiality but only the activities from
which substance may be inferred . . . because they are predicates." [10]
"One can think something only through predicates, with the exception of the ego." I can know "substantiality only in one case; and
that is whenever I intuit myself . . ." [11] "In myself I immediately

8. M.-H. 97 (probably after 1781).
9. Cf. Reiche, *Lose Blätter,* p. 155; M.-V. 55.
10. II, 337; M.-V. 133; Reflex. Nr. 1287, 1291, 697, 1046.
11. M.-H. 84-85, 92 (perhaps after 1781).

intuit substantiality. The self expresses not only substance but also substantiality."

While we know only the outer relations of bodily elements of matter as it is given, here what is within is apparently given with the substantial unity which represents itself.[12] Only the consciousness of myself is intuitive and not discursive.[13] What is decisive here is the contact of the knower with his own spontaneity, as opposed to the usual kind of knowing which always experiences only accidents as the effect of substantial spontaneity through receptivity. Only "through the *verbum activum,* the ego" can we recognize that something is a subject and not a predicate. "The representation of our free activity of the self is such that, since we are not affected, it is therefore not appearance but apperception." [14] A kind of "primordial intuition" appears to be present here.

The Critical period, as is known, broke with this conviction, and the opposition of appearance and thing in itself was transferred from the given of predicates to the effect of a substantial spirituality and substance itself to the self-knowledge of the subject. What was decisive in this for Kant was the dependence of all mental experience of finite subjects upon what is given by the external world. However much we are essentially spontaneous subjects, the material of the representations "with which we engage the intellect" (e.g., in spontaneous acts of attention) originates primarily from the external world. With this alone, accidents—objective things—place themselves before the pure substance of spontaneity. The element of affection infringes upon what is spiritual. The pure spontaneity of the Leibnizian monad, which is only apparently inhibited from within, is for Kant an artificial and false construction which misconstrues the essential element of real interaction in all changes and occurrences in finite substances. Something else is added—especially the problem of freedom and the growing insight of the impenetrability of one's own ethical structure for every finite subject. (Nobody can be sure of the exclusive purity of his motives. Circumstances of desires and drives are often hidden behind a self-certain ethical spontaneity that is merely illusory.) Thus we do not grasp ourselves as substances and things in ourselves because we do not

---

12. Cf. Reiche, *Lose Blätter,* pp. 26-27.
13. M.-V. 133, 135.
14. Reflex. Nr. 1048, 952.

make ourselves in the way the notion of a genuine primordial intuition would have to require. Here, also, that opposition and final separation of knowing subject and thing in itself are dominant.

It cannot, to be sure, be asserted that self-knowledge is merely equated with the knowledge of outer reality. Kant continues to hold that an immediate consciousness of spontaneity, a grasping of substantiality and thereby of the thing in itself, is present apart from the grasping of what is given and thus present apart from mere expressions of substance. That is in part explicit and in part only implicit in his doctrine of transcendental apperception and of the subject of freedom and ethical consciousness.[15]

From these observations certain recurrent and frequently attacked descriptions of the thing in itself in the *Critique of Pure Reason* become completely clear and obvious. When the Inaugural Dissertation says that phenomena do not express the "inner and absolute quality of the object,"[16] the correlative concept is well known to us: phenomena exhibit to us only the exterior side of the presented substances; and this is relative to us. Seen in this way, there is also no difficulty when the *Critique of Pure Reason* designates things in themselves as "the absolute and inner cause of outer and corporeal appearances," even though the thing in itself is always called the inner ground of the givenness of nature.[17] The great difficulties that result for the concept of the thing in itself as the cause—Kant says "transcendental cause"—of appearances result from purely epistemological and especially from a position immanent to consciousness do not concern the metaphysical foundation of Kant's system. It will be shown in another place that the concept of causality (the pure category of causality free from the temporal determination that makes it into causal law with its special manner of determination, and thus into causality according to natural causation) has and completely retains its validity for things in themselves. It will be shown that, according to Kant's conviction, it is not a formal error to speak in a metaphysical context of the causation of our representations by external things in themselves. Seen

15. This is further discussed in an article of the author in the Kant *Festschrift* of Königsberg University: "Persönlichkeitsbewusstsein und Ding an sich in der Kantischen Philosophie" (appeared separately, Dietrich'sshe Verlagsbuchhandlung, Leipzig, 1924).

16. H, 39v.

17. Kr. 331 [A 394-395]; 242f. [A 348]; V, 388; Opus post. (Adickes, 594)

in this way, the infamous term "affection" is to be taken seriously. The outer sense is in the forefront here, too: it gives us nothing internal except simply "the relation of an object to the subject, . . . not what applies to it in itself." [18] Things in themselves are not given to us—indeed, they can "be given to us perhaps in no way at all." The "perhaps" can be explained by that problematic view of a mystical participation in an intellectual intuition.[19] What loses every difficulty in our connection is that the impenetrability that appears to us in spatial form (and, with it, every determination of phenomenal matter) is designated as an effect or activity that must have its cause and therefore cannot be conceived as a thing in itself, let alone as the primordial being.[20] Once Kant says expressly that the common understanding assumes "something unperceivable and self-active" behind the objects of the senses.[21] These are centers of force of which we know through sensuous experience only the properties that are, as it were, turned toward us. These properties are still modified in a definite way by "the way in which we are affected by objects." Empirical realism and the realism of things in themselves are, for Kant, not so widely separated as it appears on an epistemological view. Common sense, science, and philosophy move in the same direction. Although this expression is really reserved in the *Critique of Pure Reason* for the permanent in appearance, it cannot be surprising when the thing in itself is occasionally called "substance" whenever the discussion turns on the substratum that is at the basis of appearances.[22] Thus even the category of substance has a transcendent significance in addition to its immanent use.[23] Even the specific term "the substantial" occurs.[24] And the thought is always the same: knowledge which is determined by receptivity and affection must *eo ipso* be limited to appearances. "It is an observation the assertion of which requires no subtle reflection but about which one can assume that the most common understanding can make it: that all representations that come to us

18. Kr. 72, 73a, 255f. [B 67-68, B 68-69, A 284-285=B 340-341]; IV, 282 (Proleg.).

19. Kr. 85 [A 63-64=B 88-89].

20. Kr. 485 [A 617-618=B 645-646].

21. IV, 452.

22. Kr. 85 [A 63-64=B 88-89].

23. E.g., V, 99, and continually in the *Critique of Pure Reason*.

24. Kr. 242, 248 [A 264-266=B 320-322, A 273-274=B 329-330].

without our choice (as those of the senses) give us objects to know in no other way than that in which they affect us; whereby what they are in themselves remains unknown to us."[25] In the Critical period, also, "appearance" designates primarily and above all this: the totality of that which rests on the relation of things in themselves to our receptivity.[26] A genuine ontological relation is at the foundation of every case of finite knowledge and imposes on its content the character of the merely relative (relative to the subject-substances and their capacity to be affected) and can never be given for being itself. Appearances are "to be regarded as accidental modes of representation of intelligible objects by such beings that are themselves intelligences"—as it is stated once in the middle of the *Critique of Pure Reason*.[27] That makes our knowing, in so far as it is receptively conditioned, in no way worthless: the properties that we experience in this way are to be regarded "as something that is genuinely given." "The predicates of appearances can be ascribed to the object itself"—but only "in relation to our senses." [28] Things in themselves cannot "wander over into my capacity of representation." Thus our representation can never be completely similar to the thing in itself; and Kant expressly explains that he can associate no sense with such an assertion of similarity. For him it is ontological nonsense, but for that reason it is "completely in accord with the relation that our sensibility has to objects." [29] Our knowledge does not exactly copy things in themselves but nonetheless stands in a relation to them of complete representation. That in experience which is receptive provides us with properties of being—which takes on a special significance in Kant's system of *Critiques* in the problem of special laws and the whole matter of teleology. But from this there comes no insight or knowledge in the primary sense of the word; namely, knowledge of being in itself which could be given only in pure spontaneity. In addition to the dependence upon a given, a positive spontaneity must also come into play so that there could exist such knowledge for us as beings which are coordinate with and dependent upon things. Only in this way does

25. IV, 451.
26. Kr. 73 [B 68-69]; IV, 286.
27. Kr. 451 [A 566-567=B 594-595]; the cautious phrase at the beginning of the sentence changes nothing of interest to us.
28. Kr. 73 [B 68-69].
29. IV, 289-290.

the concept of "appearance" become complete for *knowing* and not simply attending, receptive beings. Genuine knowledge is knowledge *a priori*, which, however, is "impossible for us regarding all things of which we are not ourselves causes." [30] God knows everything through Himself and *a priori;* "but finite beings cannot of themselves know other things because they are not their causes, with the exception only of mere appearances, which they can know *a priori.*" [31] Thus, in this domain of appearances—this peculiar domain where a reception of beings given relative to us functions with the spontaneous effect of our inner powers—we are "in part creators." [32] Man is *Kosmostheoros,* who himself creates the elements of knowledge of the world *a priori* out of which he conceptually fashions the vision of the world while at the same time being an inhabitant of the world.[33] As God is the creator of things in themselves, man is the *principium originarium of appearances.*[34] And man has here his analogy to the divine Ideas of totality, his archetypes, in which he moves *a priori* from *the whole to the parts,* from the possible to the real: space and time, the essential forms of receptivity.[35] The soul as cognitive substance thus contains "in itself the real condition of all possible appearances." "Just as the *noumenon* in us is to appearances, so the highest intelligence is in relation to the *mundi intelligibilis"* (that is, to the things in themselves).[36] Here the subject (every subject) "posits" and "makes" objects as a result of an original, essential spontaneity present in him and thus knows them also *a priori* through forms of totality and general laws. For in one respect man "makes" himself here and therefore has knowledge *a priori* of himself: he posits himself as an object of his inner experience.[37] But this "making" pictures the self only as *object,* the self in appearance: so this knowledge *a priori* is not an insight into the thing in itself. There are other elements of this self-making that lead us closer in the consciousness of spontaneity to the thing in itself in *its* spontaneity, its *genuine* in-

30. R.-V. 96. "One comprehends only as much as one can himself make or bring about through concepts." V, 384.
31. Reflex. Nr. 929.
32. Reflex. Nr. 1117.
33. Op. Post. (Adickes, 756, 771)
34. Reflex. Nr. 1160, 1161.
35. Reflex. Nr. 966.
36. Reflex. Nr. 1133.
37. Cf. Op. Post. pp. 627, 645ff.

ternality. They are, first of all, the self-consciousness of transcendental apperception in every thinking being; then there is the consciousness of an end in itself of every ethical person as a consciousness of a purpose in itself, not "for" another, practical consciousness of the being in itself of the substantial subject over against all that is relational in the givenness for others. This goes deeper than the ego of inner experience as that which has already become an object of observation occupied with material given from the outside. But this does not belong here any longer.

All finite knowledge must therefore bear this limitation out of ontological necessity and thereby the dual character, the peculiar tension between positing spontaneity that "prescribes" laws (but which does not immediately grasp the laws of being) and ontological receptivity. But, again, this does not mean knowledge and always remains tied to that which expresses itself to us, that in being which is relative to us. The tendency of pure spontaneity toward the thing in itself is retained only in a specific sense by the reason of the finite subject—which even in the common understanding requires the unconditioned of the thing in itself, of things in so far as we do *not* know them.[38] Thus the concept of a thing in itself can be the central concept of the *Critique of Pure Reason*. Reason does not express itself first in Ideas of a world-totality. Rather, it attests its kinship to and derivation from intellectual intuition from the very beginning in the indispensable conception of the thing in itself. The "Idea" of the soul in the Dialectic, like the unconditioned character of the moral end in itself, represents only a special application of the unconditioned—both of which are approaches which are possible and which we are enjoined to attain.

The motive of so-called synthetic properties is one which, from Kant's earliest works onward, moves toward the critical doctrine of the limits of knowledge. The conception of synthesis in Kant is not primarily epistemological, for the question about synthetic judgments *a priori* is developed in connection with the ontological problem of real connections. Similarly, in the later metaphysics of the Kingdom of Ends, the synthetic judgment *a priori* of the categorical imperative has no less significance than that of the ontological law governing any supersensuous community of rational beings. Kant's pluralistic concept of the world (from the early

38. Cf. Kr. 20 [B 20-21].

Monadologia physica to the late domain of personal ends in themselves in the Kingdom of Ends) is bound from the very outset to
see the most important problem of ontology in the fact of connection, in the combining functions by which substances which are
in themselves isolated are bound to the world. This matter cannot
now be pursued. For our interest, it is enough to know that just
that natural force of all substances—physical, psychic, and intellectual—represents the interconnected totality of things as a community of reciprocal cause and effect. If finite knowledge can never
grasp the internal character of substance but rather only the relation to accidents (and substance only through passive reception of
accidents or grasp the forces themselves only through their effect),
it is clear that all finite knowledge can grasp the synthetic elements
of the given world only according to its active being (through
closer examination, for example, of its causal regularity), but never
according to the manner of its causation, according to its inner possibility. This line of thought begins very early in Kant. The assumptions of gravitational force or attraction serve to explain the great
movements of the world structure "only as the law of a general
phenomenon recognized in experience, of which one does not know
the cause. . . ." "Only through experience can one come to understand that the things of the world . . . have such a power; but one
can never grasp its possibility." Similarly, we know only the "various appearances of life in nature and their laws"; but we do not
know the "principle of this life." In general, inner possibility can
never be made clear, comprehended, or understood in cases of *"the
primary relations of causes and effects."* [39] What is given by experience (and perhaps also the discovery of the law) is all that finite
knowledge can attain. Here, too, the discursive limitation of our
reason shows itself, its dependence upon external reality, which it
cannot spontaneously comprehend.[40] Here begins Kant's consideration of causation as the ontological, synthetic ground of connection
as opposed to all merely logical-deductive relations which are intelligible to reason by mere concepts.[41] Here also begins the collapse
of logical rationalism. The real ground of the connection cannot
be perceived by reason, whatever the relevant causation of force

39. II, 20, 322, 323, 351; cf. also X, 69.
40. M.-V. 225.
41. Cf. II, 203, 294f.

might be (whether purely material, psychic, or intellectual).[42] The fundamental forces and relations of all things are not open to us. They are realities which, as regards their possibility, are unknown.

In the same vein the *Critique of Pure Reason* also speaks of "basic synthetic properties," "basic forces," as well as "riddles of nature," that we cannot grasp.[43] The possibility of every kind of change and causation necessarily remains inscrutable to us. That applies even to those natural properties like weight which are most familiar to us. Weight is a synthetic property; that is, one which does not belong to the individual body as such but rather shows itself first in the connection of substantial forces. Therefore, the judgment "All bodies are heavy" is synthetic. We do not know the causes but only the effects and the law of attraction.[44] The metaphysical tendency of this observation is the same for the Critical as for the pre-Critical Kant. On the one hand, the battle is directed against a rationalistic exaggeration which claims to have comprehended these basic forces and, for this reason, thinks itself justified in rejecting *a priori* all other possibilities of causality (causality through freedom, specifically organic natural forces, mind-body interaction). The inner possibility of freedom of the will, for example, is for us so intelligible because it represents a basic force.[45] Similarly, the *commercium* between body and soul is a "primary force," a "fundamental relation." [46] That we ourselves grasp the mechanism of material natural occurrences only in their appearances, not in their causes and "inner grounds" [47]—this critical insight was supposed to preserve us from the dangers of a false and dogmatic-cum-rationalistic metaphysics which wants to argue the great irrational aspects of the world of freedom, organism, and the mind-body relation out of existence. (Examples of such metaphysics are the dangers of Determinism or Fatalism, as in Spinoza; of metaphysical mechanism, as in Democritus or Epicurus; of the artificial hypotheses of the pre-established harmony or Occasionalism, as in Leibniz and Malebranche.) On the other hand, the arbitrariness of a wandering, poetic metaphysics was to be avoided, which simply

42. M.-H. 118.
43. Kr. 373 [A 449-451=B 477-479].
44. Cf. R-V. 88a.
45. M.-V. 314.
46. Reflex. Nr. 1330; also II, 322f., 370; X, 68-69.
47. See *Critique of Judgment*, V, 395.

postulates corresponding occult forces wherever irrationalities appear and thus thinks an explanation has been offered. Kant's critical metaphysics opposes both types: it neither interprets things out of existence nor postulates hypotheses according to need. Rather, it remains aware of the essential distance from being in every attempt at interpretation and explanation. "True metaphysics knows the limits of human reason; and among these is the hereditary defect that it cannot deny: that it simply cannot and may not conceive *a priori* any fundamental forces . . . [R]ather, it can do nothing further than reduce them, so experience teaches, to the smallest possible number and seek the fundamental force—as far as physics is concerned—in the world and—as far as metaphysics is concerned—outside the world." [48] But we know only two kinds of causality: material causality according to natural laws and the intelligible causality of free, purposive action. We know the law of both (the law of attraction "in the world"; the law of morality "outside the world"). The former is familiar to us through sense experience, while the way in which the law of freedom is given or presents itself is more complicated. But we do not thereby understand the "how" of these forces and relations of forces. Nor can we somehow assert that they (or even one of them) are the only ones possible. We cannot form *a priori* "the least concept of the possibility of dynamic relation"; and the concept of causality, "the category of the pure understanding does not serve to produce such things but only to understand them when they are encountered in experience." [49]

One should not think that a useful metaphysical hypothesis has been given whenever one introduces "new basic relations of cause and effect," when one simply assumes a purely intellectual community of substances, attraction without contact, or organic life forces.[50] The special access which practical reason opens up to the noumenal and the unconditioned does not lead us into the inner "how" of the *causa noumenon*.[51] "All human insight is at an end as soon as we have arrived at fundamental forces or fundamental powers." [52] Even the *Critique of Practical Reason* retains this. A

48. VIII, 179-180; cf. from the pre-Critical period II, 371, 416.
49. Kr. 587 [A 770-771=B 798-799]; cf. 205 [A 222-223=B 269-270].
50. Cf. Kr. 588 [A 771-773=B 799-801]; X, 69; II, 370.
51. V, 46, 49.
52. V, 46-47, 49.

practical relation of will between rational beings as things in themselves (ends in themselves) presents itself here. And this really carries in itself the character of the original and the unconditioned. The basic forces themselves, however, which form this relation (and the form of their law is rationally accessible only to us)—these we do not grasp. Thus the absence of logical contradiction in some kind of hypothetical fundamental forces alone does not prove its real possibility at all. But on the other hand, for this very reason the possibility of freedom cannot be denied *ab initio* and be metaphysically invalidated through the application of other, ostensibly rational and intuitable causal relations. From the ontological necessity that finite (receptive) knowers can be given only effects and appearances results the methodological necessity for every critical metaphysics: neither to deny the irrationalities that are given to us through experience or in another way, nor simply to accept them as a special mode of being and endow them with secret "forces." Rather, they are to be, as it were, encircled through the most precise exhibition of what can be grasped by us and through the sharpest separation of that from what is no longer knowable in them. Paradigm cases of this are Kant's treatment of freedom and the organism.[53]

II

To the distinguishing characteristics of the Kantian system belong not only his opposition of appearance and thing in itself (and the Critical attitude toward the irrational, which is necessary for all finite knowledge) but also the thesis that space and time lie on the side of appearance, that they—and just they—are characteristic of the "for us" of what is given and do not pertain to their being for themselves. Kant's philosophy is intended as critical idealism. The transcendental ideality of space and time is its basic assertion; and the concept of "appearance" is determined by it. For this the driving metaphysical motives next to and prior to the epistemological justifications (for example, the familiar arguments of the transcendental aesthetic) must also be exhibited.

At one point the merely descriptive characterization of space

53. For the issue of organism cf. VIII, 180ff.; V, 395.

and time touches what has been so far considered. What we know of things is said to be only what is relative to us, not what they are in themselves. That all our spatial and temporal determinations (especially all observation of motion) remain essentially relative conforms very well to this. This hovering of all the data of experience in mutual relativity makes the suspicion obvious that space and time are typical ways of determining what relates to us. In this sense Kant says over and again (precisely in connection with the terms so far considered) that space, time, and spatio-temporal matter yield "nothing but relations," only "external relations" and "nothing that is purely internal," no "internal" determinations of things.[54]

But this is only incidental. The genuinely decisive factors in the critical-cum-idealistic devaluation of space and time lie deeper. Above and beyond such relations of their essential features to the basic epistemic thesis, they are situated in quite definite positions and considerations of Kant's original and lasting metaphysics. First, let us consider space.

All of modern philosophy since the great rise of natural science finds itself in a peculiar opposition, which the great systems—each in its own way—attempt to overcome. The central reality is for all of them the intellectual: an absolute (*res cogitans infinita* of Christian theism) which is grasped in a purely intellectual way and the life-centers of conscious beings, of psychic subjects, which are in themselves purely spiritual. Now out of the spiritual tendencies of Neoplatonism (but with especially great force in the philosophy of the fathers of the Christian church) this had become the genuine riddle of metaphysics: how the spatiality of the visible cosmos could be reconciled with the spiritual ground of the world and the (similarly spiritual) principal contents of the world. Already at that time and then in the Middle Ages certain movements attempted a solution by devaluating what was spatial and material.[55] For the

54. Cf., e.g., Kr. 72 [B 67-68]: "since nothing except mere representations of relation are given us through outer sense, it can contain . . . only the relation of an object to the subject. . . ." Similarly, for inner sense and temporal relations, Kr. 242, 255f. [A 264-266=B 320-322, A 284-285=B 340-341]; VIII, 153; Reflex Nr. 782; Op. Post. (Adickes, 78)

55. Cf. on this point my book concerning *Die grossen Themen der abendländischen Metaphysik und der Ausgang des Mittelalters*, Berlin, 1922, Chap. III: Seele u. aussenwelt.

modern period the conflict came more sharply to a head in that just this spatial and material cosmos became with modern science not only the sensuously most impressive and, as it were, the most sublime of what is really given, but also the primary object of all visible scientific knowledge, of the entire cognitive interest for the scientist oriented to exactitude and the mathematical method.

From Cusanus and Giordano Bruno on, the new pathos about infinity is associated with this and particularly with the spatiality of the universe. Motives that had driven the natural consciousness of the world and then the cosmological speculation of all peoples (particularly of the Greeks) to the spatial cosmos as the all-inclusive and obviously primary reality are very much strengthened at this time within the context of a mode of thought whose central interest and sense of reality promoted a metaphysics of the inward and the spiritual. A new "scientific" naturalism emerged out of the overpowering insight into the rationality and apparently unlimited rationalizability of the spatial and material. And this threatened to destroy the primacy of the spiritual, which, although it is immediately certain and closest to us, remains indefinite, just as vague as the "substantial forms" of a superceded view of nature. Not only sensuous intensity and superiority but also ideal structure and essence appeared to belong solely to the spatial and material cosmos. The "eternal truths"—those are the mathematical and the geometrical, are they not? For the natural philosophy of bygone times —yes, even for the Renaissance—the spatial and temporal can have a secondary standing as distinct from forces and substances that might not only be so very removed from the mode of being of the spiritual and intellectual. With the new mathematical and mechanistic science these two factors in the world break apart; and just the geometrical and spatial—the purely mechanical—is the essential, the rational, and what reveals structure. The conflict took on especial importance for the great modern metaphysicians because they directly participated in the new scientific work. Now whoever remains aloof, like Berkeley, and does not feel the entire weight of the newly set task, can speak out in opposition to the threatening scientic naturalism for the frank assertion of an absolute metaphysics of spirit through a radical idealism, for which the entire external world (and thus the entire world of the new science) is regarded as mere appearance, a symbolic embodiment of an immediate and purely spiritual intercourse between God and man, between primordial spirit and finite spiritual beings. Or again: only those who (like Hobbes or Spinoza) are willing to deny the ontological primacy of the spiritual either completely or in part are able to look for a solution of the conflict in the direction of naturalism. And only who remains with the duality of claims, leaving the final unification to mere religious conviction, can (like Descartes) teach a dualism with the superstructure of a *res infinita* that is only *cogitans*. The entire weight of the question rests on spirits (as with Leibniz, Malebranche, and Kant). For Kant, the metaphysical nature of space was from very early a central problem. For the pupil of Newton the world and space are quite inseparable things. Space appears as the all-inclusive principle for the infinite multiplicity and variety of the contents of the world. The metaphysical world-order is above all a spatial one; and the rationality of this total order supplies the genuine foundation for all dogmatic rationalism of this early period. Not only human existence but also the spiritual and the moral in general are fitted into this order. The distance from the middle of the world determines the levels of distinctness and freedom for cognitive and volitional beings. The naturalism regarding space of the mechanistic natural philosopher dominates the field. Also the enthusiasm for infinity (which is perpetuated later in the familiar words of "the starry heaven above me") refers predominantly and fundamentally to the infinite spaces and worlds in an actually infinite world-space.

But for Kant just as for all his predecessors from Cusanus on,[56] the infinity of the world is the consequence and expression of the infinite spiritual principle that not only lies before the beginning of the world as its creative ground but, at the same time, remains the principle of the preservation of the world. The doctrine of infinity in natural philosophy leads immediately and necessarily to *Theologia naturalis*. Thus space is for Kant—in the spirit of Newton—the "infinite extension of the divine presence."[57] And thus the conflict is already there.

In a short passage the conflict is already present in the early work: the Godhead is said to be equally present in all of world-

56. Cf. my book *Über die grossen Themen*, etc., Chap. II: Unendlichkeit im Endlichen.
57. I, 306.

space. "Wherever natures are which can work themselves beyond dependence upon creatures to community with the highest being, it is equally close." Only he who "knows how to free himself from creaturely existence" is able to find himself closer to this original source of perfection than anything else in all of nature.[58] The concept of universal presence strives beyond spatiality and a dependence upon space. "Equally close" and "closer"—these point to another order and disposition of the world. It is a community which is quite different from spatial community and which unites the natures which free themselves from creaturely existence with the primordial being. The later two-worlds theory, the duality of the starry heavens and the moral law and domain, mildly suggests itself.

Indeed, Kant's development goes away from a naturalistic and rationalistic theory of space in favor of that other irrational concept of the world of the Kingdom of Ends, completely separated from all relation to space and accessible to us only through the law which finally superceded the former view. The critical turn of 1770-1781 marks the final victory of the metaphysics of spirit and inwardness over the metaphysics of naturalistic rationalism. The ideal structure of the spirit (the *a priori* of morality) shrinks that of the spatial and mathematical to an intellectual function of quite a special kind. Kant's great turn of life, seen metaphysically, is also a link in the great chain of struggles which the spiritual metaphysics of Christianity has had to carry on against the metaphysics of the cosmos since the end of antiquity. Through the restriction of the merely naturalistic and rationalistic habits of sensuous experience, as well as the significant necessities of mechanistic science, the critical restriction of theoretical reason was to hold the way open for the recognition and the philosophical comprehension of an ontology of spirit and its relations. The battle of the *Critique of Pure Reason* against the proofs for the existence of God, for example, is aimed at the naturalistic conception of God as primarily relating to nature (God as prime mover or as Demiurge, God as *ens realissimum* in a Neoplatonic sense, natural theology, or a proof that is cosmological or ontological).[59] Only moral theology, grounding itself on the spontaneous volitional reality displayed in moral action and with its different categories, is able to point to the primordial spiritual

58. I, 329-340.
59. Cf. V, 483, 485, 183; Kr. 26 [B 30-32]; Op. Post. (Adickes, 775).

principle through the personal concept of being in itself and the absolute core of the unconditioned end in itself. The personal spontaneity of morality, of the power of freedom, prepares a narrow way to the absolute for a searching reason, while all merely objective and theoretical knowledge, with its categories applicable to nature, sees itself tied to a domain of relations which, seen metaphysically, is very limited. Similarly, the section on the paralogisms battles against the concept of "soul" as natural substance (as an enduring individual thing with varying properties) and for a deeper view of the element of endurance and identity of a developing being given with the ego and the personality. This is a tendency whose positive fulfillment can only bring about a practical-dogmatic metaphysics. Indeed, the element of concrete personal endurance and substantiality in the flow of psychic moments accrues here to the conception of the ego which is absent from merely empty apperception. For here there is an enduring development of an identical, free subject.[60] Spiritual immortality, for example, may not be looked upon as a special case of the indestructability of all natural substances (as it was seen, in a certain sense, by Leibniz). And the mere reflection on the knowing subject still does not do justice to the demands of the problem: transcendental apperception (this I, he, or it which thinks in me) remains, when it is taken in itself, in the indefiniteness of a "consciousness in general" without the fulfillment of an individual personality which results only through self legislation. Similarly, the four antinomies battle only for the conception of a spiritual conception of creation and against the objections of the outer temporal flow and the Law of Sufficient Reason conceived naturalistically. They battle for freedom against the contradiction of a spatial continuum; and they battle for a spiritual as opposed to the cosmological principle of the absolute. In addition, they are for the "true infinity" of the spiritual world and against the merely quantitative infinity or finitude of the cosmos. They are especially for the infinity of spiritual relations as opposed to the infinity of, say, spatial reality as it is presented to us.

It is clear that, with the gradual victory of this departure from the natural to the spiritual concept of the world, the metaphysical question about the relation of space and everything that is spatial to spiritual reality was bound to become increasingly prominent.

60. Cf. V, 133.

The concept of the infinite extension of the divine presence, which was accepted with such pathos in the beginning, becomes problematic. A local omnipresence shows itself to be a flat contradiction. Nothing can be present in several places at once; nothing can stand in an external relation to itself, or, for the standpoint of one place, see itself in another. The divine omnipresence cannot obtain in a presence in all places. There could then be only a part of the omnipresent being in every one of these places. Omnipresence can be asserted only according to power (*virtualiter*), not according to position (*localiter*). Otherwise the *ens originarium* would suffer a limitation that would be incompatible with his essence and would not be compensated by the infinity of space.[61]

The concept of the primordial being admits nothing spatial. "Impenetrability, extension, and the like cannot be the properties of what has understanding and will." Thus the paradox results, that the *ens realissimum* cannot contain all realities.[62] Further, for our thought about the world—which is usually naturalistically oriented —the concept "of the infinite Spirit is purely negative and consists in the fact that one denies the properties of matter in it that are incompatible with an infinite and necessary substance." [63] Spatial reality cannot be conceived as a determination of the *ens realissimum* ("a confusion that up until then was uncommonly dominant") but in any case only as a "sequence." [64]

But the difficulties are not removed. Conceived as a sequence, space, when it is understood as infinite reality, reduces the primordial being to a form of being that is incompatible with its absolute spirituality. Or should the comparison that the *Physical Monadology* draws between the spatial effect of an essentially non-spatial monad as the extension of the external presence of this element, and the world-whole as the *ambitus* of divine presence (with the division of both regions of space the substance is not divided along with them) —should this analogy really be taken seriously? A naturalistic pantheism would be the unavoidable consequence. This is also the decisive metaphysical doubt of Kant about the reality of space (even

61. II, 414, also 297; M.-H. 113; M.-V. 302f.; R.-V. 85, 184ff.
62. II, 85.
63. II, 321a. Cf. the later noumenon understood negatively and the positive access of practical-dogmatic metaphysics to the infinite spiritual being, which shows absolute inner necessity in volition.
64. II, 85.

if it is only a derivative reality as an objective emanation and phenomenon of monads): the reality of an infinite spatial whole to
which the divine spiritual being is to be everywhere related moves
in the direction of pantheism. The Newtonian connection between
God and space through the concept of the *Sensorium Dei* makes
the primordial being—which is to be considered independent—a
kind of world soul which stands in reciprocal *commercium* with
the matter of the world and thus becomes itself dependent. "Space
is possibility of community; if God were in space, He would be
dependent." [65] All dogmatic metaphysicians of the time took this
way out—whether it was Crusius, who considered location as one
of the infallible determinations of existence in general; or Mendelssohn, who regarded space as a condition of the existence not of
God but of finite and derivative beings.[66] Newton's questionable
fomulations gave rise to the danger of open pantheism as it was
taught by Spinoza in the combination of the spiritual primordial
being and spatial infinity. "If I were to assume space as a being in
itself, Spinozism would be irrefutable; that is, the parts of the
world would be parts of the Godhead. Space would be the Godhead; it would be unitary, omnipresent; nothing outside of it could
be thought; everything would be in it." [67] After the successful completion of transcendental idealism, this motive comes out quite
clearly in the *Critique of Practical Reason:* "Thus, when one does
not assume the ideality of time and space, Spinozism is the only
thing left, where space and time are essential determinations of
the primordial being itself; the things which depend upon him
(including ourselves) are not substances but merely accidents which
inhere in him." [68] Thus it is no peculiar slip of the critical epistemology when the considerations of the Transcendental Aesthetic
conclude with a passage about natural theology, with the thesis (and
the argument): when one makes time and space into forms of
things in themselves, "then they would also have to apply to the
existence of God." [69]

As regards the Critical solution itself, it must first be remarked
that even the pre-Critical Kant (following Leibniz and in this al-

65. M.-V. 302, R.-V. 186f.
66. II, 76; V, 101; M.-H. 31.
67. M.-H. 101, after 1781.
68. V, 101-102.
69. Kr. 74 [B 70-71].

ready an opponent of Newton) had devaluated space to a phenomenon in a quite definite sense. Space is *expers substantialis* and is itself affected only through relations of force of psychical (non-spatial) elementary substances. Space is not the highest condition of the possibility of the system of reality, but rather the divine being; space and everything spatial are only a sequence, only the outer phenomenon and secondary but nonetheless real product of the community of substances constituted by God's virtual omnipresence (that is, the presence of force in all monads).[70] In this way the spatial world presents itself here as the phenomenon of divine omnipresence.

It is clear that the difficulties mentioned above are not removed by such a concept of objective phenomena. The spiritual primordial being remains the indirect creator of space, directly related to the perception of space, since space possesses real, even if only derivative, reality. Only with the *Dissertation* of 1770 is the conflict settled. Even the way of Malebranche is rejected, above all because of the danger of a mystical pantheism. The concept of appearance as subjective, which is also present in Leibniz (Kant himself later regarded his theory of space and time as a consequence of what Leibniz meant),[71] according to which space is not the condition of the possibility or the objective product of things in themselves but rather only the condition of the possibility of our finite intellect, the essential conditioning form of our specific subjectivity in that cognitive and metaphysical transition of substantial effects on intelligences [72]—this new concept of appearance leads beyond the earlier duality. While it was said before that it is conceivable that other world-forces in their interaction could produce other kinds of space [73]—the turn is now subjective in character; it is conceivable that other finite beings might have other ways of intuiting an "outer" than ours. From now on space means the combination of substances in their sensuous representation. Everything without us must *appear* to us in space but not, as Crusius thought, *be* in space. Space has only empirical reality, possessing a determinative necessity only for our representation. In themselves, space and time are

70. I, 17, 21f., 23f., 408, 479f.; II, 81.
71. VIII, 203, 207ff., 249.
72. Cf., e.g., M.-H. 97f.
73. Kr. 55 [A 26-27=B 42-43].

only *entia imaginaria;* the cause of the world is not affected at all by it.[74] The concepts of virtual omnipresence and the phenomenon of divine omnipresence (both designations are retained up until the *Opus Postumum*) [75] take on a new sense which is freed from the old difficulties. The presence of divine power has nothing to do with that which is ontologically located, not even by an indirect way of constituting it by some kind of secondary relation to intuition. "One really ought not to say that God has created appearances but rather the things that we do not know to which a corresponding sensibility in us has been assigned." [76] Thus we cannot become sensuously conscious of the divine omnipresence; our spatial sense would always distort this consciousness and make it that of a pantheistic containment. "We cannot become conscious of ourselves as in God; rather, if we were in him, God would be conscious of us as of his own determinations, and we would not be conscious of ourselves at all." [77] But that correspondence obtains because sensibility and spatial perception represent only a subjective form in which we grasp really given things in themselves and their community and interaction. Thus space remains the subjective phenomenon of divine omnipresence. The real world-system of things in themselves founded by the primordial being and His to-us-unknown power is at any rate given to us as an appeaarnce in the sensuous dress of an infinite space and infinitely many interconnecting spatial worlds. The element of uniqueness—which is inimical to the concept of an extramundane and independent being—is detrimental only to the picture of spatial appearance. But, on the other hand, this picture has genuine (representative) contact with the real connection and ground of things in themselves. While it earlier sounded objective: "Space is the phenomenon of existence of all things through an infinity (that of the primordial being),"[78] space is now only a subjective thing, which is, however, represented as something real (empirical reality) and thus becomes "the effect of the feeling of omnipresence"—in this way representing even now a kind of consequence of the dependence of the existence of all things upon

74. II, 398; M.-H. 31; 98ff.; M.-V. 112f.
75. II, 410, M.-V. 303, 338-339, 113; Op. Post. (Adickes, 233a)
76. Reflex. Nr. 1131.
77. Reflex. Nr. 345.
78. Reflex. Nr. 1339 (surely before 1770).

the One.[79] "Because things are all there through One, they constitute a unity. When this unity is represented sensuously, it is space.
Thus, space is a phenomenon of divine omnipresence, not an organon, as Newton thought . . . when this space is represented intellectually, it is the omnipresence of God." [80] Effects are symbols
of causes; thus space, through which things are represented as really
and necessarily combined through a common ground, is a symbol
of divine omnipresence or the phenomenon of divine causality.[81]
The entire pathos of antiquity concerning spatial infinity thus retains its limited sense: what stays is that we are in contact with the
effects of the infinite being in the infinity of worlds and worldsystems—only this sensuous contact is merely a symbolic mode of
representation, not an adequate ontological picture.[82] The pathos
of the "starry heaven above me" in the *Critique of Practical Reason*
retains its full sense even after everything spatial and material has
been made subjective with respect to its form. We can even suspect
of the late Kant—in very close connection with certain speculations
of the early period—that the purely spiritual infinite community of
intellectual beings with one another necessarily and generally connects every one of us with all observable worlds.[83] This entire infinity of worlds which represents itself spatially is for Kant's solution of the conflict not illusion (as it is for the idealism of Berkeley)
but appearance. All appearances refer to being in itself.

But in this way the theology of spatial naturalism is superceded.
It is no longer a rarity that the *ens realissimum* does not reckon the
reality of space to its properties. The primordial being is not the
object of outer intuition, not the object of sensibility.[84] With moral
theology, which (proceeding from an entirely different fact) opens
up a way to the primordial being, "the disturbing condition of space
and extension" falls away.[85] This still enables us "to conceive divine
omnipresence as existence in all places, in order to grasp its

79. Reflex. Nr. 403.

80. M.-V. 339.

81. Reflex. Nr. 339; apparently (contrary to B. Erdmann's assumption) after
1770. See also Reflex. Nr. 406, M.-V. 113.

82. Cf. Kr. 488 [A 621-622=B 649-650].

83. V, 162. Cf. with this peculiar passage Reflex. Nr. 107: "whether we
stand in any relation at all through the representation of space to all creatures in
general."

84. M.-H. 101.

85. V, 483.

immediate presence for extended things"; but we can no longer attribute this determination to God as something which is perceived in Him.[86] Another and deeper understanding of the presence of the primordial being reveals itself in morality: a presence not of outer intuition but in internal being, in the voice of duty, in the "moral law within me." [87] The fact that "in Him we live, move, and have our being" must be freed from sensuous representation of space and the pantheistic tendency which is bound up with it. We may think of the relation of our limited existence to the *ens realissimum* as a one-sided analogy and, so to speak, as a lame comparison, as, for example, that all figures are possible only as various ways of limiting infinite space. We are not allowed to form an explanatory concept from this sensuous embodiment of that idea. Strictly speaking, the limitation of the *ens realissimum* is something which is completely different from division." [88] "The omnipresence of God is the closest presence; that is, God contains the substantiality and the spiritual part of substances." It is, therefore, immediate and close, but not local. The most perfect being cannot be thought as spatial; its presence cannot be thought according to the immediate but nonspiritual way of the Newtonian mutual attraction of all things.[89] The concept of the world in the *Metaphysics of Morals* (community of spirits under a supreme lawgiver) makes us familiar with a relation of dependence and an ordered system that have nothing of that pantheistic containment and that merely accidental existence of all finite things in the universal substance. With this attitude, separated from categories of nature and spatial form, the system of nature (as teleology of nature) takes on another complexion. What rationalistic metaphysics had to miss was accomplished by practical-dogmatic metaphysics, to which the three *Critiques* were to give a propaedeutic. This was, to be sure, accomplished with important limitations regarding the intelligibility of the structure of things.

Closely connected with the foregoing motive is the opposition that from the outset shows itself between Kant's pluralistic concept of the world and the monistic structure of the spatial continuum. It is the same motive that forced Leibniz to the phenomenality of

86. V, 484.
87. Cf. Op. Post. (Adickes, 778: "This Idea is the feeling of the presence of the Godhead in man.")
88. M.-V. 339; Kr. 459.
89. R.-V. 185.

space.[90] For Kant, too, this pluralism is determined from the outset primarily through the fundamental conviction of the independent, substantial reality of all individual egos; secondarily, however, through the conviction of the mechanical inexplicability of organic unity. The lines of thought which lead to the concept of the physical monads as pre-spatial centers of force enter here also. One of the motives which was influential from quite early to the end of Kant's life is marked by this opposition. It concerned Kant from at least 1756 as the tension between metaphysics and geometry; and in the great revolution of 1769-1770 it played the decisive role.[91] The *Inaugural Dissertation* begins with the consideration of two possible concepts of the world: the world as *compositum substantiale* (the aggregate and community of simple substances; the parts are the ground of the possibility of what is composite); and the world as a continuum which as a totality is the ground of the possibility of the parts and which itself does not consist of simple elements. Space and time seem to require the latter form of being; and its essential divisibility to infinity excludes any reconciliation with the first concept of the world. The idealistic solution of the conflict reduces the spatial *mundus sensibilis* to appearance; the two worlds amount to two kinds of knowing, of which only the abstract and intellectual are applied to the world in its being in itself. In the *Critique of Pure Reason* the second antinomy battles against the fact that space resolves all simple substances into an infinitely divisible continuum. Its intention is to ground the ontological possibility of simple things that cannot be sought in space itself. Especial weight lies upon simple spiritual substances; in 1770 it had lain on immaterial substances, which, according to Kant's idiom, are not non-spatial things in themselves but spiritual substances.[92] In 1789 Kant also emphasized that "no other way out remains than to grant that bodies are not things in themselves and that their mode of sensuous representation . . . is nothing but the appearance of something which [can] contain what is simple as a thing in itself." [93]

---

90. For the historical connection cf. Reflex. Nr. 1120, and Reiche, *Lose Blätter*, p. 173.

91. I, 477ff.; see also the discussion of the question in the *Untersuchung über die Deutlichkeit* . . . , III, 279, 286ff.

92. Cf. II, 398; Kr. 385, 386 [A 466-467=B 494-495; A 467-469=B 495-497].

93. VIII, 209.

The opposition must become especially significant just to the degree to which the intelligible world takes, in opposition to nature, a central position. The pluralistic structure of the spiritual world always gave Kant the decisive argument against every monistic world-view (such as Spinozism or egoism). For the question of this ontological community of personal ends in themselves it is of special importance to know that space cannot be the ground of the possibility of the substantial totality of things. Seen from any spiritual conception of the world, the spatial continuum represents itself rather as a principle of division. Space in the extension of its places always has a limited and negative element which makes it into something incompatible with the highest being.[94] For the interests of the spiritual world and its deeper connections one observation has particular value in opposition to the dogmatic-rational doctrine of space: we do not know how community of substances (grounded, as they must be, through a common dependence upon a primordial being) is possible. All rational beings seem "to stand in a community which accords with their nature, and which does not rest on the conditions through which the relation of beings is limited, and where the distance of plans and ages which constitute the great schism in the visible world and destroys all community disappears." [95] Another mode of connection is demanded and sought here; and practical and dogmatic metaphysics has come upon the synthetic law of this community. Thus, in that passage referring to the starry heaven, the order and community of spiritual beings are no longer placed in a spatial connection; rather, the exact opposite occurs: the connection of every rational being with all visible worlds is grounded upon the truly infinite community of the spiritual and personal world with its not merely accidental but general and necessary connection.[96] Here belongs also Kant's battle, carried on since 1765,[97] against the spatial element in the conceptions of heaven and hell that, despite all opposing spiritualistic tendencies, appeared ineradicable up into the eighteenth century. Even Kant's late philosophy of religion opposed such a spatial-

94. Cf. R.-V. 47.
95. II, 332; even *before* the consequence that the Critical solution draws from this fact.
96. V, 162.
97. II, 332a.

cosmological narrowing of the concept of the world.[98] It is not another place, a community with other things (for example, on other planets), to which those conceptions of the religious life point, but rather to a different mode of perception, a separation from the sensuous-spatial condition of our knowing. "The other world remains the same as far as the objects are concerned; it is not different as regards substance, except as it is perceived in the intellect. . . ." [99] The "other" world is deeply bound up with our present existence. We touch it, as it were, with each of our deeds.

The third of the metaphysical objections against the reality of space proceeds from the problem of the soul and its relation to matter. This question arises early for Kant and does not disappear again. The clearest formulations are given in the period around 1765. For example: "In my opinion everything depends upon finding the *data* of the problem: how the soul is present in the world constituted of material natures as well as those of a different kind. One should find in such a substance the power of outer efficacy and the power to endure receptivity from without, of which the union with the human body is only a special variety." [100] "The way in which a spirit can be present in space has not yet been given." [101] Moreover, it is important to know that, with "those of a different kind," the question always arises for Kant about intellectual beings in general; that is, not only about other human beings but about possibly higher and purely spiritual intelligences which exist apart from the body. For Kant the problem of space and the spirit is always connected with that of space and the soul.

In the first work of his youth, Kant regards this as certain: spiritual substances stand in direct causal relation (*influxus physicus*) to material substances. An insurmountable difficulty is thereby presented only for a purely mechanical conception of nature, which recognizes only forces of motion and no other, inner, forces of substances. Kant himself, however, answers the question of that causal connection simply as follows: "that the soul must have outward effects simply because it is in a place." [102]

98. VI, 128a; the conclusion of the quotation (which for the young Kant would not be true at all) is meant ironically.
99. M.-V., 256ff.
100. X, 68.
101. II, 293, 312.
102. I, 201.

But here lies the difficulty; what does the inner nature of spiritual existences have to do with an external existence that is spacial? At what place or point of space is my soul? Where is its position in the body? In the context of these questions it is a certain alleviation, but not a solution, when space is regarded as an objective phenomenon resulting from the forces exerted by substances, as already in this early work, in which Kant draws the conclusion (which is for him apparently very important and which he says that no one had drawn) that things (i.e., spiritual beings) can really exist which are nowhere present in the entire world. And this is said to follow because place and location result only in outer relations, and it is not necessary for a substance to stand in relation to other things.[103] In regard to the objective phenomenon of space, it becomes necessary to distinguish two basic kinds of substances (monads), which constitute something extended in their interaction, and the spiritual unities that are not present through impenetrability in space (which is effected by psychic monads and filled with matter).[104] Spiritual substances could thus occupy a space in connection with the body without "filling" space. The space of their immediate presence is not a point but a space: the body with whose material elements the soul interacts. Accordingly, the soul does not have its location in a particular place in the body but rather in the entire body.[105] To overlook this distinction between the two kinds of substances would have to lead to overt materialism. The questionable interaction may not, therefore, be conceived as material in character—as accomplished through impenetrability; rather, we must conceive it in such a way that the spiritual essence of matter is closely present and does not influence "those forces of elements with which they are related, but rather the internal principle of their condition." [106] Moreover, Kant constantly rejected, in addition to materialism, the spiritual tendency of Leibniz's theory of monads. It will not do to conceive of the unknown interior of physical monads simply according to the analogy of what we know about what is in us.[107]

It is clear how much that is questionable still remains in this and, at the same time, how little is accomplished for the question con-

103. I, 21f.
104. Cf. for example II, 293, 326-327. M.-V. 228f.
105. II, 323f.
106. II, 328.
107. Cf. my book about *Kants metaphysischer Weltbegriff.*

cerning the mutual connection of spiritual substances completely detached from space. For it cannot be satisfactory when the *Nova Dilucidatio,* in the face of that merely isolated possibility of a being which is nowhere present in the world, toys with the thought that there could be several systems of relations (since they do not depend upon space but rather space depends upon them), and that there could therefore be several worlds in a metaphysical sense.[108] To be sure, the conception here tends toward a Kingdom of Ends as opposed to our spatial-material world; but it still stands dubiously close to that suggestion out of the early work, according to which different relations of forces could bring about other kinds of space. The essential separation of the concept of a spiritual world order from all spatial representation is still by no means clear. Only the critical-idealistic solution changes the situation completely. Space is in no way the prototype or even only the most basic expression of the world-system, but rather just the sensuous-subjective mode of representation of a world-system—only in a quite definite way. The question about the location of the soul in the body becomes senseless when spatial relations themselves apply only to outer in-intuition. The soul perceives itself only through the inner sense. How could one also want to observe it through the outer sense— in an external relation to something external? "Just as little as an eye can perceive itself, so likewise can the soul perceive itself externally." "But when the soul is not an object of the external senses, the conditions of external existence will not apply to it . . . since it is not an object of outer intuition, it is not in space." Only by analogy can we say that it is in space; "in a similar way one says that God is in a church." The spatial body denotes only an element in the subjective mode of representation of its non-spatial position in the world.[109] "*Sedeo animae*. What is simply an object of inner sense cannot be an external object. Accordingly, the substance of the soul cannot be subject to the conditions of external intuition but is merely the subject of its influence [the body]." [110] "I as soul am determined by the body and stand in community with it. I as intelligence am not in a place; for the place is a relation of outer intuition; as intelligence, however, I am not an external object that

108. I, 414.
109. M.-V. 227f.
110. Reflex. Nr. 1298.

can be determined in reference to the relation. . . . Thus I shall not be able to determine my place immediately; but I as soul determine my place in the world through the body; but I cannot determine my place in the body; for otherwise I should have to perceive my-self in an outer relation." The cognitive principle in me is "distin-guished from what can be only an object of outer sense." The presence of the soul is not local but spiritual.[111] The locality is not a condition of the existence of the soul, not applicable to it im-mediately but rather mediately, derivatively, and contingently. And all beings that cannot be objects of outer sense to one another are divorced from space as the very condition of outer intuition.[112] The forms of sensuous knowledge that are necessary for us are not conditions of the possibility of things themselves. There can be not only other forms of intuition but, above all, other modes of connection than those which appear familiar and rational to us. All the difficulties *de substantiarum immaterialium . . . locis in universo corporeo, de sede animae,* etc. fall to the ground because they rested on a false dogmatism about space.[113]

With this the path is prepared for another concept of the world and for another concept of the possibility of several worlds: the totality of all moral persons (to whose being in themselves we have a direct access as distinct from the phenomenal limitations of all natural knowledge) stands over against and sets itself above the physical-spatial cosmos in the extension of the concept of pur-pose from ethics to nature. In his naturalistic and pre-Critical period, whenever Kant worked with the conception of an analogy of the spiritual world, its systematic constitution, and the ethical influences of spiritual beings with universal gravitation (although he did not venture to assert this as a serious opinion), the critical systems can quite innocently take nature and natural law as the model of the moral domain and its organization, since in that sys-tem space and spatial gravitation themselves indicate only the phe-nomenal connection of a deeper being in itself.[114] Now there is no longer a danger that the spiritual community of rational beings and the formal structure of the Kingdom of Ends—whose law we our-

---

111. M.-V. 132, 255f.; M.-H. 101.
112. II, 419.
113. II, 414.
114. Cf. *Kr. d. prakt. V., Abschnitt,* "Von der Typik der reinen praktischen Urteilskraft" and also the *Grundl. z. Met. d. Sitten.*

selves grasp in its unconditional character—are distorted into something sensuous and spatial.

Parallel and closely connected with the problem of space from Kant's early period—as so often in the history of metaphysics and finally with Leibniz—is the question concerning the being of time. What is most decisive here is the irreconcilability of succession with the essence of the primordial being. It is impossible for the *ens illimitatum* to stand in the separation between past and future; absolute reality of time would have to lead to a non-entity such as the God of Spinoza, that, according to Kant's interpretation, is subjected to interminable changes. Even divine foreknowledge cannot pertain for God to something in the future. For him everything is real (that is, present).[115] Time, like space, contains an element of negation. Time, like space, is a principle of separation that, "when it is regarded absolutely, destroys all deeper community through the separation of the ages."[116]

Such lines of thought find their broader extension in discussions from the Critical period, when the new solution removes the difficulties. "The deficiency of never being completely what one strives to become (future) is inseparable from the existence of a being in time" is just as incompatible with the primordial being as the thought that a part of His existence is already behind Him (past), that a definite year can be experienced only after another has already been experienced.[117] The eternity of the primordial being cannot be infinite temporal duration (*sempiternitas*). The spiritual relation of the *ens illimitatum* to the world cannot be influenced by the temporality of the world. "Things are temporally differentiated only with regard to themselves but not in regard to God; for God is not in time; thus time is not for Him the condition of the perception of things." The divine presence cannot be conceived in any other way than as a present intuition of all eternity, in the full infinity of its future developments.[118] This conception is just as unavoidable and in itself necessary as it cannot be carried out by us. It appears to our temporally limited representation as a flat *contradictio in adjecto*.[119] The questions come to a head in the conception

115. II, 74, 297.
116. II, 232.
117. M.-V. 67, 303; R.-V. 83.
118. M.-V. 312.
119. Reflex. Nr. 371; M.-V. 312f.; R.-V. 84.

and problem of the creation, this solely adequate Idea of the origin of the world (*systema liberae productionis* against *syst. inhaerentiae* and *syst. emanationis*—in other words, against Spinozism and Neo-Platonism) despite the anthropomorphistic tendencies and reductions which are mostly associated with it. "If time were the mode of being of things in themselves, the causality of the cause of the world would be a causality of the beginning of the world in time; and there is therefore not a first and necessary cause." [120] The entire antinomy of time arises, as far as its difficulties for the concept of creation are concerned, not through this confusion of intelligible cause with sensuous beginning; out of the false tendency "to infer from the impossibility of an infinite series of given causes in the sensuous world to a first cause." [121] Without himself knowing the historical connection accurately, Kant applies here the critical probe to the peculiar contradiction of those scholastic proofs for the existence of God that wanted to retain the old Aristotelian proof from the impossibility of an infinite series in the context of their new conviction of the actual infinity of the divine being. For Kant the creative and conserving principle has nothing to do with temporal beginning. God originates the entire series, whether it be finite or infinite, temporally limited or eternal in the sense of *sempiternitas a parte ante*.[122] "A beginning of sensibility contradicts itself because the sensuous is then viewed as bounding upon the intellectual." [123] What is temporal is viewed as really emerging from what is timeless and eternal (and thus having a beginning). The spiritual and infinite being cannot itself be conditioned with respect to the existence of things; nor can it be the cause of time and space.[124] All the pathos concerning the infinity of time can only indicate the sensuous projection of a true and fundamental infinity of being on a temporal plane that is not itself real. And this view remains equally influential from a very early period, where an infinity of the future was for Kant the primary infinity, into the doctrines of

---

120. Reiche, *Lose Bl.* 208; Reflex. Nr. 376.
121. M.-V. 87; Kr. 480 [A 609-611=B 637-639].
122. Cf., e.g., M.-V. 85; M.-H. 43; Kr. 480; Reiche, *Lose Bl.* 234; Reflex. Nr. 1431: "God created the world from eternity . . . but did not create an eternal world." Nr. 1432: "The world lasts eternally . . . at every time."
123. Reflex. Nr. 387.
124. V, 101.

the infinite progress of all spiritual development in Kant's late period.[125]

But that is just the critical solution. Time is *aeternitas phaenomenon* (and therefore it is infinite); the intelligible endurance of a thing, when it is measured temporally, is only a subjective appearance of time.[126] Temporal as well as spatial determinations are mere conditions of relation. Our temporal view of things and of ourselves is itself possible only through a more basic connection of things which itself points back to the intelligible endurance of the creative and conserving *vis infinita*.[127] Endurance in time is only the sensuous-subjective mode of appearance of a *duratio noumenon*. The sensuous-temporal form is itself the only "means possible for us to represent existence as quantitative." [128] Here also it is only practical-dogmatic metaphysics that decisively removes the error of making the conception of the "first" mover and the "beginning" of creation into something sensuous. And this is done by holding the conception of creation of the *systema liberae productionis,* not on the basis of natural experiences of time or objective processes of time, but rather to understand (if not to intuit) it on the basis of the freedom of the ethical subject. The personal category or principle of free causality—this purely spontaneous and internal positing of the will that is unaffected by time—replaced that natural causality and succession which had been unjustifiably expanded and dogmatically carried over to things in themselves.

The other great metaphysical doubt about the reality of time proceeds, as is well known, from the concept of freedom.[129] The metaphysical and not only the ethical emphasis of this question—the issue about its status within a naturalistic and rational view of the world—formed an essential part of Kant's development from very early. The solution of the *Nova Dilucidatio* (with, as Kant later said, its concept of merely comparative instead of absolute freedom) became obviously unsatisfactory. A continual concern with

125. Cf. my book about *Die grossen Themen der abendl. Metaph.,* p. 118; also *Kants metaph. Weltbegriff.*

126. M.-H. 115f.; II, 410.

127. II, 410; Reflex. Nr. 403, 404.

128. V, 117.

129. Those lines of Kant's thought which are in themselves better known and belong in this context must not, of course, be omitted. It also seemed necessary to emphasize more strongly certain elements in this question which are frequently overlooked.

this question can be seen in many a passage in the pre-Critical work.[130] And this problem had finally to move into the forefront of Kant's interest out of its originally special position with the increased shift from the natural cosmos to the world of spiritual inwardness. There can be no doubt that this issue played a decisive part in the critical-idealistic revolution, even though this is peculiarly less evident in the relevant texts (e.g., the *Inaugural Dissertation*) than the influence of other metaphysical questions.[131]

We are here concerned only with the conflict of freedom with time. But for this question, too, the little-regarded fact is important that the original and most general opposition for Kant is not between natural law and freedom (which is in the foreground of the *Critique of Pure Reason*) but rather in temporal determination in general and freedom. The antinomy of freedom in Arabian and Christian metaphysics pertains to the conflict between divine presence and free decision of finite, created beings at a particular time. And with Fichte it is not the opposition between freedom and natural law but rather the conflict between eternal foreknowledge and individual freedom out of which his idealistic view of freedom emerges.[132] Similarly, for Kant the freedom of a dependent wordly being, subject to divine foreknowledge and pre-determination, indicates the genuine and fundamental riddle.[133]

An ultimate question of existence is broached which is for us in the end absolutely insoluble: how can there be *actus originarios,* absolute spontaneity in the *ens derivativum,* in a *causatum alterius?* How can created beings be free? [134] That there are in reality finite substances—cases of finite activity—is for Kant a final certainty which is grounded in an indisputable fact of reason. This defies all attempts at explaining it away, as through an *a priori*—constructive and rational definition of substance like that of Spinoza.[135] But no mortal, no finite understanding, attains to the knowledge of how this can be. But whatever philosophical knowledge can ac-

---

130. II, 110f., 282, 370.
131. Cf., e.g., Reiche, *Lose Bl.,* 224: "The source of the critical philosophy is morality in regard to the accountability of actions." Cf. also V, 101.
132. Cf. my book about Fichte (Munich, 1923, bei E. Reinhardt), pp. 16ff.
133. Cf. I, 405; also II, 369: "Freedom and Predetermination."
134. VI, 142; VIII, 263-264; *Preisschrift über die Fortschritte,* etc., pp. 196-197; M.V. 206, 313, 336.
135. R.-V. 79.

complish here as in the other ultimate questions—that is the critical
removal of those limitations in our attitude that would have us
represent the incomprehensible as also impossible in itself. Naturalistic dogmatism lives on this constant confusion. With regard to
our present problem, it is the reality of time on the basis of which
he wants to argue the freedom in dependent beings out of existence. Indeed, if the temporal determinations in human actions were
not "mere determinations of man as appearance but of the thing in
itself, freedom could not be saved." "Therefore, unlike those who
still persist in viewing time and space as determinations which
belong to the being of things in themselves, I do not neglect to
avoid fatalism." Even for someone who considers time, like space,
to be real, Spinozism is the only thing that remains. And such
Spinozism is fundamentally better founded "despite the absurdity
of its fundamental idea, than the theory of creation, when . . .
temporally existent beings . . . are regarded as being themselves
substances." We have, then, only to choose between abandoning the
freedom of finite substances and abandoning the reality of time.
Only on the assumption of the ideality of time can the principles
of freedom and creation of finite substances be held without contradiction and be reconciled with each other. "The separation of
time and space from the existence of things in themselves which is
accomplished in the critique of pure speculative reason is of great
importance." [136] The metaphysical question of freedom is side-
tracked when one tries, as Kant himself had done once in the
Nova Dilucidatio, to solve it through the determinism of inner
grounds: "a deception, just as if the difficulty consisted in reconcil-
ing determinism with freedom—which nobody thinks of doing;
rather, the difficulty is this: how pre-determinism, according to
which random events have their causes in prior time (which, together with what it contains, is no longer in our power) can exist
together with freedom, according to which the action as well as
its opposite must be in the power of the subject at the moment of
the event." [137] Only the doctrine of the ideality of time avoids the
obvious impossibility—without, to be sure, giving a genuine intuition of freedom. With the metaphysics of morality that keeps itself
free from representations of nature one comes at least somewhat

136. Cf. Op. Post. (Adickes, 824-825); VIII, 263.
137. Cf. V, 94ff.; 97f.

closer to the great riddle of a free finite being: it is something strange and permanently irrational but nonetheless inescapable that moral law, conscience, and goodness of deed as the most original expressions of the freedom of my person represent at the same time the effect in me of divine causality.[138]

Thus time is the real *punctum saliens* in the more special con- the question of predeterminism.[139] It is not, as the antithesis of the flict between freedom and natural causation which is bound up with third antinomy in the naturalistic limitation of its position would have us believe, lawlessness which freedom entails. Rather, freedom opposes only the allegedly universal validity of temporal law, the necessary connection with what has gone before. Freedom en- deavors to separate from a temporal mode of representation that cannot conceive an absolute beginning the principle of a beginning that is necessary for the metaphysics of the spiritual (for creation or transcendental freedom as well as for the freedom of the will of finite beings).[140] Nature itself cannot make an absolute begin- ning intelligible. Reason, which is bound solely to natural law and the being of nature, fails with the problem of the origin of the world. Here, too, only practical metaphysics, from the standpoint of its principle of freedom and volition that is conceived of as timeless and subject to another, timeless lawfulness, gives the empty theoret- ical Idea a real and metaphysically adequate fulfillment from the very beginning.

Thus the double emphasis of the "reality of the concept of free- dom unavoidably [draws] the doctrine of the ideality of objects of perception in space and time in its wake." [141] That freedom itself does not in that case become reasonable and intelligible is no re- proach but rather unavoidable: it is, indeed, a basic force; we also know nothing of the internal "how" of the natural causality of experience.[142] The entire doctrine of the metaphysics of morals concerning intelligible character and radical evil does not intend to make intelligible the inner structure of the finite volitional being itself but rather intends to let the peculiar issue concerning spiritual realities become intelligible only through the critical separation of

138. Cf. Op. Post. (Adickes, 824-825); VIII, 263.
139. Cf. V, 94ff.; 97f.
140. M.-V. 208, 265, 304f.; Reflex. Nr. 1480; Kr. 374 [A 450=B 478].
141. Reiche, *Lose Bl.*, 217.
142. Kr. 372 [A 450=B 478]; M.-V. 314.

freedom from temporal naturalism and the naturalism of temporal causality. That applies to the questions that arise with the separation of time from being in itself for so many fundamental concepts of moral and religious life. But does not the thought, accepted by Kant himself, of inner reversal and "re-birth" presuppose interminable changes and thus time? Further, is the same presupposition not made with the requirement of moral development and especially with the infinite progress that is so expressly emphasized in Kant's doctrine of immortality and his philosophy of history? [143] When the doctrine of transcendental apperception separates the temporally determined and objective ego from the spontaneous subject of apperception as a principle for which "the representation of time and thus of change" no longer has any application; when this spontaneous subject, "which modifies and changes itself," as that which *makes* the change but which itself is not supposed to be subject to change—how, then, is there to be a spiritual life and a progressive movement? Can one really so crudely set the "subjects that represent appearances to themselves" over against the appearances and events of outer and inner nature? Can one separate subjects that represent appearances to themselves as those beings which, although they represent to themselves what occurs, have nothing which occurs in themselves? [144] Is it feasible to transfer the timelessness of God to finite spiritual things ("not only the being that is in itself necessary but also everything that is intellectual is unchangeable")? [145] Here, too, time is not illusion but appearance. Temporal relations represent in their sensuous limitation real aspects of being itself. Kant's opposition is to development and life (and change in this sense), but only to the specific determinative concept of time of sensuous and scientific experience. The infinite permanence of the immortal soul is something different from the eternity of God; it is truly a series which only God views synoptically.[146] It is our sensuous limitation that is able to represent to itself such a series and permanence only as temporal. Only endurance that is measured temporally is a phenomenon. If we try to rid ourselves of the representation of time, everything will appear to us

143. Kr. 63 [A 37-38=B 53-55]; Reiche, *Lose Bl.*, 124.
144. Reflex. Nr. 1189.
145. Reflex. Nr. 377.
146. Cf., e.g., V, 123, and innumerable other passages in the *Critique of Practical Reason* and in the philosophy of religion.

equally rigid and petrified. "For a being which can become aware
of its existence and the quantity it has (as endurance) only in time,
such a life—if it is otherwise to be called 'life' at all—must appear
akin to destruction." [147] The expression "unchangeable" can be
understood only in a polemical sense against temporal change.
"What I call 'unchangeable' is considered only under the aspect of
time. Accordingly the *intellectualia* are neither changeable nor unchangeable." But what "corresponds to changes *in intellectualibus,*
we do not know." [148] Moreover, the denial of temporal occurrence
in subjects concerns only passive succession in the manner of association, not the subject's spontaneous life activity. Thus Kant can continually hold not only an infinite progress through new duties and
actions, and assert that this striving is a continuous approximation
toward mystical rest and self-possession as the true spiritual existence and life of finite beings. While doing this, he can remain
with the language of the temporal and frankly speak of "future
times and all worlds" and of "incalculable future." [149] The entire
temporal pathos concerning infinity present in his early period thus
retains its full sense in the practical-dogmatic metaphysics of the
Critical Kant—only the entire emphasis on the infinity of cosmic
developments has been transferred to the infinity of a spiritual
occurrence.

The metaphysical motives that led Kant to the critical limitation
of knowledge are by no means exhausted with what has been
treated. What would have to be included is the entire series of
fundamental elements in the world whose structure, according to
Kant, must remain for us and our rational, finite knowledge forever inscrutable, but whose peculiar and indisputable reality is for
him metaphysically certain. Such realities are, among others, life
(the organism), the actual infinity, the teleology of the world,
moral repugnance, moral character, and the absolutely necessary
being. But these questions must be discussed elsewhere.

147. VIII, 334.
148. Reflex. Nr. 387 and 1164.
149. VI, 69, 75; VI, 490a.

Part III

Kant's Theory of the Synthetic-Analytic Distinction

KANT'S distinction between synthetic and analytic judgments houses a family of problems, not the least of which concerns what exactly that doctrine is and how it is to be set off from very different but superficially similar views about that distinction which are current today. Lewis White Beck argues that, unlike certain current views of the analytic, a Kantian analytic judgment is not stipulative; that, unlike other current views, it is not certified to be analytic because it states something that is true by definition; and, finally, that, unlike still other views, the Kantian synthetic judgment *a priori* cannot be reduced to judgments that are stipulative or true by definition.

Beck draws most of his evidence for the foregoing conclusions from a consideration of Kant's theory of definition. The distinction is drawn between analytic and synthetic definitions. Now this distinction is based on the prior distinction between analytic and synthetic predicates. For Kant an analytic predicate is a partial concept of a thing thought in the *definiendum;* a synthetic predicate is what Kant calls a determination (*Bestimmung*), and it assures the definiendum an application to reality. When a definition contains only analytic predicates, it serves to distinguish one thing from another, but it does not show that the concept defined has what Kant calls objective reality. To know, however, that the *definiens* contains synthetic predicates or determinations is to know that the concept under definition has objects which correspond to it in reality.

This gives Beck the evidential basis for his account of Kant's distinction between synthetic and analytic judgments. First of all, no analytic judgment is stipulative because, for Kant, such judgments are relations of concepts, not words. The only relations which we are able to alter in such judgments are the words used to express them; we cannot alter the relations of concepts. This follows from the fact that Kant is concerned to talk about concepts or marks (*Merkmale*), not words or verbal expressions. Secondly, Kant does not certify the analyticity of a judgment by reference to a definition. He appeals rather to the predicate contained or thought within the concept defined. To appeal from what is thought within the subject concept of an analytic judgment to a definition to tell us what is thought within the subject concept is circular: we must appeal to what is thought within the concept in question in order to know that the definition is adequate. Thirdly, we cannot reduce Kant's synthetic judgments *a priori* to analytic judgments simply because all synthetic judgments contain synthetic predicates; and a synthetic predicate applies to the world and thus adds more to the subject concept than can be discovered by analysis. Hence, on Beck's account, even if you do attempt to reduce synthetic *a priori* judgments to analytic judgments by an appeal to a definition, what you will be appealing to is a synthetic definition; and this in turn will merely reproduce the character of the synthetic judgment you were trying to reduce to an analytic judgment.

The foregoing argument will not help Kant explain why synthetic *a priori* judgments are not merely covert analytic judgments. For the argument is an extended repetition of what was to be proved. You have not shown that synthetic judgments cannot be reduced to analytic judgments merely by pointing out that synthetic judgments rest upon synthetic definitions. The logical properties of the latter are just those of the former; and it is about those logical properties that we are asking; hence an appeal to synthetic definitions here is circular.

But Beck gives another and much stronger argument to prove the irreducibility of synthetic judgments. It is this. Let us permit anybody holding that all synthetic judgments are covertly analytic to include the predicate concept of any synthetic judgment in the definition of the subject concept. The result of this is to constitute a complex concept in which a cluster of simpler concepts is united. But how do we know that the referents of the concepts combined in this cluster are invariably associated with one another in experience? We do not find this out from an examination of the definition, for it is because we are antecedently assured that the concepts can be combined that we include them in the definition in the first place. The only way left for us to justify the inclusion of one concept in another, then, is by an appeal to the combination of their referents. And propositions stating this must, accordingly, be synthetic. For any definition you choose, you can always ask how the concept defined applies to the world. And answers to this question must always be expressed in synthetic propositions.

Beck's account of Kant's synthetic-analytic distinction raises two issues. One of the principal reasons for Kant's insistence that synthetic judgments are irreducible is the presence in synthetic judgments of determinations or synthetic predicates. But the distinction between a synthetic and an analytic predicate appears to trade on a confusion between syntactical and semantical relationships. A synthetic predicate is one about which we know that it applies to the world. But why should this be a reason for saying that no such predicate can be contained in the subject concept of the proposition in which it appears? To show that a predicate has application is to show something about its relation to the world. And this relation tells us nothing about whether such a predicate is or is not syntactically related in certain ways to other concepts. Thus what I am asking is whether Kant's distinction between two kinds of predicates is enough to guarantee the irreducibility of synthetic to analytic judgments. And I believe there is reason for thinking that it is not.

The second issue here is Beck's argument that every effort to reduce synthetic propositions to those which are true by definition must be self-defeating. Whenever we assert that the concepts combined in the *definiendum* have objects corresponding to them we are asserting a synthetic proposition. Thus Beck is right to insist that there are some propositions which cannot be reduced to analytic propositions. But this has a curious consequence for Kant's theory of syntheticity: the only genuinely irreducible synthetic judgment is an existence claim. Thus, to say that the concepts combined in a definition have objective reality is to say that there are objects falling under them. And this kind of claim does not relate one concept to another but rather a concept to an object in the world. But the kind of judgment about which Kant wants to say that it is irreducibly synthetic is a relation between two concepts. Thus Beck will have succeeded in supporting Kant's claim that synthetic judgments are irreducible only at the cost of changing Kant's theory of what a synthetic judgment is.

The analytic-synthetic distinction is also at the root of the transition from the Metaphysical to the Transcendental Deduction. In the Metaphysical Deduction Kant lists what he calls the forms of judgment. And his task is then to move from this list to the list of categories. One of the problems in this move is to show how the forms of judgment can also be the forms of the synthetic judgments that constitute the Analytic of Principles. And this has not been explained until it has been explained whether the forms of judgment are merely the forms of analytic judgments or the forms of both analytic and synthetic judgments. If these forms are inherent solely in analytic judgments, then Kant obviously cannot argue that the list of categories can be derived from the list of the forms of judgment. For the categories appear in the synthetic judgments *a priori* which make up the Analytic of Principles.

This same point can be put somewhat differently. The issue here centers around the following passage in the *Kritik,* where Kant says that "the same function . . . which gives unity to the different ideas *in a judgment* also gives unity to the mere synthesis of different ideas *in an intuition"* (A79=B104). This is the bridge between the Metaphysical and the Transcendental Deduction; we are told that the same functions that are listed in the forms of judgments are the functions that are listed in the Table of Categories. If they are not the same, then the Metaphysical Deduction would not give us a clue to the categories. But are they the same? If the forms of judgment are restricted to analytic judgments, then they manifestly are not the same; for the categories appear in synthetic judgments, while the forms of judgment would govern only analytic judgments.

Many have thought that the forms of judgment were in fact only the forms of analytic judgments. And Paton gives two arguments to show that such a claim is false. For one thing, if the forms of judgment gave us only the forms of analytic judgment, then we would have to say that synthetic judgments would not be judgments at all; they would lack such properties as quality, quantity, relation, and modality, the absence of which would erase judgment entirely. For another, the view that the forms of judgment do not extend to synthetic judgments rests on a confusion of "analytic" with "discursive" and "synthetic" with "intuitive." It is first pointed out that for Kant all synthetic judgment demands intuition. It is further pointed out that for Kant all thought is discursive as opposed to intuitive. And then the conclusion is drawn that all thought is analytic, since "discursive" is opposed to "intuitive." But Paton exposes this for the confusion it is: synthetic judgments are dis-cursive in that they involve relations of concepts; they are, how-ever, no less discursive because they refer to intuition. Thus, to say that all thought is discursive does not imply that all thought is analytic.

I have one reservation about Paton's arguments. While he suc-ceeds in showing that the forms of judgment in the Metaphysical Deduction must encompass both analytic and synthetic judgments, has he in fact shown—what he takes to be a direct conclusion from this—that the categories are the same concepts as those listed in the functions of judgment? I do not think he has shown this. Consider, for example, the concept of the categorial judgment. Now this ap-pears as one of the functions of judgment in the Metaphysical De-duction, for it is the concept of the relation between subject and predicate concepts in the judgment. But is this the same concept as that which appears in the corresponding place in the list of cate-gories? The corresponding category is that of inherence and sub-sistence. But the function of judgment and the corresponding cat-egory are concepts of very different things: the former is a concept of a relation in a judgment; the latter is a concept of a relation in the world between an object and its properties. And if they are concepts of such different things, then in what sense can they be called the same concept? It is no answer to this question to say, as Kant does, that the categories are just the forms of judgment as they are applied to a sensuous manifold; for the concept of the subject-predicate relation is still the concept of a relation of con-cepts and not of a relation between things in the world even after this addition has been made. It would thus seem that, while Paton's argument is fatal to a narrow application of the forms of judgment to analytic judgments, it still does not show in what sense the functions of judgment and the categories are the same concepts.

While Paton is concerned to defend the identity of the functions of judgment and the categories, Lovejoy assails the coherence of Kant's theory of the functions of judgment. And this is just one more outgrowth of Kant's theory of the synthetic-analytic distinc-tion. The classification of judgments into analytic and synthetic presupposes Kant's entire theory of the characteristics of judgment. And if this theory is incoherent, so is any distinction which is elaborated in terms of that theory. This is the import for the synthetic-analytic distinction of Lovejoy's paper on the table of judgments. Lovejoy argues that the entire classification is incoherent. Let us take the major divisions of that classification in turn and review Lovejoy's arguments.

1. *Quantity:* Here Kant distinguishes universal, particular, and singular judgments; and he says that the basis of this distinction is the amount of knowledge conveyed by the judgment: we are told something more by a universal than by, say, a particular or a singular judgment. Lovejoy objects that, on this principle of division, Kant is committed to introducing as many classes as there are quantities of things. And the only reason, Lovejoy suggests, why Kant retained a classification of three kinds of quantity is that he confused two principles of classification. He confused, that is, the principle of division between the whole of a class and any part (the proportion of the class being talked about) with the quite different principle of how many things are being talked about. According to the first principle, a threefold division is defensible; but, according to the second, such a division is arbitrary.

2. *Quality:* Here propositions are divided into affirmative and negative. But Kant also introduces the infinite judgment, which is neither affirmative nor negative. His reason for doing so is that we learn something from the infinite judgment that we do not from either of the other two kinds. And this is so because the predicate of an infinite judgment does not limit the subject class, which remains infinite even after the predicates are added. Lovejoy objects here that this is not reason enough for setting infinite judgments off from affirmative and negative judgments; for the subject classes of both these kinds of judgments remain infinite even after the predicates are added. There is no reason, therefore, for Kant's threefold classification here.

3. *Relation:* Here Kant divides all judgments into hypothetical, disjunctive, and categorical. Lovejoy objects to such a division, pointing out that disjunctive judgments are reducible to hypothetical judgments. Thus "A is either B or C" is reducible to "If A is B, it is not C; and if A is not B, it is C." But if disjunctive judg-

ments are constructible out of hypotheticals, then what justification is there for making a threefold classification of judgments according to relation?

4. *Modality:* Kant tells us that the modality of a judgment designates only the value of the copula in relation to thought in general. Lovejoy points out that this can mean either (a) the subjective degree of confidence we have in asserting a proposition, or (b) the relation of conditionality between one proposition and another. But this ambiguity renders the whole classification incoherent. If we take Kant to mean (b), then the problematic judgment is reduced to the hypothetical or the disjunctive judgment under relation; and, further, the assertoric judgment is reduced to the categorical judgment under relation. This comes about because the modality of a judgment is identified with properties of a judgment and not with the attitude of the person asserting it. The incoherence here is caused by Kant's professing to use (a) but actually using (b) in classifying the modality of judgments.

The cumulative effect of Lovejoy's arguments is to show that the principles governing the construction of the table of judgments do not render the classification plausible. And so long as the coherence of the table is in question, the theory of judgment Kant offers will be obscure; and so long as that theory is obscure, the precise character of the synthetic-analytic distinction in Kant will remain obscure. Yet is the whole table so obscure as Lovejoy alleges? Consider Lovejoy's criticism of quantity. We can grant that Kant is trading on two very different principles of classification and, further, that the assumption of the one makes the classification Kant offers arbitrary. But Kant's argument can be reconstructed by assuming that the principle according to which the classification is not arbitrary is the dominant one. The same point can be made in the context of modality. What Lovejoys argues there is that Kant professes one criterion of division but in fact uses another. We can, however, argue that the dominant criterion is the one according to which modality is the subjective degree of confidence we have in asserting a proposition. And, on that assumption, the incoherence disappears. I do not, of course, deny that there are many difficulties of this sort running throughout the classification of judgments; all I am suggesting is that the incoherence that results from them can be removed by holding that one of the principles of division is dominant. And one reason for holding this is that it removes the incoherence.

The final problem which the synthetic-analytic distinction in Kant brings with it is the defense of specimens of synthetic judgments *a priori*. A paradigm case of such a judgment is the Second Analogy. Here Kant's problem is to prove the proposition that every occurrence presupposes something which it follows according to a rule. That such a proposition needs a special kind of proof is for Kant evident: the predicate term is not contained in the concept of occurrence; hence, the demonstration of the proposition cannot be accomplished by an application of the Law of Contradiction. Nor can the proposition be demonstrated by an appeal to experience; for what the proposition tells us is, on Kant's account, something that is universally and necessarily true.

How, then, does Kant seek to prove the proposition? Kant bases his demonstration on the distinction between two kinds of succession. Every object, he observes, presents itself to us successively; thus both our apprehension of stationary and that of moving objects is successive. Yet some successions are present in the object while others are due only to the subjective apprehension of the object.

Kant gives two examples to illuminate this distinction. We apprehend a stationary object like a house successively by apprehending first one side, then another. But we also apprehend an object like a ship moving downstream in like fashion. Yet there is a difference: the apprehension of the house is reversible, while the apprehension of the ship is not. We cannot, that is, alter the sequence in which the ship presents itself, although we can alter the sequence in which the house appears to us by changing the order in which we apprehend its parts. Now irreversible sequences are properly causal in that each stage in the sequence follows the other necessarily according to a rule. But there is no such rule governing the sequence of stationary objects like a house.

But how did Kant take this distinction between two kinds of sequence to prove the Second Analogy? On the requirement Kant lays down, we can show the Second Analogy to be true if we can show what right we have to combine the subject and predicate concepts independently of particular experiences. And this right is established when it is shown that the referents of the subject and predicate concepts of the proposition can be combined in pure intuition. The proof depends, accordingly, on the existence of irreversible temporal sequences, for they justify the *a priori* combination of the subject and predicate concepts of the Second Analogy.

Lovejoy counters the foregoing demonstration with three ingenious arguments. First of all, what Kant has demonstrated is merely that there is a distinction between our apprehension of stationary and moving objects. That a series of presentations is irreversible tells us something about a moving object, while the reversibility of a series is a sign of a stationary object. But Kant has not proved that the distinction between reversibility and irreversibility is the same as that between a purely subjective and an objective sequence. The reversible-irreversible distinction applies equally to our dreams and our non-dream states. For the apprehension of moving objects in our dreams has the same property of irreversibility that Kant attributes to objective occurrences like boats moving downstream. Thus, Kant has not shown that irreversibility is the invariable characteristic of objective sequences and hence of properly causal sequences.

Lovejoy's second objection runs like this. When Kant distinguishes between reversible and irreversible sequences, what he succeeds in establishing is that stable objects are dependent upon the movements of an observer, while a moving object must be observed in a single order. But this is just an explication of two concepts: that of a changing and a stable object. But both of these explications give us analytic, not synthetic, propositions. It is no answer to this objection to say that Kant's demonstration turns not on the explication of the concepts of two kinds of object but upon the application of the notion of a rule-governed event to our experience. For the same objection can be raised to the use which Kant makes of the reversible-irreversible distinction. What Kant succeeds in showing is that all occurrences or happenings which are to rank as events must be irreversible. And this is shown by an explication of the concept of "event" as distinguished from "happening" or "occurrence"; and this explication, like that of two kinds of objects, issues in an analytic proposition. What it tells us is not that all phenomena in nature must follow one another according to a rule but only that our concept of "event" contains the concept of "succession according to a rule."

But worse is to come. Kant has shown that there are sequences in our experience that are irreversible. But this is quite different from proving—what, for Kant's purposes, must be proved—that my perceptions of a given phenomenon are necessarily uniform in repeated instances. This point can be illuminated by considering Kant's example of the moving boat. We cannot reverse the order of the boat's movement: if we see it moving from a position upstream through successive positions downstream, we cannot reverse the order in which we apprehend the voyage. Yet this applies only to a single ship on a single occasion. It does not apply to the behavior of all moving ships. If Kant is to prove the latter, he must give an argument which will enable him to move from what he has shown about the behavior of the ship in his example to the behavior of all moving ships. If he cannot supply such an argument, he will not have shown that the Second Analogy is universally valid of experience.

Let us take Lovejoy's arguments in turn and ask what reply is open to a defender of the Second Analogy. Regarding the claim that Kant confuses the reversible-irreversible distinction with the distinction between subjective and objective occurrences, there are two ways in which Kant's argument could be supported. You could argue that all Kant is doing when he proves the existence of irreversible sequences is to give the necessary but not the necessary and sufficient conditions for distinguishing causal from non-causal sequences. Thus Kant can admit that our dreams can contain irreversible sequences, because his argument does not require him to distinguish between dream and waking states. One piece of evidence for this way out of the difficulty Lovejoy raises is to be found in Kant's notion of a necessary succession *according to a rule*. That a causal sequence be regular is a demand that is not fulfilled by irreversible sequences. For all irreversibility provides is that the sequence cannot be apprehended in reverse order; and this is not the same as the requirement that it be apprehended according to a rule. This suggests that Kant himself intended irreversibility to be only the necessary condition of causal sequences.

But there is also a second way of meeting Lovejoy's difficulty. You could simply deny that Kant needs to equate "objective" with "waking state" and "subjective" with "dream state" in order to prove the Second Analogy. To say, for example, that there are irreversible sequences in our experience makes no claim that such sequences cannot occur in our dreams. When Kant says that causal sequences are objective, all he need be taken to mean is that they must be apprehended in a certain sequence; and this does not preclude apprehending them in dream states. Accordingly, all that we need do is say that what is subjective is the fact that I can choose to apprehend non-causal sequences in any order; what is objective in causal sequences is the order of their apprehension. And this is not a matter of my choice. The distinction between subjective and objective apprehension is not, on this reading, the same as that between a dream and a waking state.

Lovejoy's second objection—that the Second Analogy is an analytic judgment—cannot, I think, be answered so easily. What must be done to answer it is to show exactly how Kant's demonstration that there are irreversible sequences in experience relates to the syntheticity of the Second Analogy. Let us suppose that there are such sequences and that they can be called properly causal. Why is this a reason for believing that the Second Analogy expresses a synthetic rather than an analytic proposition? That there are such sequences in experience is perfectly compatible with the analyticity of the Second Analogy. And it is no answer to this to say that the concept of "occurrence" or "happening" (*"Alles, was geschieht . . ."* or *"Alle Veränderung"*) does not contain the concept of "necessary succession according to a rule." For what must be explained is why the argument purporting to show that the Second Analogy is necessarily and universally true cannot be construed as evidence for the conclusion that the Second Analogy is an analytic proposition.

Lovejoy's third objection to the proof for the Second Analogy is that it is based on an illicit move from the characteristics of Kant's example to the alleged characteristics of all phenomena of similar kind. But this objection, I believe, overlooks the importance of the Aesthetic for understanding the Transcendental Analytic. What Kant thinks he has shown in relating causality to irreversibility is something about transcendental time relations. And whatever he can show about such relations is universally true just because time is a universal condition of sensibility. Thus, in order to show that the move that Kant makes here is illicit, you must show either that the conclusions about time in the Transcendental Aesthetic are unsound or that the properties in virtue of which the voyage of the ship is irreversible depend upon properties the ship itself has, rather than the temporal relations in which it appears.

KANT'S THEORY

OF DEFINITION

Lewis White Beck

§

I

In most contemporary writings on the distinction between analytic and synthetic propositions, an analytic proposition is defined as one that follows from an explicit definition by rules of formal logic. If, as is usual, it is assumed that all definitions are nominal or stipulative, and further that all *a priori* propositions are analytic, it follows that the necessity of an *a priori* proposition is linguistic in origin and scope.

The original distinction between analytic and synthetic propositions, however, was drawn by Kant, who did not make any of these three assumptions. Confusion arises through discussing, in Kantian terms, a distinction whose modern usage differs widely from that of the author of the distinction; discords are produced by Kantian tones in otherwise empiricistic harmonies. Sometimes one or more of the three doctrines mentioned above is attributed to Kant himself,[1] or more often it is argued that the Kantian doctrine is important and plausible only when seen as anticipating and

1. Three widely scattered specimens are: (a) "La notion kantienne du jugement analytique semble d'exiger que les concepts soient d'une part absolument susceptibles d'une définition unique, rigoreuse et sans aucune ambiguité, et que d'un autre côté leurs définitions soient susceptible d'être analysées sans qu'on aboutisse à des jugements synthétiques" (Paul Tannery, *Bulletin de la Société Française de Philosophie*, 1903, p. 124); (b) "Kant scheint bei der Einteilung der Urteile in analytisch und synthetisch von der Fiktion auszugehen, dass auch

preparing the way for the more recent doctrines. Either of these tactics keeps Kant's own doctrines from teaching us anything important and distinctive by obscuring what was unique and original in them but has since been forgotten or neglected.

My purpose here is to try to show the relationship between Kant's own views of definition and of analytic judgment. I shall suggest that the interpretation of his analytic judgments as those based upon definitions is without historical warrant. This raises the question whether modern disputes about the possibility of *a priori* synthetic propositions, in which the theory of definition plays a decisive role in the formation of criteria for analyticity, are really discussions of the problem to which Kant devoted the first *Critique*.

II

To define, according to Kant, means to present the complete concept of a thing within its limits and in its primary or original character. A complete concept is one with a sufficiency of clear predicates for the entire concept to be distinct; and the predicates stated are primary or original in the sense that they are not derived from other predicates included in the definition. The predicates must, in other words, be primitive and coordinate; no derivative and subordinate predicates are admissible in a definition, for otherwise, the definition would require proof.[2] If a definition does incorrectly contain derivative predicates—properties instead of *essentialia*—it is lacking in *precision*. Definition is a "sufficiently distinct and precise concept (*conceptus rei adaequatus in minimis terminis, complete determinatus*)." [3]

The definition of "definition" that Kant gives here leads him to deny the name "definition" to many sentences commonly so called. It is reached partly by an analysis of usage and partly by a decision which makes the concept more precise: "There are definitions of concepts which we already have but which are not correctly named.

die nicht-mathematischen Begriffe definiert werden können" (K. Marc-Wogau, *Theoria*, XVII, 1951, 150); (c) "The distinction . . . is easy and clear as long as we deal with merely stipulated or nominal definitions, as Kant seems to have supposed we could" (R. E. Gahringer, *Journal of Philosophy*, LI, 1954, 435).

2. *Critique of Pure Reason*, A 727-B 755, note.
3. *Vorlesungen über Logik*, § 99.

In these cases, it is not that the meaning of a word is analyzed, but that a concept, which we already possess, is analyzed; and then it must be particularly shown what name properly expresses it." [4]

Kant distinguishes two major and independent divisions of definitions: into analytic and synthetic, and into nominal and real.

A definition is analytic if it is of a given concept; synthetic if of a concept made or synthesized by the definition itself.[5] The former makes a concept distinct, the latter makes a distinct concept.[6] Under each of these major divisions, there is a subdivision: the concept defined may be given or made *a priori* or *a posteriori*.[7]

An analytic definition states the original analytic predicates of the thing defined. An analytic predicate is a partial concept of a thing actually thought in the concept of the *definiendum*.[8] Thus an analytic definition is an analytic judgment containing no subordinate predicates. A synthetic definition, however, contains synthetic predicates, predicates whose union first establishes a distinct concept of the *definiendum*.

The other major division is between nominal and real definition. Kant does not draw this distinction as one between the definition of a word and the definition of a thing; because he regarded the concept, rather than thing or word, as the *definiendum* he was prevented from using this formula of the distinction. Rather the difference lies in the content of the *definiens* and in the methodological function of the two kinds of definition. A nominal definition states the logical essence of the concept of the thing, or serves merely to distinguish this thing from others. If it does only the latter it is called a diagnostic definition, in contrast to a definition stating essential primitive predicates.[9] The logical essence, stated in nominal definition, is the original primitive concept of all the *essentialia;* [10] the diagnostic definition may state only the irreducible minimum of some easily recognized attributes or properties,

---

4. *Reflexion* 3003. (All references to the *Reflexionen* are by number, as established in the edition of the Prussian Academy, vols. XIV-XVIII.)

5. *Vorlesungen über Logik*, § 100.

6. *Ibid.*, Einleitung, viii (Cassirer ed., VIII, 376); *Reflexion* 2929. All subsequent references to pages in the *Vorlesungen* are to the Cassirer edition.

7. *Vorlesungen über Logik*, § 101.

8. *Ibid.*, p. 372.

9. *Reflexionen* 2994, 3003.

10. *Vorlesungen über Logik*, Einleitung, viii, p. 374.

sufficient as a criterion in a dichotomous classification by a pass-fail test.

A real definition not only puts one word in place of others, but the *definiens* contains a clear mark by which the object can be recognized and by virtue of which the defined concept is shown to have "objective reality"—by which it is shown that there is a defined thing.[11] (The diagnostic definition does this, but not by stating the diagnostic symptom as an *essentia* of the thing.) Real definition, therefore, is a part and not merely a tool of knowledge. Real definition states the real essence constituted by real predicates, not merely by logical predicates included ("already thought in") the concept of the subject.

A synthetic predicate is a determination (*Bestimmung*) not contained in the subject-concept but enlarging it; it is not found by analysis. It determines a thing, not merely its concept. "Anything we please can be made to serve as a logical predicate; the subject can even be predicated of itself; for logic abstracts from all content. But a *determining* predicate is a predicate which is added to the concept of the subject and enlarges it. Consequently it must not be already contained in the concept." [12] A real definition, therefore, is always a synthetic judgment, even though the real definition, *as definition,* may be analytical and is analytical if the concept is given.[13]

Real predicates are never arbitrarily synthesized into a logical product called the essence; in every case the determinations are not purely conceptual but intuitive representations. General logic is concerned only with the logical essence or predicates; or, rather, in abstracting from all contents it treats determinations as if they were logical predicates. But knowledge of things requires knowledge of and through determinations, not merely the mouthing of their names, and this knowledge is knowledge of the real possibility of the object through a specific determination as both its *ratio essendi* and *ratio cognoscendi*.[14] We find the logical essence by reflecting

---

11. *Critique of Pure Reason,* A 241-2 n.
12. *Critique of Pure Reason,* A 598-B 626 (tr. Kemp Smith); *Reflexion* 4055.
13. *Reflexionen* 2955, 2994.
14. *Vorlesungen über Logik,* Einleitung, viii, p. 374. *Ratio essendi* is, of course, to be understood not as having a bearing on the thing itself, corresponding to the "real essence" in Locke; for Kant, like Locke, admits ignorance of that. But *ratio essendi* may be applied also to the object of knowledge; and when its *ratio cognoscendi* and *ratio essendi* in part coincide, there is *a priori* knowledge.

on the predicates which constitute or are made to constitute the nominal definition; for real essence, we seek data from experience or intuition to determine whether and under what condition the object is really possible.[15]

This difficult and obscure matter is involved in the distinction between general and transcendental logic, and it cannot be made intelligible within the limits usually imposed on discussions of definition in formal logic. Kant is saying that in a real definition we do not merely equate a word with a logical product of arbitrarily chosen logical predicates, but we make at least a problematical existential judgment and state the conditions under which this judgment could be verified so that the *definiendum* will be seen to have "objective reference." There must be, in the *definiens,* some determination or compound of determinations that can be "cashed" in possible sensible (intuitive) experience. Its absence is the reason why all definitions in speculative metaphysics are only nominal. Its specific epistemological character is the reason also why general logic does not deal with (or at least does not distinguish) real definitions, since general logic disregards the transcendental difference between a predicate and a determination; and neglect of this difference is, finally, the reason why logic, when used as an organon in metaphysics, develops into dialectic.

The notion of real definition is not only excluded from general logic by Kant (though he dealt with it in his Lectures, which far exceeded the bounds he set up around the field of general logic), but is challenged on other grounds by most modern writers who reject the ontological distinction between essence and property.[16] They admit, in any specific case, the distinction between an essential and an accidental definition, though on pragmatic not ontological grounds. Kant, in accordance with a tradition going back at least to the *Port Royal Logic,*[17] uses the distinction between nominal and

15. *Critique of Pure Reason,* A 218-B 265. Kant insists on the distinction between the two meanings of possibility as early as the *Einzig möglicher Beweisgrund* . . . (Akademie ed.), II, 77-78, the most important point always being that existence is not a logical predicate. There are many things logically possible that are not really possible, because the non-conceptual condition that would show them to exist is not possible. Thus "a two-sided plane figure" is logically but not really possible, while a "two-sided triangle" is not logically possible (*Critique,* A 221-B 268). The only kind of possibility subject to formal definition is logical (*Critique,* A 244-B 302).

16. Cf. Richard Robinson, *Definition* (Oxford, 1950), pp. 154-155.

17. Part I, ch. xii.

real definition to designate this other, quite different, distinction: a real definition is one from which other properties can be derived, while a nominal definition suffices only for "comparisons" and not for "derivations." Thus, "The circle is a curved line all of whose parts can be made to coincide" is described by Kant as a nominal definition despite the fact that it prescribes an applicable test; he means that it is a definition that contains a predicate already derived, not an *essentia;* but instead of pointing this out, he calls it nominal.[18]

Having now set up the major divisions, I turn to the specific types of definitions resulting from the two independent divisions. They may be most easily seen from the following table.

	Analytic		Synthetic	
Nominal	Logical definition		Declaration	
Real	*A priori* Exposition	*A posteriori* Description	*A priori* Construction	*A posteriori* Invention

1. *Analytic nominal definition.* Kant says little about this, and even that little is confusing. Because it is in any case of small importance to our inquiry, I shall not undertake to examine the various confusing statements he makes, but merely list the passages for the interested reader.[19]

2. *Synthetic nominal definition.* Such a definition is a stipulation or a "declaration" of an intended usage, the concept being created by the definition. Since they are not determined by experience or by analysis of a given concept, Kant says that such definitions are *a priori* synthetic, not realizing, perhaps, the inappropriateness of this adjective to what is not a proposition or judgment proper.[20]

18. *Reflexion* 2916; cf. *Reflexion* 2995. He does, however, point out the real infirmity of this definition in the *Critique,* A 732-B 760.

19. *Vorlesung über Logik,* § 106, Anm. 2; *Reflexionen* 2918, 2931, 2963, 3004.

20. *Reflexion* 3007. Such a definition—in the case under discussion, it happens to be Kant's definition of analytic judgment—cannot be in error. *Über eine Entdeckung* (Akademie ed.), VIII, 232. All references to this essay are to pages in vol. VIII of the Akademie edition.

3. *Analytic real definition.* A definition of this type states the defining predicates of a given concept known to have objective validity, and it contains the synthetic predicate (*Bestimmung*) which gives the defined concept this objective reference. Nevertheless, upon investigation it turns out that any attempt to state such a definition fails to meet the formal requirements of definition, with respect either to completeness or precision.

If the concept is given *a priori,* we cannot be sure that we have a complete analysis of it into its coordinate predicates. A concept given *a priori* may include "many obscure representations, which we overlook in our analysis, though we are constantly making use of them in our application of the concept." Therefore the completeness of a proferred definition is never more than probable, and rather than call such an indefinite analysis by the name "definition," Kant calls it an "exposition." [21]

If the concept is given *a posteriori,* its analysis suffers from the same infirmity mentioned above in discussing the definition of an *a priori* concept. Such a concept has no precise and complete analysis, for the concept itself is not a fixed union of predicates. It is variable, depending upon the scope of the experience we classify under it. Kant in one place says that it cannot even be nominally defined.[22] A statement of the attributes and properties of a thing meant by an empirical concept is at most a description, which is not held to rules of precision and completeness; description provides many truths which serve as the "material for definition," [23] the definition itself being only an ideal.

4. *Synthetic real definition.* It is obvious from the very name what falls here: such a definition must not only make a concept, but must show its real possibility by including the *Bestimmung* which is its *ratio essendi* and *cognoscendi*.

If the synthesis is of pure concepts, the real determination must be a character of pure intuition; if of empirical concepts, the real determination must be an empirical intuition. The synthesis of pure concepts is a construction. Construction is the presentation of a concept through the spontaneous production of its corresponding and verifying intuition. Concepts, if pure, can have an *a priori*

---

21. *Critique of Pure Reason,* A 729-B 757.
22. *Reflexion* 2992.
23. *Vorlesungen über Logik,* § 105, Anm. 3.

representation only in pure intuition; and such representation is definition as this occurs in mathematics. If the concept is empirical in its components, we have the presentation of an actual empirical intuition not through the productive imagination alone but through a change effected in the real world. A definition of such a concept may be genetic, telling us how to make a corresponding object,[24] and the devising of the object is proof that the concept has real objective possibility and is not chimerical. Kant calls such a definition (as of a ship's chronometer) a "declaration of a project" [25] or an "exposition of appearances." [26] Since "exposition" and "declaration" are both used in other senses, I have called this, in the table, "invention."

In mathematics, we make a concept by synthesis. "The mathematician in his definitions says, *Sic volo, sic jubeo.*" [27] But in spite of the modern sound of this statement, mathematical definitions for Kant are real, not nominal. Mathematical entities are not arbitrary logical products of compatible logical predicates; the concepts have objective validity (in pure intuition) shown through the presentation of the corresponding determination. If the presentation is a product of the productive imagination, the construction is called schematic or pure, as of a figure (no matter how roughly drawn) used in a geometrical proof. Such a figure is not used empirically, and the actual drawing of it is not a part of the science of mathematics but belongs to art. Kant calls the empirically made sketch "technical construction," [28] and, indeed, it is like the "invention" of any empirical object. Mathematics is the only science able to construct its concepts *a priori,* and only by construction can we achieve completeness and precision in knowledge. Therefore mathematics is the only science which contains proper and strict definitions.[29]

Kant often speaks of synthetic definitions, including mathematical definitions, as *willkürlich.* The word *willkürlich,* ordinarily

24. *Reflexion* 3001.
25. *Critique of Pure Reason,* A 729-B 757.
26. *Vorlesungen über Logik,* § 102.
27. *Reflexion* 2930; see also *Untersuchung über die Deutlichkeit der Grundsätze* . . . (Akademie ed.), II, § 1; (Beck tr., p. 262)—hereafter referred to as *Prize Essay,* the first number referring to the page in the Akademie edition, the second, in parentheses, to my translation (Chicago, 1949).
28. *Über eine Entdeckung,* 192 n.
29. *Critique of Pure Reason,* A 729-B 757.

translated as "arbitrary," does not, however, suggest the caprice sometimes understood in the word "arbitrary"; "arbitrary" does not mean "random." Arbitrariness, as it is now commonly interpreted, is not a feature of mathematical knowledge as Kant interprets it; mathematical concepts are limited by the fixed conditions of intuition, just as empirical concepts are synthesized under the limits imposed by the actual content and order of empirical data. Kant contrasts *willkürlich* with *empirisch,* not, I think, with *notwendig.*[30]

III

I shall now consider the role that definitions play in the progress of knowledge, as this is described by Kant.

The search for definitions of empirical concepts is justified by the technical demands for communication in relatively unambiguous language. We need to "fix" the meaning of a concept from time to time, and we do so by nominal definition or declaration. Such definitions, if made too soon or especially if taken too seriously as a part rather than as an instrument of knowledge, distort inquiry by permitting logical analysis to usurp the place of empirical amplification. "What useful purpose," Kant asks, "could be served by defining an empirical concept, such, for instance, as that of water? When we speak of water and its properties, we do not stop short at what is thought in the word 'water' but proceed to experiments." [31] Description suffices; definition which aims at being more than nominal is a useless presumption.

Turning from empirical to rational knowledge, Kant insists upon a sharp distinction between the methods proper to mathematics and those of philosophy. The mathematician begins with definitions and proceeds by a synthetic method (involving constructions) to his conclusions; his definitions cannot be false, and their only fault may be lack of precision, which is progressively corrected.[32] The philosopher, on the other hand, must begin with concepts already given to him, though confusedly and without sufficient determinateness. The thing meant is not intuitively clear in the sign, as in the

30. *Vorlesungen über Logik,* § 103 Anm.
31. *Critique of Pure Reason,* A 728-B 756 (tr. Kemp Smith).
32. *Reflexion* 2979.

concepts of mathematics,[33] all of which are subject to construction in intuition. The symbols, such as a set of points representing a number, have their meaning "on their face"; whereas the philosopher must use his symbols only as poor representations of richer concepts. These he must analyze in order to compare their segregated characteristics with those originally intended by a ready-made concept used to render unanalyzed experience intelligible. A definition reached by synthesis in philosophy could only by accident be a definition of a concept which originally posed the philosophical problem to us.

In mathematics there are few unanalyzable concepts, and they can be used with assurance according to explicit rules without any need for analysis. Analyses of concepts, if made at all, belong to the philosophy of mathematics rather than to mathematics itself. In philosophy, on the contrary, there are many unanalyzable and indefinable concepts, but we do not begin our work with them. We discover what they are only by the analysis of given concepts, which are not entirely clear and distinct. Thus (if he is fortunate) the philosopher ends where the mathematician begins, to wit, with indefinable elementary concepts and definitions of the concepts given in the beginning. Definitions in philosophy, therefore, are not the conditions of knowledge; they are what we hope to conclude with, not the raw material with which we begin.

From these textual inquiries, we can conclude that definition does not play the dominant role in Kant's philosophy that it does in later theories of analytic judgment. In only one field, mathematics, does Kant admit strict definitions, and in mathematics it is possible to decide indubitably what is analytic and what is synthetic. In empirical knowledge, definition is only loose and informal, and we should expect what we do find, namely that decision on the character of specific judgments is variable and without great importance. It is *a priori* judgments outside of mathematics that Kant is chiefly concerned to establish, and of their concepts definition is impossible. Yet it is with respect to these judgments that it is of fundamental importance to distinguish the apriority of formal logic (analytic) from the apriority of transcendental logic (synthetic).

Definition is not essential to certainty in knowledge. Quite apart

33. *Critique of Pure Reason,* A 734-B 762; *Prize Essay,* 278 (264).

from Kant's belief that not all *a priori* knowledge is analytic, he does not even assert that analytic judgments are necessarily consequences of definitions. Though he indicates [34] that analytic judgments are deducible from definitions, this statement occurs in the reply to Eberhard, in a context supplied by his opponent; it is not his characteristic way of stating the nature of analytic judgments. Definition would be a sufficient, but is not a necessary, condition for analytic judgments; we may have *a priori* knowledge of undefined concepts provided we can either exhibit the concept in pure intuition (schematize it to give a basis for synthetic judgments) or give a partial analysis of the concept.[35] And in three places,[36] at least, Kant describes the way logical certainty in knowledge is gained, showing clearly that definition is given a secondary role. He tells us that we begin by analyzing concepts, expressing the analyses in analytic judgments, and only then organize these analytic judgments into definitions. Even so, definition requires a completeness and precision that is often an unattainable ideal; yet its absence does not jeopardize the analytic judgments already made.

The *Critique of Pure Reason* is supposed to answer the question, How are synthetic judgments *a priori* possible? But if it is not possible to decide objectively whether a given judgment is synthetical or analytical, the entire *Critique* seems to be wasted effort. Can we make synthetic judgments and know that they will, as it were, remain synthetic while we examine their apriority? Or do not definitions grow and so extend their sway that a judgment once known only empirically can, under better definitions, come to be logically necessary? Can we not agree [37] that a "synthetic *a priori* judgment" is a judgment with an ambiguous term, and that when we remove the ambiguity by definition we either remove the apriority or the syntheticity?

This presupposes that analytic judgments are determined by definitions, and it at least suggests that definitions are arbitrary in such a manner that we have a choice as to whether the judgment in question will be made analytic or synthetic. Expressed in other

34. *Über eine Entdeckung*, 229.
35. *Critique of Pure Reason*, A 731-B 759; *Prize Essay*, 285 (271); *Vorlesungen über Logik*, § 109 Anm.
36. *Prize Essay* 282 (268); *Falsche Spitzfindigkeit der vier syllogistischen Figuren* (Akademie ed.), II, 61; *Prolegomena*, § 2, c, 3 (Beck ed., 18).
37. With H. W. Chapman, *Mind*, n.s., LXI (1952), 391.

ways, this is one of the oldest and probably the most common of all criticisms of Kant's theory. The difference which he thought was fundamental seems to be a subjective, shifting distinction, dependent upon how much one knows at a given time, and how one formulates what one knows. Very early in his use of the distinction, Kant seems to have anticipated this objection,[38] though he gave no answer at that time, and for many years used the distinction as though completely oblivious of the objection.

He does not seem to have realized its full force until he prepared his reply to Eberhard. Even then, in the published reply he does not come to grips with the problem; but in the working paper prepared under his direction by Schultz there is a passage [39] which deals with the shifting of the line between the two types of judgments by the modification of definition. The passage is obscure, but I will try to describe what I think Kant would have said had he put it into shape for publication.

Kant invites his opponent to add any attributes he wishes to a concept, so that whatever it is he wishes to prove he can prove by deduction, i.e., analytically. But then Kant asks him: how did you come to include in the concept precisely those attributes you needed in order to render previously synthetic judgments analytic? He cannot reply that he is giving a definition of the concept unless he can show that he is obeying the rules of definition in formal logic. That is, he must be able to show that the newly introduced attributes are logically independent of the old, yet invariably attached to the subject in experience, so that the conjunction of the old and new attributes has the same denotation as the original concept. A narrower denotation will not do, for that means that a new concept has been introduced, not that an old one has been defined. Now in order to know the identity of the old and new denotation, he must know the connection of the independent attributes before stating them in a new definition; he must know this synthetically, for if they are analytically related the rule concerning the precision of definition is broken. Hence, definitions devised for the purpose of rendering synthetic judgments analytic are not real definitions, or in making them we must already know with certainty the synthetic judgment they were designed to establish as analytic. If they are

38. *Reflexion* 3928, dating from the late sixties.
39. *Rezension von Eberhards Magazin* (Akademie ed.), XX, 408-409.

not real but only nominal definitions, then the problem of synthetic *a priori* knowledge (which Kant calls the metaphysical problem) is not touched by this exercise in logic.[40]

IV

In contrast with the views mentioned at the beginning of this paper, sometimes erroneously attributed to Kant, we have found that Kant's views on the relation between definition and analytic judgment are as follows. While a judgment logically implied by a definition is analytic, analytical judgments are not necessarily or even usually known or justified by deduction from definitions. Analytic judgments are made by analysis of concepts which need not first be established by definition. Definition is a late stage in the progress of knowledge, being preceded by the analysis of given concepts, expressed in analytic judgments. Because definition is a secondary and more or less adventitious element in Kant's theory of the criteria of analytic judgment, the view that synthetic propositions can be rendered analytic by a change in definition is foreign to the distinction as Kant established and used it, and does not contribute to a solution of his problem of justifying *a priori* judgments whose necessity is not that of formal logic.

40. I have translated this passage and discussed the issue of the variability of the synthetic-analytic decision in "Can Kant's Synthetic Judgments Be Made Analytic?" *Kant studien,* XLVII (1955), 168-181.

CAN KANT'S SYNTHETIC

JUDGMENTS

BE MADE ANALYTIC?

Lewis White Beck

§

In the sixties, when Kant had first drawn his distinction between analytic and synthetic judgments, he made the following note: "If one had the entire concept of which the notions of the subject and predicate are *compars,* synthetic judgments would change into analytic. It is a question of how much arbitrariness there is." [1] This question has been asked repeatedly since that time, and the clear and unmistakable trend of the answers has been that the decision whether a specific judgment is analytic or synthetic is arbitrary or at least is dependent upon variable conditions of how much the judger knows about the subject of the judgment and on his arbitrary decision of the choice and formula of his definitions.

In recent discussions of the distinction, analytic judgments are those that follow from explicit definitions by the rules of logic; and definitions are nominal or stipulative, to some degree arbitrary. If it is further argued, as is often done, that all *a priori* judgments are analytic, it follows that the distinction between *a priori* and *a posteriori* is likewise a shifting, arbitrary distinction.

Kant, who first asked the question, seems to have decided very

---

1. *Reflexion* 3928. The numbering of the *Reflexionen* and all page references to the works of Kant are, unless otherwise noted, those of the edition of the Prussian Academy.

early that the line of demarcation between these two types of judgment was not variable or arbitrary. The purpose of this essay is to inquire into the reasons for his decision and to indicate some of its implications for his philosophy as a whole.

I. ANALYTIC AND SYNTHETIC JUDGMENTS

Judgment, for Kant, is a synthesis of representations, having objective validity. The synthesis must be in accord with some objective, normative rule, and not merely illustrate some contingent law of association. A representation, functioning in the synthesis of judgment, is not just a brute given mental content, but is a mark of an object, its meaning fixed by a rule. Abstraction from the given complexity of representations in consciousness, and the generalization that a particular kind of representation is the mark of a particular kind of object, are necessary in converting raw representations into marks which can be manipulated in knowing.[2] Concepts are such marks functioning in knowledge; they are representations under an analytical (abstractive) unity through which they are discursive and not merely given sense contents. As concepts, they are not given; they are made concepts by being involved in a special attitude of intention and the interpretation of data. All that we directly have of an object is such marks. Our original consciousness is a congeries of raw materials for concepts, and the business of consciousness is to refine and organize these representations, assigning to some of them the role of subjects and to others that of predicates in judgments which are their objectively valid syntheses[3]; only as predicates of possible judgments do *Vorstellungen* serve as concepts, and only as containing representations under themselves do concepts refer to objects.[4]

Besides the analytical unity by which *hic et nunc* representations are made to serve as marks under a discursive concept (e.g., this *quale* at this time is seen as an example of a specific quality also instanced in another *quale* at another time) in order that there be judgment there must also be a synthetical unity through which the

2. *Reflexion* 2881.
3. Cf. *Reflexionen* 3920, 4634.
4. *Critique of Pure Reason*, A 69-B 94.

concepts (and their corresponding representations) are referred to the same object.

This object may not be given at all, or if given it is given as only a still further complex of representations which refer to "the same object" only by virtue of some precedent synthetical unity. The synthetical unity, which is a form and not a content of experience, is not given but is prescribed to experience by a rule that requires a common focus of meaning of the several concepts that appear in a judgment; if one such object is not meant by the various concepts, the synthesis of the concepts is a comparison, a setting of them side by side, and not a judgment. This common object is called by Kant X, and the rule of synthetical unity means that the terms in a judgment (concepts derived through the analytical unity of representations) such as A and B, must be regarded as marks of X. Then through A and B, we know X, and the cognition of X through A or B is a concept of X.[5] A and B are, epistemologically, predicates of X, but one of them is made to serve as the logical subject and the other as the logical predicate. The one called subject is directly related to X, the one called predicate is indirectly related to X in the judgment, though its occurrence in experience may be direct evidence of the existence of X (usually it is the wider concept, and is applied to a specific X only through the mediation of the subject concept).[6] Thus, to summarize and make specific: when X is known through two concepts related to each other in a synthetical unity, then a judgment whose form is given by a category or rule of this synthetical unity is established. If the rule is, for instance, the category of inherence and subsistence, the judgment reads, "There is an X such that X is A and X is B."

If B is related to A directly by being included as a part of its connotation, so that "X is A" implies logically "X is B," the judgment is analytic. In an analytic judgment, reference to X is otiose, and we say simply, "All A is B" where A and B are "partial concepts" of X, and B is a constitutive part of A. But "All A is B" is an elliptical expression, since A is a complex concept containing B. Fully expanded, therefore, the analytic judgment is the tautology, "All A.B is B."

When B is a concept of X because it is a *nota notae* of X, i.e.,

5. *Reflexion* 3920.
6. *Fortschritte der Metaphysik* (Cassirer ed., VIII), p. 245.

a mark or constituent of *A,* we can speak of the judgment as one in which the certainty of the connection of subject and predicate is "through identity." [7] If the identity is explicit, the judgment is inconsequential. The important case is the one in which the identity is implicit, so that its explication "widens our knowledge *formaliter"* though not *materialiter. B* may be "covertly contained in the concept" [8] and not thought "so distinctly and with the same (full) consciousness" as *A.*[9] It is an "analytic attribute" of *A* contained in it and elicited from it by logical analysis.[10] But it is essential that it be "contained in" *A,* so that the judgment is explicative, not ampliative, and independent of further experience of the X of which both *A* and *B* are concepts.

Now if the decision on analyticity of a specific judgment could be based on a definition of the subject, it would be easy enough to determine whether the judgment is analytic. But Kant rejects this procedure, because he holds that "definability" is a stricter condition than "analyzability," and that we can therefore make analytical judgments with concepts we cannot define. It is, in fact, through organizing analytic judgments that we gradually approach to definition,[11] which is the end, not the beginning of knowledge.

Since Kant has so restricted the scope and value of definition, these statements about the inclusion of one concept in another are exceedingly obscure. It seems that, without a stated definition, they can be understood in part only psychologically or phenomenologically. Speaking for the phenomenological interpretation is the emphasis upon what is "actually thought" in the subject; speaking for a logical interpretation is the fact that analytic attributes may be uncovered and brought to light only by sustained inquiry, and are not present, in any phenomenological sense, in the thought of the concept of the subject.

If we investigate each phrase in these passages, the possible con-

---

7. *Vorlesungen über Logik,* § 36. Kant objects to calling them identical judgments, however; cf. *Über eine Entdeckung . . . ,* p. 244.

8. *Critique of Pure Reason,* A 7/B 10.

9. *Prolegomena* § 2 a.

10. *Über eine Entdeckung . . . ,* p. 228f.

11. *Prolegomena,* § 2 c 3; cf. *Vorlesungen über Logik,* § 109 Anm.; *Über die Deutlichkeit der Grundsätze,* p. 282 (Beck trans., p. 262); *Falsche Spitzfindigkeit,* p. 61. I have studied the relation between Kant's theory of definition and the distinction between the analytic and synthetic in some detail in "Kant's Theory of Definition."

fusion of the two meanings is not removed. For instance, "contained in" (*enthalten in*) was a logical term used by Kant's contemporaries to describe predicates belonging to all individuals denoted by a concept.[12] But Kant obviously does not mean it only in a logical sense, for then synthetic attributes would be contained in the subject concept, which he denies; "contained in" seems to have reference to the subjective intension, and thus to have at least psychological overtones. But the words "actually thought in the concept of the subject" are elsewhere given a strictly logical meaning, since Kant says that what is really thought in a concept is "nothing other than its definition." [13]

I think we have to suspect here a fundamental failure on Kant's part to distinguish the logical from the phenomenological aspects of thought. Where definitions or fairly complete analyses are available, he thinks of the distinction between analytic and synthetic judgment as logical; where they are not, but are rather the objects of search, he has recourse to a phenomenological criterion, by virtue of which he seeks definitions through analysis of what, in the plainest sense, is "actually thought" in a concept or even "contained in" a complex experience subject to subsequent analysis.[14]

While we cannot speak of two definitions of the analytic, and can at most say that the analytic has both a logical and a phenomenological dimension, we can discern two criteria for analytic judgment. Kant, in apparent disregard of their differences, uses first one and then the other as it suits his purposes, perhaps in the conviction that their answers will in any specific case be the same.

(i) The logical criterion of analytic judgment is its conformity to

---

12. Vaihinger, *Commentar zu Kants Kritik der reinen Vernunft*, I, 258. "Contained in" is contrasted with "contained under"—*Reflexion* 3043. The latter, used in describing synthetic judgments, seems to mean for Kant what Vaihinger says was commonly meant by "contained in." Cf. also *Reflexionen* 2896, 2902.

13. *Critique of Pure Reason*, A 718/B 746.

14. A paper by Robert S. Hartman, "Analytic and Synthetic as Categories of Inquiry" (*Perspectives in Philosophy*, Ohio State University, 1953, pp. 55-78), has the special merit of singling out the two kinds of analyticity, one of which it calls definitional and the other expositional, and distinguishing both from "analytic" in the sense of descriptive of what is "contained in" an experience of an empirical object. Hartman's paper presents very clearly the processes by which analytic judgments lead to definitions, and definitions then establish a new and stricter criterion of analyticity. Another study of the process by which an analytic judgment may become synthetic is K. Sternberg, "Über die Unterscheidung von analytischen und synthetischen Urteilen," *Kantstudien* XXXI (1926), 171-201.

the law of contradiction, a necessary condition of any judgment and a necessary and sufficient condition for an analytic judgment. The test is applied as follows: substitute in a judgment synonyms for synonyms, or an analysis or definition of the subject concept for the subject itself. Then the contradictory of this judgment will infringe the law of contradiction if the original judgment is analytic. And as the contradictory of a self-contradictory proposition is necessary, the original judgment is necessary.

In applying the logical criterion, a definition in the strict sense is not required, for it is from the analytic judgments in informal exposition that we first gain the definition. All that is needed is a partial analysis of the subject concept. The absence of definition may at most prevent only the decision that some specific judgment is *not* analytic,[15] for what is mentioned as the predicate may be an unnoticed analytic attribute that we would have noticed had we possessed a full definition. But no criterion is infallible; even given a strict definition, the pertinancy of a specific attribute as analytical may be a discovery of the most difficult and surprising kind. It is in such cases that there will be the greatest divergence between decisions made on this and those made on the phenomenological criterion.

(ii) The phenomenological criterion is the issue of an inspection of what is found introspectively to be really thought in the concept of the subject. Though we have seen that what is "really thought" is said to be a definition, and that the mention of predicates not thought "with the same (full) consciousness" suggests a very wide range of predicates that might pass the logical but fail the phenomenological test, still it is clear that Kant was not free from a psychologizing, introspective tendency in his decisions on what is analytic and what is synthetic. The *Port Royal Logic* [16] demanded "moderate attention" to see whether the predicate is "truly contained in the idea of the subject," and not a completely articulated logical system as a criterion for this decision; the same kind of "moderate attention" seems to provide a criterion for Kant. He repeatedly asks himself and the reader what he thinks when he thinks a particular concept, and though undoubtedly one may think much, by casual association, which is not "contained in the con-

15. Cf. *Vorlesungen über Logik,* § 109 Anm.
16. Part IV, Ch. VI.

cept," what he does *not* think is *not* included in the content of the concept.

Just as he has previously distinguished between what is contained in and what is contained under a concept, so also he distinguishes what "lies in" a concept and what "belongs to" it.[17] There seems to be here a tacit distinction between two kinds of concepts, one being a concept of a highly refined analytical or abstractive unity, subject to strict definition, and the other being a looser complex of representations, more or less loosely held together and expandable through the accretion of new experience or subject to restriction in content through the supervention of a definition.[18]

I now turn, for the space of one paragraph to Kant's description of synthetic judgments, after which I shall come back to these two criteria of analytic judgment. The following material is essential for evaluating the issues raised by the two criteria.

B may be related to A indirectly by virtue of the fact that both are predicates of the same X. Then the concept A does not include the concept of B as a part of its logical essence, and to relate them to each other in judgment requires reference to the X of which each is a partial concept. There are three kinds of X which serve to mediate between A and B. (i) X may be a schema of an object in general (of a thing, cause, etc.). (ii) X may be a determinable intuition of space or time or both, which A and B both refer to and make determinate. (iii) X may be a datum or *concretum* of experience, "the complete experience of the object which I think through the concept A." [19] In the former two cases, the judgment will be valid regardless of the empirical content of the concepts, and in the first case there is established the kind of judgment which appears in "metaphysics as science." Failure to provide a schema without the conditions of space and time and to put the thing in itself in the

17. *Critique of Pure Reason*, A 718/B 746; but cf. *Vorlesungen über Logik* Einl. VIII (Cassirer ed., p. 373), where attributes belong to the essence, so far as they are derived from it.

18. The confusion between these two meanings of "concept" has been discussed by Koppelmann, "Kants Lehre vom analytischen Urteil," *Philosophische Monatshefte*, XXI (1885), 65-101; and by H. Ritzel, "Über analytische Urteile," *Jahrbuch f. Philosophie u. phänomenologische Forschung*, III (1916), 253 bis 344, at 261-76, 324. The full significance of it, as representing the interpenetration of two stages of inquiry dominated respectively by the analytic and the synthetic method, is ably worked out by Hartman, *op. cit.*

19. *Critique of Pure Reason*, A 8; omitted in B.

role of the X makes synthetic judgments impossible except of objects of possible experience. The second is the situation with respect to mathematical judgments, where X is a construction. In the third alternative, the judgment is *a posteriori*. But in each case it is a synthetic judgment, since the predicate is not found by analysis of the logical subject. If X is (as is actually the case) a subjective condition for the synthesis of A and B, the resulting synthetic judgment is, in the transcendental sense, only subjectively valid; though we can say still that the predicate is a part of the real and not of the nominal essence. In the same sense, an analytic judgment is objectively and even transcendently valid, not being restricted to the conditions of synthesis placed upon the X.[20]

From this account of the origin of synthetic judgment, and from the two criteria mentioned above, it is clear that the distinction between analytic and synthetic judgment is not one of formal logic, for formal logic abstracts from the meaning of all terms.

II. VARIABILITY OF THE DISTINCTION

Eberhard interpreted an analytic judgment as one the predicate of which is an *essentia* of the subject, and a synthetic judgment as one whose predicate is an attribute derived from an *essentia*. But Kant denies that this is his meaning, for he holds that "derived from" is equivocal. If the attribute is derived by logical analysis, the judgment is indeed analytic whether we *knew* that the attribute was "contained in" the subject concept or not; but there are other attributes, synthetic attributes (*Bestimmungen*), that are not contained in the logical essence, even though they might be associated with it in our minds, e.g., as weight with body. They are derived not by logical analysis but by construction or exhibition of a corresponding intuitive object. From such an experience the attribute can as it were be read off, though it is not a *nota notae* of the subject concept but a *nota* of the real object. It is this kind of synthetic predicate which is a part of the *ratio essendi* of the object, and it gives the concept of the subject and all its judgments whatever objective validity they have.

Though Eberhard was a mediocre thinker much of whose argu-

20. *Reflexion* 3950.

ment is vitiated by being based upon patent misunderstandings of Kant, he did nevertheless ask a difficult and important question, "How do we decide what is 'actually thought' in a concept?" Unless a definite and plausible criterion can be given that is exempt from the vagaries of the phenomenological criterion and of the logical criterion when Kant attempts to employ it unarmed with definitions, then an important member of the structure of his philosophy must be given up. Modern writers, reacting against both psychologism and phenomenology, wanting a behavioral rather than an introspectional criterion if a significant logical criterion cannot be given, have directed their main attack on the possibility of maintaining the distinction, in any particular instance, without a complement of definitions.

Rather than considering the views of those who give up or relativize the distinction for the reasons just mentioned, however, it will be more profitable to consider the views of a critic who admits a sharp distinction between analytic and synthetic, yet who does not base it on the test of nominal or stipulative definition. A critic this close to Kant is likely to be more instructive, at this juncture, than one more radically opposed to Kant. The criticism I shall consider is that by C. I. Lewis, which is in part an infinitely improved version of some debating points raised by Eberhard. Kant's cognizance of these arguments, admittedly in a more primitive form, makes a study of them especially worthwhile for an understanding of Kant himself.

Lewis argues as follows. The notion of a necessary but non-analytic proposition such as "Every event has a cause" is based on an equivocation. For "event," as a concept which does not contain "having a cause" as a part of its meaning, is not the same as the concept of "event" which does contain the concept "having a cause." Part of Kant's argument is based on the former and simpler concept, and here Kant rightly infers that the proposition is synthetic. But the argument that the proposition is *a priori* is based on the second, richer, concept. We can, according to Kant, think without contradiction an uncaused event; hence the relation expressed in the judgment is synthetic; but we cannot imagine, represent, or know an event as objective without relating it to another event by a rule of causation; hence the judgment is known *a priori*.

The equivocation is that "event" in the second case means "phenomenal event in objective space and time," while in the first case it is not so restricted. If this restriction is made explicit, however, the relation between the restricted concepts is seen to be analytic. The second Analogy of Experience seems to be synthetic only because the word "event" is not usually given the restricted meaning. The term needs to be fixed by definition before one can pronounce the judgment to be analytic or synthetic; and in defining it, we must be sure to include in its meaning everything needed to determine the objective applicability of the term in question: ". . . Anything which is essential to the temporal character of an event must be included in the adequate concept of it as a temporal event. . . . A definition which does not logically entail all characters essential to what is defined, is faulty." [21]

Kant's reply to this kind of criticism, as it appeared in its first crude form, or rather Schultz's reply written under Kant's supervision, makes two responses.

(i) Two different propositions, one of which is analytic and one synthetic, may be expressed by the same sentence, for the same word in the sentences may refer to two different concepts, one narrower and one broader.

(ii) Closely related to this is the assertion of the "fixity" of a concept. A concept cannot be arbitrarily widened through the accumulation of information. It can be replaced by another called by the same name; but of any given concept it can be decided what is implicit in it to be explicated in analytical judgment and what does not lie in it at all. When one changes a definition, which may change the status of many judgments the judgments are changed not merely in status but in meaning and validity. Definitions should not, therefore, be arbitrarily changed; a new one must pass the same kind of test of "realness" that the old one originally passed and later failed, if it is not to be merely stipulation without objective reference. We cannot convert empirical knowledge into *a priori* knowledge simply by refining our language:

> Let one put into the concept of the subject just so many attributes that the predicate which one wishes to prove of the subject can

21. *An Analysis of Knowledge and Valuation,* pp. 161-162. I have given a fuller exposition of Lewis' views (without discussion of the point raised here) in "Die Kantkritik von C. I. Lewis und der analytischen Schule," *Kantstudien* XLV (1954), 3-20.

be derived from its concept merely by the law of contradiction. The critical philosophy permits him to make this kind of analytic judgment, but raises a question about the concept of the subject itself. It asks: how did you come to include in this concept the different attributes so that it [now analytically] entails synthetic propositions? First prove the objective reality of your concept, i.e., first prove that any one of its attributes really belongs to a possible object, and when you have done that, then prove that the other attributes belong to the same thing that the first one belongs to, without themselves belonging to the first attribute. The whole question of how much or how little the concept of the subject is to contain has not the least bearing on the metaphysical question: how are synthetic *a priori* judgments possible? It belongs merely in the logical theory of definition. And the theory of definition without doubt requires that one not introduce more attributes into a definition than are necessary to distinguish the defined thing from all others. Hence [in a good definition] one excludes those attributes of which one can demand a proof whether and on what grounds they belong to the former attributes [that *are* included].[22]

Put in our own words, Kant is saying that a definition which will change a synthetic into an analytic judgment must be either nominal or real. If nominal, it does not in the least affect the cognitive status of the original judgment; while it may make the original sentence formally analytic, it does not give to the knowledge it expresses any logical or epistemic necessity it previously lacked.[23] And if the definition is a real one, we must know the necessary conjunction of independent, coordinate attributes in order to make it; and this conjunction is precisely what was stated in the synthetic judgment whose status is now being disputed. All that is effected by such a procedure, we might say, is that the locus of *a priori* synthesis is shifted.

22. *Rezension von Eberhard's Magazin,* pp. 408–409.

23. In this, Lewis is in agreement with Kant. In criticizing those who identify the *a priori* and the analytic, and then define the analytic in terms of linguistic rules or procedures, Lewis writes: "If implications of conceptions of this sort should be well worked out, it must appear that they are fatal to the thesis that what is *a priori* coincides with what is analytic; since the notion that what may be known true without recourse to sense experience, is relative to vocabulary or dependent on conventions of procedure, is not credible" (*op. cit.,* p. 36).

III. INDEFINABILITY OF THE CATEGORIES

Thus far I have considered only Kant's explicit answers to the criticism that the analytic-synthetic distinction is variable. I now examine Kant's reply in its general philosophical bearings.

I have already mentioned that there are in Kant's writings two quite different species of concept. In one case, like that of "water," the word is "more properly to be regarded as merely a designation than as a concept of the thing," [24] and its meaning does vary with experience. In the other, the concept is fixed either by definition, or fixed because it is a *pure* concept which, while not subject to definition, is not subject to revision by the accumulation of experience. In the latter case, Kant believed that a fixed decision could be made concerning what was and what was not included in it, even at a time before a stated definition had been reached. The rationalistic tradition in which Kant wrote fixed many of the most important concepts by "implicit" definition and common use or by nominal definitions that had become well established.[25] Thus Kant could confidently decide that a given proposition is analytic without the necessity of referring to a "rule book" of stipulative definitions. We, in a more conventionalistic period, are usually puzzled by some of his decisions and can only feel that Kant and his contemporaries were committing what Whitehead called the "fallacy of the perfect dictionary"—when the dictionary could not, in principle, exist for Kant at all. But the more important point is that the concepts with which Kant is most concerned, viz., the categories, are not fixed by definition and need not be fixed in this way. They are fixed because, as pure, they are not susceptible to experiential modification.

Let us consider what Kant was attempting to do with these concepts. It had been shown by Hume that they could not be given objective validity by definition, and though Kant might have given a richer, more determinate definition to such a concept as cause, a

24. *Critique of Pure Reason,* A 728/B 756.
25. Cf. J. H. Hyslop, "Kant's Treatment of Analytic and Synthetic Judgment," *Monist,* XIII (1903), 331-351, which emphasizes Cartesian and Newtonian conclusions as they "infected" the concepts Kant used.

still more extended Humean argument would have been fatal again to its claims to objective validity. Definition and proof of objective validity are not the same except in mathematics, which, for quite peculiar reasons, does not have to meet the Humean type of criticism. Assuming a broader definition, a proof of the objective validity of its analytic consequences is still called for if Hume's criticisms of the rational structure of empirical knowledge are to be met. Given the broader definition, of course, antecedently synthetic judgments become analytic. So long as the definitional component is expanded *ad lib,* any *a priori* judgment can be shown to be analytic. But apriority is not dependent upon this kind of analyticity; the analyticity of such a judgment is not a condition of its apriority but a subsequent, factitious addendum to it. That is, there must be recognition of some special dignity of function of a specific proposition that makes it worthwhile to devise a language in which it will be necessary; but the linguistic necessity is established subsequent to this recognition.

Kant did not simply suppose that causality had objective meaning; he tried to show that it did, and in doing so he found that he had to add to the concept of sufficient reason determinations which neither Hume nor the rationalists had suspected; he had to give a new interpretation to "possible experience" as the mediator between the terms of such a judgment. To have suppressed this interpretation for the sake of a formal definition of cause which would render the second Analogy of Experience analytical would have distorted the whole procedure of the critical philosophy, and would have left unanswered the reiterated question, how can *this* judgment, based on definition, be valid objectively?

Kant thought that real definitions should come at the end of inquiry, not at the beginning. One might expect, therefore, that the contribution of the *Critique of Pure Reason* might have been seen as a new set of definitions subsequent to which *a priori* judgments previously called synthetic would now be called analytic. Why did Kant not see his work in this way, but obstinately regarded the Analogies as synthetic judgments—in spite of the fact that he might have seen the logical classification as tentative, dependent upon the richness of the concepts?

There were several reasons why Kant did not do this. Among

them was his respect for tradition; more important was his recognition that Hume's objections to the rational foundations of empirical knowledge could not be met by new definitions. And a still more fundamental reason is to be found in his repeated denials of the definability of the categories: the definitions which some might think would serve for this reduction of all *a priori* knowledge to analytic knowledge cannot be given. Definitions, however elaborated, are still conceptual relations; but what is needed is some way to get a concept into relation with an object, and to do it in an *a priori* fashion. Concepts alone, however richly furnished with predicates, do not establish contact with things; only intuition can provide this contact. We can indeed conceptualize and name the requisite intuition; but in doing this, we treat it like a universal concept, and as such it fails to establish the objective reference. It always leaves open the question: does *this* complex universal apply? The category, whether it can be defined or not, must be schematized—must be provided, in Lewis' terminology, with a sense meaning as well as a linguistic meaning. Kant is profuse in his definitions of pure categories, but these definitions are nominal.[26] Schematizing a category is very different from defining it:

> There is something strange and even nonsensical in the notion that there should be a concept which must have a meaning but which cannot be defined. But the categories are in a unique position, for only by virtue of the *general condition of sensibility* can they have a definite meaning and relation to an object. This condition, however, is omitted in the pure category, for this can contain only the logical function of bringing the manifold under a concept.[27]

without specifying the concept or the condition of its application to a specific manifold.

No philosopher has emphasized more than Kant the fundamental difference between sense and understanding while at the same time asserting their complementary function. This fundamental difference is essential here. It is not the *concept* of an intuitive condition, which might be added to a concept or included in its definition, that gives full meaning to the category; it is the *condition of sensibility*

26. *Critique of Pure Reason*, A 244/B 302.
27. *Ibid.*, A 244-245; omitted from B. Italics supplied.

itself,[28] the condition of its actual use in specific circumstances according to rule. This is a transcendental addendum, a real predicate, a synthetic predicate, a *Bestimmung,* an element in the *ratio essendi* as well as the *ratio cognoscendi.* It is not just another attribute without which the definition is "inadequate." Make the added condition a conceptual amendment to the definition, and the entire question is postponed: we would still have to ask, "How does *this concept* have *a priori* objective application?" [29]

IV. THE STATUS OF MATHEMATICAL JUDGMENTS

Because Kant does admit definitions, in the strictest sense, only in the field of mathematics,[30] it is easy to admit a sharp distinction between analytic and synthetic judgments here; in fact, mathematical definition has been taken as establishing the paradigm of the analytic-synthetic distinction.[31] Granting the sharpness of the distinction between analytic and synthetic here, most competent critics of Kant are in agreement that he was in error in saying that mathematical judgments are synthetic. It is said that what kept him from seeing that they are analytic was the lack of adequate mathematical definitions, definitions not available until much later. Professor Lewis characteristically writes: "It would be ungrateful and unjust to blame Kant for not foreseeing that, from genuinely adequate mathematical definitions, the theorems of mathematics might be deducible." [32] Obviously, deducible from definition and analytic are here regarded as equivalent notions.

28. The difference between a concept of an intuitive condition and the intuitive condition itself is formally like that between the concept of existence and existence itself. Kant's criticism of the ontological argument, *mutatis mutandis,* could be used here against the view (expressed by Lewis, *op. cit.,* p. 162, middle paragraph) that the *concept* of space suffices, if we assume, with Kant, that mathematics is knowledge of something real.

29. There is still another argument in the *Critique* (A 245, abesent from B) against the definability of categories, to wit, that such definitions are circular. I do not think the argument is valid; but inasmuch as it applies, if at all, to the pure as well as to the schematized categories, it is not relevant to our purposes here.

30. *Critique of Pure Reason,* A 729/B 758.

31. "Kant scheint bei der Einteilung der Urteile in analytisch und synthetisch von der Fiktion auszugehen, dass auch die nichtmathematischen Begriffe definiert werden können."—K. Marc-Wogau, "Kants Lehre vom analytischen Urteil," *Theoria,* XVII (1951), 140-154, at 150.

32. *Op. cit.,* p. 162.

This, however, as we have amply seen, is not what Kant meant by "analytic." In the *Prolegomena* he wrote:

> As it was found that the conclusions of mathematics all proceed according to the law of contradiction . . . men persuaded themselves that the fundamental principles were known by the same law. This was a great mistake, for a synthetical proposition can indeed be understood [*eingesehen*] by the law of contradiction, but only by presupposing another synthetical proposition from which it follows, never by that law alone.[33]

From this we see the following: (i) Mathematical theorems may be synthetic even if proved by the law of contradiction, i.e., by strictly logical procedure. Deducibility is not a sufficient condition for analyticity. To be analytic, in Kant's meaning, a proposition would have to be proven by the law of contradiction *alone,* i.e., its contradictory would have to be *self*-contradictory; but in mathematical proof by strict logic, the contradictory of the proposition contradicts some *other* assumed propositions. (ii) A proposition will be called synthetic if among its premises is a synthetic proposition, such as an axiom, or a mathematical definition, i.e., a synthetical definition which can be exhibited in a construction. (iii) Mathematical axioms (fundamental principles) are synthetic since they are not established by the analysis of a given concept, but only by the intuitive construction of the concept, which will show the necessary presence of attributes not included in a logical definition of the subject.[34]

The theorems, therefore, can be called synthetic even though they are strictly (analytically, in modern usage) demonstrable. The famous discussion of the example, "$7 + 5 = 12$," two paragraphs later, is quite independent of the grounds given in the quotation for calling the theorems synthetic. It is, in fact, inconsistent with it. In the quotation, Kant is conceding that a theorem does follow from premises by strict logic; whatever may be the nature of the premises, the internal structure of the proof is logical. But in the discussion of "$7 + 5$" Kant is arguing that a theorem does not follow logically even from synthetic axioms, but that intuitive construction enters into the theorem itself and its proof. These two

---

33. *Prolegomena,* § 2 c 1 = *Critique of Pure Reason,* B 14.
34. *Über die Deutlichkeit* . . . , p. 277 (Beck trans., 263); *Über eine Entdeckung* . . . , pp. 229ff.; *Critique of Pure Reason,* A 730/B 758.

theses—that an intuitive synthetic element is present in the primitive propositions, and that an intuitive synthetic process is present in demonstration—are independent of each other. Because a mathematical judgment is often synthetical by the phenomenological criterion, Kant seems to have supposed that there were good logical reasons for calling it synthetic. Of these two theses, only the first is of any moment in the epistemology (not the methodology) of mathematical knowledge, but it is only the second of the theses that could be corrected by the use of what Lewis calls "genuinely adequate mathematical definitions."

The real dispute between Kant and his critics is not whether the theorems are analytic in the sense of being strictly deducible, and not whether they should be called analytic now when it is admitted that they are deducible from definitions, but whether there are any primitive propositions which are synthetic and intuitive. Kant is arguing that the axioms cannot be analytic, both because they must establish a connection between concepts, just as definitions do, and because they must establish a connection that can be exhibited in intuition. And this is what is denied by the modern critic of Kant.

I think Kant is obviously right in saying that there cannot be a system of nothing but analytic propositions; there must be some complexes to analyze, and these must be stated synthetically. But if the postulates are not analytic, this does not mean that they are synthetic *propositions,* i.e., synthetic statements expressing truths. A stipulation can "establish" synthetic relations, but it does not thereby qualify as a proposition. If it be assumed that mathematics is a game, then the analytic-synthetic distinction is of no importance in discussing the postulates, because the premises are not propositions at all but are only stipulations or propositional functions.[35]

Kant did not espouse the game theory. Mathematics was for him objective knowledge. That is why he regarded the axioms as propositions, not proposals. Were they mere relations of ideas, in Hume's

---

35. Kant says that mathematical definitions are *willkürlich,* which is usually translated as "arbitrary." But the connotation of "random" present in "arbitrary" is not present in Kant's word "arbitrary," for Kant makes the antonym of "arbitrary" not "necessary" but "empirical." *Vorlesungen über Logik,* § 103 Anm. *Willkürlich* has reference to the volitional character of a synthetic definition, a rule for the synthesis of a concept; but a mathematical concept is synthesized only under given conditions of intuition, and is therefore not arbitrary in the modern sense of this word.

sense, they could be made as "adequate" as one wished, yet the question of how they could be objectively valid would remain untouched. But for Kant, real mathematical definitions are possible, because the definition creates the object. This sounds like stipulation again; but the object is not an arbitrary logical product of subjectively chosen independent properties. To define a mathematical concept is to prescribe rules for its construction in space and time. Such a definition is a synthetical proposition, because the spatial determination of the figure is not a logical consequence of the concept but is a real condition of its application. The real property is joined the logical properties synthetically, not analytically.

Objections to Kant's views of mathematics, therefore, cannot be removed merely by the substitution of more adequate sets of definitions and postulates, as if being a better mathematician would have corrected Kant's philosophy of mathematics. *The syntheticity of mathematical knowledge in Kant is not a consequence of the inadequacy of his definitions.* It is an essential feature of his entire theory of mathematical knowledge, by which the identity of mathematics and logic was denied. Mathematical knowledge in his view of the world has objective reference, and this is obtained not through definition but through intuition and construction. His mathematical definitions are real; what is deduced from them may be, in modern but not Kantian terminology, analytic propositions. But the propositions admitted as theorems by Kant are not like the analytic propositions of modern mathematics or the relations of ideas of Hume, for they have a necessary relation to experience through the synthetic, intuitive character of the definitions and axioms. Even propositions which Kant admits are analytic belong to mathematics only if they can be exhibited in intuition.[36] Whatever improvements in Kant's definitions might have been introduced for the sake of making the theorems analytic in his sense would have cost a high price in setting mathematics apart from the discussion of the conditions of possible experience. And had they been seen as analytic, Kant's long and deep concern with mathematics would not have positively contributed to his interpretation of the problems of empirical knowledge. For Kant saw in mathematics a clue to the objectivity of all *a priori* knowledge, both analytic and what he considered to be synthetic. This is indeed the sense of the

36. *Critique of Pure Reason*, B 17 = *Prolegomena* § 2, c 2.

Copernican revolution: even empirical objects are constructions; and their necessary conditions are geometrical. Had Kant radically sundered mathematical knowledge from the intuitive *a priori* structures of empirical knowledge, as he criticizes Hume for doing,[37] both would have been rendered unintelligible to him. The question is thereby raised whether, in introducing modern amendments into Kant's theory of mathematics (perhaps for the purpose of "saving what is essential in the critical philosophy"), we do not at the same time overlook or destroy everything distinctive in his theory of empirical knowledge.

---

37. *Prolegomena* § 2, c 2; *Kritik der praktischen Vernunft*, p. 51 (Beck trans., pp. 101-102.

THE KEY TO
KANT'S DEDUCTION OF
THE CATEGORIES

H. J. Paton

§

I

If there is any doctrine on which Kantian commentators are agreed, it is the doctrine that for Kant the forms of judgment are the forms of analytic judgment only. The question then arises, How can the forms of analytic judgment be a clue to the categories, which are principles of synthesis? To the question in this form there can be no answer. It is irrelevant to appeal, as some do, to the fact that all analysis presupposes synthesis. We are forced to conclude that the metaphysical deduction of the categories lacks even elementary plausibility, that it is another example of Kant's pedantic devotion to "Architectonic" and is to be explained as due to the childish desire to find parallels between formal and transcendental logic.

It may seem a foolhardy and futile thing to question a doctrine so widely accepted.[1] I will not venture to say outright that it is false, for in the immense mass of Kantian literature there may be

---

Professor Paton wishes to have this essay prefaced by the statement that, in Section III, he is mistaken in so far as he takes a crucial passage in the Metaphysical Deduction to be concerned with the difference between analytic and synthetic judgments.—ED.

1. The acceptance of the doctrine is neither so widespread nor so unqualified in Germany as it is in this country.

evidence sufficient to establish its truth. I do, however, assert that the evidence usually brought forward is inadequate for this purpose, that there is evidence working in the opposite direction, and that a very different view is at least worthy of consideration. And in spite of the prevailing attitude toward Kant, which varies from pitying patronage to petulant rebuke, it seems to me as rash to attribute this extraordinary doctrine to the founder of the critical philosophy as it is to suppose that his commentators may be mistaken.

It will hardly be denied that the doctrine in question is an extraordinary one. The more we reflect on it, the more extraordinary does it appear. If it means anything, it means that the forms of judgment as known to formal logic are the forms of analytic judgments and are *not* the forms of synthetic judgments. We should expect that the forms of judgment would be the forms of all judgments, or the forms of judgment in general, or of thinking in general. This is how Kant himself habitually describes them. For example, just before introducing the Categories,[2] he describes the previous table[3] of forms as giving us the logical functions (that is, forms) *"in all possible judgments."* This ought to mean that the forms of judgment are the forms *both* of analytic *and* of synthetic judgments, and indeed there would be no point in calling them forms of judgment unless they were so.

We may well ask how any other view can be considered as even a possible view. To assert that the forms of judgment are not the forms of synthetic judgment is to assert something that is perilously near nonsense—in fact (not to put too fine a point on it), it is nonsense. It means that a synthetic judgment is neither universal nor particular nor singular; that it is neither affirmative nor negative; that it is neither categorical, nor hypothetical, nor disjunctive; and that it is neither problematic, nor assertoric, nor apodeictic. One can only say that if this, or anything like this, is true, no synthetic judgment has ever been, or ever will be, made, and that the very idea of a synthetic judgment becomes as meaningless as the idea of

2. A79 = B105. (The first edition of the *Kritik of Pure Reason* will be referred to throughout as A, the second edition as B. The numbers in brackets refer to the complete Edition of the Prussian Academy.)
3. A70 = B95.

a square circle. If synthetic judgments do not partake of the forms of judgment, they are not judgments at all.

No doubt it is possible that a doctrine which is in itself nonsense may have been held by Immanuel Kant. Nevertheless, there is a presumption against attributing nonsense to one who has earned some reputation as a thinker. The presumption will be greatly strengthened if it can be shown that the rejection of this nonsensical view makes the Metaphysical Deduction cease to be the broken-backed thing which it is usually represented to be. This point will be considered later, but even without it we may say that the evidence ought to be carefully scrutinized, and indeed that it ought to be clear beyond all dispute, before we surrender ourselves to the ortho-dox theory, supported though it be by so many venerable names.

II

The orthodox theory could never have become so firmly established unless there were evidence, or what looks like evidence, to support it. It is, however, difficult to say what precisely the evidence is, since the commentators accept the doctrine without question and consequently do not gather together the passages upon which they rely. The arguments in favor of their theory are embedded in dis-cussions which do not face the question directly; they have to be extracted by means of inference. In the writings of Kant himself I am acquainted with one passage only (occurring, however, at a very critical stage in his argument) which may seem to offer direct evidence of the kind required; but there are many statements in his works which can easily be mistaken for such evidence, and which often are so mistaken. It is necessary, even at the risk of tediousness, to touch upon some of these misconceptions. I propose to deal with mere misunderstandings in this section and to reserve the more serious evidence for the following section.

(1) Kant is no revolutionary in regard to formal logic; many of his statements about it might have come direct from Aristotle; and the weakness of his argument from the modern point of view is that, like his contemporaries and predecessors, he accepted Aris-

totelian logic as, within its own sphere, complete and final. I do not think anyone will maintain that Aristotle regarded the forms of judgment as confined to analytic judgments, but it seems to be believed that in holding this doctrine Kant was, as in other respects, merely continuing an established logical tradition.

What is the evidence for such a belief? It is true that some thinkers regarded analytic (or identical) judgments as the ideal of knowledge, but this has nothing to do with the forms of judgment as such. I have sought in vain for the required doctrine in Leibniz, in Baumgarten, in G. F. Meier, and in Kant's own lectures on logic. Furthermore, in the so-called *Streitschrift gegen Eberhard* [4] Kant appears to resent the statement that Wolff and Baumgarten had made clear the distinction between synthetic and analytic judgments, and to claim novelty for his view in this respect. If there is any truth in this, it is manifest that the exclusive concern of formal logic with the forms of analytic judgments can be no part of the existing logical tradition. On the other hand, if this exclusive concern is an innovation made by Kant himself, it is amazing that he does not refer to it more explicitly.

(2) Transcendental logic, as opposed to formal logic, deals with synthetic *a priori* judgments. It does not follow from this that formal logic deals only with the form of *analytic* judgments, just as it does not follow that formal logic deals only with the form of *empirical* judgments. Formal logic deals with judgment in general, that is, it deals with the forms of judgment without regard to the matter. The difference between empirical and *a priori* judgments is a difference of matter only, and these judgments have the same forms. So too, I suggest, synthetic and analytic judgments have the same forms.

No one has yet asserted, so far as I know, that the forms of judgment do not hold of empirical judgments. Yet that is the necessary consequence of the prevailing theory, since analytic judgments (for Kant) are all *a priori*. This in itself seems to me a sufficient refutation of the theory.

(3) Formal logic is for Kant the logic of *discursive* thought. It is easy to misunderstand this statement and to suppose that if for-

mal logic gives us the forms of discursive thought, it gives us the forms of analytic thought (or judgment), and of that alone.[5]

Discursive cognition is cognition through concepts, while intuitive cognition is cognition in intuition. The intuition refers directly or immediately to the object, while the concept refers mediately to the object by means of intuition. *All human thinking is discursive;* that is to say, we do not possess an intuitive understanding or intellectual intuition which would create its own object in the act of thinking. Apart from what is given to us in intuition by means of sense, human thinking would be without an object and would be empty. This is a commonplace of the Kantian philosophy.

If we consider cognition or knowledge (*Erkenntnis*) as opposed to mere thinking (*Denken*), we can say that for Kant it always (in human beings) involves both thought and intuition; that is, it involves both a discursive element and an intuitive element. We sometimes, however, describe cognition as discursive or as intuitive, according to the element which is most prominent in it.[6] Thus mathematical cognitions can be described as intuitive, while philosophical cognitions are described as discursive.[7] The reason is that philosophy (even Kant's philosophy) has to work with mere concepts (although always in relation to a possible experience), while mathematics can construct *a priori* in intuition objects corresponding to its concepts.

There are no exceptions to this rule, although the Mathematical Principles are said to have intuitive certainty[8] (*Gewissheit*) and evidence (*Evidenz*),[9] while the Dynamical Principles have discursive certainty. Kant is, however, careful to make clear[10] that even the principle of the Axioms of Intuition is itself not an axiom but is obtained by means of concepts and so is discursive. His general position is established beyond a shadow of doubt in the Transcendental Doctrine of Method and may be summed up in his own

5. Prof. Kemp Smith seems to lend support to this view, e.g., *Commentary,* pp. 176, 182-183, etc.

6. *Fortschr. d. Metaph. Beilag.* I, *Abs.* 2. *Philosophische Bibliothek,* 46C., p. 156.

7. *Logik* (IX, 23), A719 = B747.

8. A162 = B201.

9. A180 = B223. Cf. *Log. Ein.,* IX (IX, 70) where *Evidenz = intuitive Gewissheit.*

10. A732-733 = B760-761.

words: [11] "A transcendental proposition is therefore *synthetic* knowledge, through reason, in accordance with mere concepts; and it is *discursive*."

It is a very natural error to equate "analytic" with "discursive," and "synthetic" with "intuitive," on the ground that analysis works with concepts only, while synthesis demands intuition as well. It is nonetheless an error. Human cognition is always discursive *from the side of understanding;* [12] and every synthetic proposition in Kant's philosophy, including the Analogies of Experience themselves, is quite certainly a discursive, and not an intuitive proposition.

Hence, to say that logic gives the forms of discursive thought is not to say that it gives the forms of analytic judgments only. All human *thought* is discursive; and some human *cognitions* (including the very essence of the transcendental philosophy itself) are both discursive and synthetic. Indeed, I doubt whether any synthetic propositions outside of mathematics are ever described by Kant as intuitive, but it is sufficient for my purpose to show, as I have done, that some discursive propositions are synthetic.

This argument, therefore, plausible as it may seem at first sight, necessarily falls to the ground.

(4) Kant is never tired of insisting [13] that the supreme principle of formal logic is the principle of non-contradiction, and that by the mere rules of logic we can produce nothing but analytic judgments. This doctrine is supposed to reinforce the plausible error which has just been exposed, and is itself taken as implying that formal logic gives us the forms of analytic judgment only.

This alleged implication is illusory. If we accept provisionally the distinction between analytic and synthetic judgments,[14] what Kant maintains is obviously true. Supposing that any concept is given to us, we can by the principle of non-contradiction make analytic judgments, but we cannot make synthetic judgments unless we have also intuition of the object of the concept. Does any man in his senses maintain, as a necessary consequence from this obvious fact, that

11. A722 = B750.
12. *Log. Ein.,* VIII (IX, 58).
13. E.g., A150 = B189ff.
14. Mr. Joseph's attempt to turn this into another distinction (*Logic,* p. 210) seems to be explicitly rejected by Kant in the *Streitschrift gegen Eberhard* (VIII, 230).

synthetic judgments must therefore have a different form from analytic judgments, that, for example, they can be neither affirmative nor negative? If, on the other hand, this is not a necessary consequence, there is nothing in Kant's theory here which can justify us in attributing to him such manifest nonsense. We are looking for evidence that this nonsense was part of his philosophical doctrine, and clearly we must look for it elsewhere.

I should myself have thought that Kant's doctrine in this respect works in the opposite direction. It is true that the principle of non-contradiction is the supreme principle of formal logic, and that it is "the universal and completely adequate principle of all analytical cognition." [15] We can use it positively to determine the truth or falsity of any admittedly analytic judgment. But where does Kant assert that synthetic judgments are not subject to the law of non-contradiction? He says precisely the opposite, and what he says is true. The law of non-contradiction is "a universal, although merely negative, criterion of *all* truth." [16] It is a *conditio sine qua non* of *all* knowledge. Synthetic judgments must conform to the principle of non-contradiction and indeed to all the rules of logic,[17] and unless they do so they are false; but we cannot tell merely by the rules of logic whether any synthetic judgment is true.

For Kant, the principle of non-contradiction and the rules of formal logic govern all knowledge, whether synthetic or analytic. If this suggests anything, it suggests that the forms of judgment which logic studies are not the forms of a particular kind of judgment but the forms of all judgment without exception.

It is an elementary mistake to suppose that the judgments whose forms are set forth by logic are necessarily identical with the judgments which can be made by the rules of logic alone.

(5) There is another respect in which an exclusively analytic procedure is connected with formal logic. This is concerned with the production of concepts, and since it is mentioned more than once in the Metaphysical Deduction itself,[18] it acquires an importance which it would not otherwise have. The reason why it is mentioned there is to contrast the account given by formal logic of the

15. A151 = B191.
16. A151 = B190.
17. Cf. A52 = B76. Formal Logic "contains the absolutely necessary rules of thought, without which no use of the understanding ever takes place."
18. A76 = B102ff.

production of concepts with the account of the categories given by transcendental logic. We are fortunate in having Kant's own lectures on logic which expound the ordinary formal view,[19] so that there is no excuse for misunderstanding what his doctrine is.

Every concept has (*a*) matter and (*b*) form. Its form is its universality, its matter is its object. Formal logic (as always) ignores the matter and considers only the form. It explains how concepts are produced, only so far as their *form* is concerned. That is to say, accepting the fact that ideas are given to us, it explains how they can be turned into concepts,[20] or how they can be brought under a concept,[21] or how they can be given that form of universality which is demanded by judgment, and without which they could not apply to different objects. In doing so formal logic ignores the fact that the *matter* of concepts may come from different sources. The matter comes from experience in the case of empirical concepts; it comes from mere invention in the case of fictitious or arbitrary concepts; and it comes from the nature of understanding itself in the case of pure concepts.[22] The question of the origin of concepts *in regard to their matter* is considered only in metaphysics (that is, in transcendental logic).

Here, again, it is noteworthy that for Kant formal logic considers the form of *all* concepts, and this surely does something to confirm the view that it considers also the forms of *all* judgments.

Nevertheless, the procedure of which formal logic gives an account[23] is said to be analytic, so it may be well to observe what that procedure is. It consists in comparison, reflection, and abstraction. I see, for example, a spruce tree, a lime tree, and a willow. I *compare* them and observe that they differ from one another as regards their stem, their branches, their leaves. I *reflect,* however, on what they have in common, namely stem, branches, and leaves. And I *abstract* from their size, shape, and so on. In this way I attain to the concept of "tree."

19. *Logik. Allg. Elem. Abs.* I, § 1-§ 6 (IX, 91-95).
20. A76 = B102.
21. A78 = B104.
22. Cf. A84 = B116ff.
23. In A76 = B102 the procedure is (loosely) implied to be the procedure of formal logic itself, and this confusion is too often repeated by the commentators. The more correct statement is found in A78 = B104.

It is a far cry from this elementary exposition to the view that the forms of judgment are not forms of synthetic judgment.

(6) Formal logic is analytic in the sense that it analyzes [24] (*auflöst*) the whole formal procedure of understanding and reason into its elements. It is on this ground that the main part of it has, since the time of Aristotle, been called the Analytic (or Analytics). Transcendental logic has, however, also its Analytic, which is the analysis [25] (*Zergliederung*) of all our *a priori* knowledge into its elements, and indeed the analysis [26] (*Zergliederung*) of the power of understanding itself with a view to the discovery of the categories.

This kind of analysis has no connection with the problem which is being discussed.

III

Kant's doctrines in regard to formal logic have now been reviewed in so far as they indicate a connection between formal logic and any kind of analysis. It seems to me that in them there is no evidence whatever for the accepted doctrine that the forms of judgment, as given by logic, are not forms of synthetic, as well as of analytic, judgment. There is, however, much that might be (and often is) mistaken for such evidence. In particular, the fact that the thinking with which logic deals is termed discursive, may easily lead the unwary to believe that logic gives the forms of analytic judgment only. The mistake is made still more easy by another fact, namely that the principle of non-contradiction is a *sufficient* criterion of the truth of analytic judgments only, and that the only judgments which can be made by means of the rules of logic alone are analytic judgments.

Hence it is not surprising that this error (as I take it to be) should become firmly established once it had been set forth by a competent commentator. That it should be so set forth was the natural result of the one passage which offers what looks like direct evidence in its support.

24. A60 = B84.
25. A64 = B89.
26. A65 = B90.

This one passage occurs in the heart of the paragraph [27] which is the very core and crux of the Metaphysical Deduction itself. Unfortunately, this paragraph is perhaps the most difficult in the whole body of Kant's writings, and its general meaning must be considered in order to understand the particular passage with which we are concerned.

The paragraph consists of two sentences, both full of difficulty. Each throws light on the other, but we must concentrate on the second sentence, which contains the evidence of which we are in quest.

The same understanding, Kant asserts, and by means of precisely the same activities, does two things: (1) in concepts, by means of the analytic unity, it brings into existence the logical form of a judgment; (2) it brings into its ideas a transcendental content by means of the synthetic unity of the manifold in intuition in general. The transcendental content, needless to say, is the category.

The activities of which Kant speaks must be the activities of judging. All the activities of understanding can be reduced to judging.[28] If we are to have that *unity* of the manifold of intuition without which there can be no knowledge and no object, there must be judgment present as well as intuition; and if judgment (with its form) is present to unite the manifold of intuition, there is thereby introduced a category into our ideas: to this category all objects must necessarily conform.[29] That is the second statement which Kant makes about understanding and its activities, and this statement is the essence of the Metaphysical Deduction.

At present, however, we are concerned with the first statement. The other thing which understanding does by the activity of judging is, in the case of concepts, to produce the form of a judgment *by means of the analytic unity.*

This asserts (what we know already) that if we have concepts given to us, we can by mere analysis make judgments and so bring into existence the form of a judgment. The given concepts are the matter of the judgment, the determination of the way in which

27. A79 = B104-105.
28. A69 = B94.
29. A concept (it is hardly necessary to say) is called a category, only if all objects must conform to it.

they are united is the form.[30] The form of judgment is undoubtedly to be found in analytic judgments, but is there anything in the present statement to imply that it is not found in synthetic judgments?

I do not see that the statement would justify us in attributing such a view to Kant with any confidence, even if it were a reasonable view. Still less do I think it justifies us in attributing to him a view which is on examination preposterous. I believe, on the contrary, that the whole Metaphysical Deduction turns on the fact that the same form is to be found both in analytic and in synthetic judgments, and this belief is, I suggest, confirmed by the immediately preceding sentence.

Throughout the Metaphysical Deduction the word "form" is equated with the word "function." [31] The forms of judgment and the functions of judgment are one and the same thing. Their connotation may be different but their denotation is the same. In view of this the previous sentence becomes illuminating. "The same function (that is, the same form) which gives unity to the different ideas *in a judgment,* also gives unity to the mere synthesis of different ideas *in an intuition."* The reason for this is the obvious one that there is no unity in an intuition apart from judgment, and apart from the form (or function) of judgment. The statement is meaningless unless the forms of judgment in general are also the forms of synthetic judgment, for the latter alone directly involves intuition.

This view of the Metaphysical Deduction is, I believe, borne out and emphasized in the second edition of the *Kritik,* in the *Prolegomena,* and in the *Metaphysische Anfangsgründe der Naturwissenschaft.* These later expositions will be examined in the following section. What we have to consider at the moment is why in this passage Kant should emphasize the fact that the form of judgment is to be found in analytic judgments.

So far as I can judge, the reason would seem to be that if we wish to be certain of grasping the form of judgment, apart from any possibility of its being determined by the matter, we turn to the analytic judgment. Whatever be the matter given to us in concepts we can, according to Kant, always make analytic judgments;

30. *Logik. Allg. Elem. Abs.* 2, § 18 (IX, 101).
31. "Function" seems to mean the form of an activity (e.g., judgment), while "form" may be the form of a receptivity (e.g., sensibility).

whereas synthetic judgments depend upon something more, namely the presence of an intuition corresponding to the concept. Synthetic propositions increase knowledge *materialiter,* while analytic propositions do so only *formaliter.*[32] Hence there is a specially close connection between the forms of judgment and the analytic judgment, inasmuch as an analytic judgment makes only a formal difference to our knowledge. An analytic judgment can be made by a merely formal use of reason, but a synthetic judgment cannot be so made.

To say this is to admit that there is in Kant's thought and language something that gives color to the interpretation which we deny. Unless something of this kind could be discovered, the probability would be that the interpretation in question rested on evidence which had been overlooked. Nevertheless, the evidence that we have discovered is very far from justifying the statement, in its naked horror, that for Kant the forms of judgment can never be the forms of synthetic judgments. The difference between analytic and synthetic judgments is not in respect of form. It lies in the fact that the whole matter of the analytic judgment is given in the subject concept, while the synthetic judgment requires an additional matter given by direct intuition.

Another possible reason for Kant's statement is that by analysis of a concept we may produce a form of judgment which is *only* a form; that is, which has no object, no matter given to sense. Many metaphysical judgments are (according to Kant) of this nature. I do not think, however, that all analytic judgments are regarded by Kant as mere forms without matter. Furthermore, although analytic judgments take place by means of concepts only, they are, I think, intended to be about objects and not about concepts.[33]

The precise point of Kant's assertion may be doubtful. Nonetheless, one fact is clear. The assertion, even the emphatic assertion, that the form of judgment is present in analytic judgments, is not equivalent to the denial that it is present in synthetic judgments.

Hence the second sentence in this crucial paragraph does not deny that the same form is present in analytic and synthetic judgments. The first sentence seems to me to assert, or at any rate to imply, the presence of the same form in both types of judgment, and I believe it is on this identity that the whole Metaphysical Deduction depends.

32. *Logik. Allg. Elem. Abs.* 2, § 36 (IX, 111).
33. Hermann Cohen, supported by Kinkel, takes the opposite view.

IV

Kant asserts that it is the *same function* (that is, form of judgment) which gives unity (1) to ideas in a judgment, and (2) to the synthesis of ideas in an intuition. He asserts also that it is the same *understanding,* by means of the *same activities* (that is, the activities of judging), which (1) produces the logical forms of judgment in dealing with concepts, and (2) introduces the categories into our ideas. The common interpretation of this—at any rate in this country—is that Kant does not mean what he says. He is asserting an *identity,* but this is watered down by the commentators to an *analogy,* on the ground that there is no identity between analytic and synthetic judgments. It is then observed that there is also no analogy between analytic and synthetic judgments, and so Kant is rebuked on the ground that there is no such analogy, or else defended on the irrelevant ground that analysis presupposes synthesis. He is, in short, either rebuked or defended for something which he has never said.

All this confusion arises from the belief that the forms of judgment are not the forms of synthetic judgment. Set aside this error and it at once becomes clear that Kant has every right to assert an *identity* between analytic and synthetic judgments. Analytic and synthetic judgments are identical *in respect of their form.* The whole metaphysical deduction of the categories turns on the fact that *all* judgments (whether analytic or synthetic) have the *same* form. This is, I believe, what Kant is trying to say in the passage under consideration.

Kant's argument here is, however, too brief to be wholly clear. We must look for confirmation elsewhere, and of this there is no lack.

(1) In the *Prolegomena,* Kant gives us a summary [34] of the deduction. To think, he says, is to unify (*vereinigen*) ideas in one consciousness. This unification (*Vereinigung*) of ideas in one consciousness is judgment. The logical moments (that is, forms) of *all* judgments are so many ways of uniting (*vereinigen*) ideas in one consciousness. When these logical moments (or forms) serve as

34. *Prol.,* § 22 (IV, 304-305).

concepts (that is, as categories), they are concepts of the necessary unification (*Vereinigung*) of ideas in one consciousness. *This unification* (*Vereinigung*), he adds, *is either analytic* (*through identity*) *or synthetic* (*through the adding of one idea to another*).

In this passage Kant recognizes explicitly that in all judgments, *whether analytic or synthetic,* there is present an act of unifying ideas, and that the forms of judgment are the forms of this unification. It is because the *same* forms of judgment, or of unification, are present in *all* judgments, that the manifold of sense (which must be *judged* if we are to have an *object*) is necessarily subject to the categories. For the category is a "concept of that synthetic unity of intuitions which can be represented only through a given logical function (that is, form) of judgment." [35]

How could a form of judgment represent synthetic unity of intuitions, if it were not the form of synthetic judgment as well as of analytic? The forms of judgment are forms of a unification which may be either analytic or synthetic. What can this mean, unless it means that the forms of judgment are forms of both analytic and synthetic judgments?

(2) There is another Deduction of the categories in the preface to the *Metaphysische Anfangsgründe der Naturwissenschaft.* There [36] Kant asserts that "the categories are simply the forms of judgment, so far as these forms are applied to sensible intuitions." It is by being so applied that these forms first acquire objects and become cognitions. How could these forms be applied to sensible intuitions unless they were forms of synthetic as well as of analytic judgments?

The example which Kant gives to illustrate the form of a categorical judgment is "The stone is hard." Will anyone deny that this is a synthetic judgment?

(3) In the second edition of the *Kritik* Kant is as explicit as he is in the *Prolegomena.* The word "combination" (*Verbindung*) here takes the place of "unification" (*Vereinigung*). All combination is the work of the understanding [37] and not of sense, and it is so, be it noted, whether what is combined is the manifold of intui-

35. *Prol.,* § 21*a* (IV, 304).
36. (IV, 474-476)
37. B130.

tion or *concepts*. The reference to concepts suggests pretty obviously that this act of combination is present even in analytic judgments. To this act of combination Kant gives the general name of "synthesis." This combination is the one thing which is not given by the object but is an act of the spontaneous understanding. It is the condition of analysis, because apart from it we should have nothing to analyze.

This "combination" is defined as "representation of the synthetic unity of the manifold," and in a note [38] Kant calls attention to the fact that it is present *in analytic as well as in synthetic judgments.* "Whether the ideas—that is, the ideas combined by understanding in judgment—are themselves identical, so that one can be thought analytically through the other, is here irrelevant. The *consciousness* of the one (so far as the manifold is in question) is always to be distinguished from the consciousness of the other, and what is relevant here is only the synthesis of this (possible) consciousness."

It is interesting to observe that there is a sense in which synthesis is for Kant the common element of all judgments. This is too often forgotten today but is familiar to a contemporary commentator like Mellin who can say,[39] "Every judgment is a synthesis." This throws a flood of light on Kant's argument and explains how forms which belong to analytic (as well as to synthetic) judgments can be the clue to the categories which are principles of synthesis. Our concern with it here is, however, only that it involves the assertion of that identical element in all judgments which the commentators habitually condemn Kant for failing to comprehend.

It is from this point that Kant goes on to say [40] that in the logical functions (forms) of judgment combination, that is, unity of given concepts, is already thought. It is, he adds, because the categories are grounded on these logical forms that they presuppose combination.

The combination, which is here presupposed by the categories and *thought in the forms of judgment,* is, as we have seen, present in analytic judgments. Will any one deny in this context (or in any context) that it is present also in synthetic judgments?

38. B131.
39. *Encyclopädisches Wörterbuch d. Krit. Phil.,* III, 519.
40. B131.

(4) The essence of the Deduction in the second edition is, however, to be found in § 20,[41] and it fully and explicitly affirms the doctrine we have found in the first edition. All the manifold of given intuition must fall under the unity of apperception, for only so can it itself have *unity*. The activity of the understanding which brings the manifold under the unity of apperception is the *logical function* [42] (*or form*) *of the judgment*—this is true whether our ideas of the manifold happen to be intuitions or concepts.[43] Therefore the manifold of intuition (so far as it is given in *one* empirical intuition) is determined in respect of one of the logical functions (or forms) of judgment, which alone can bring it under the unity of apperception. The categories, however, are simply these *forms of judgment, so far as these forms determine the given manifold*.[44] Therefore the given manifold, if it is to have unity (and so to be an object), must necessarily fall under the categories.

Here again the argument has no meaning unless the forms of judgment are also the forms of synthetic judgment, for it is in synthetic judgment that the forms of judgment determine the manifold of given intuition, while in analytic judgments they are (sometimes at least) concerned with mere concepts. There is no word in this, nor so far as I know anywhere else in Kant, of an *analogy*. What we require is an *identity*, and that is precisely what we are offered.

(5) There is yet another deduction of the categories in Kant's uncompleted work on the Progress of Metaphysics since Leibniz and Wolff, commonly called *Die Akademische Preisschrift*. In it "composition" (*Zusammensetzung*) takes the place of "*Vereinigung*" in the *Prolegomena*, and "*Verbindung*" in the second edition of the *Kritik*. In this case also "composition" is equated with "synthesis," and the categories are once more asserted to *be* the forms of judgment,[45] "but only in so far as the forms of judgment represent *a priori* the synthetic unity of the apperception of the manifold given in an intuition in general."

41. B143.
42. There is a looseness of terminology here, because the function (strictly speaking) is the unity of the activity (A68 = B93), Kant seems to use "function" to mean also "the activity as a unity."
43. The reference to "intuitions or concepts" again suggests that the difference between analytic and synthetic judgments is irrelevant—the form being the same in both cases.
44. B128.
45. *Abt. 1. Von Begriffen a priori. Philosophische Bibliothek,* 46C, 96-98.

Furthermore, the understanding is said to show its power in judgments, and judgments are said to be the unity of consciousness in regard to concepts in general, "it *being undetermined whether that unity is analytic or synthetic.*"

All this is the doctrine with which we are familiar, and it has no meaning unless the forms of judgment are forms of synthetic, as well as of analytic, judgment.

(6) The following facts emerge from a study of the later expositions of the Deduction:

1. The Transcendental Deduction as a whole depends upon the Metaphysical Deduction, that is, upon the identification of the categories with the forms of judgment, *as applying to and uniting the manifold given to sense.*

2. This is meaningless, unless the forms of judgment are also forms of synthetic judgments.

3. Every judgment as such (whether analytic or synthetic) is an act of unification or combination or composition or synthesis.

4. The forms of judgment are forms of this unification or synthesis which is present in all judgments (whether analytic or synthetic).

5. It is for this reason that the forms of judgment can be regarded as principles of synthesis.

6. For the same reason, the forms of judgment must be forms both of analytic, and of synthetic, judgments.

These facts are in complete accordance with the interpretation which I have given of the Metaphysical Deduction in the first edition, and therefore confirm that interpretation. It is no doubt possible that in the interval between the two editions Kant's views had entirely altered, but this is explicitly denied by him in the preface to the second edition,[46] and is implicitly denied by his retention of the Metaphysical Deduction in its original form, even when the rest of the Transcendental Deduction was rewritten.

This interpretation is, I submit, the key not only to the Metaphysical Deduction but to the Transcendental Deduction as a whole.

46. B xxxvii ff.

V

The Metaphysical Deduction of the categories derives all the plausibility it has from the principle that the forms of judgment are the
same in all judgments (whether analytic or synthetic). This principle is true in itself (can any one deny it, once the issue is clearly
put?), and the weight of the evidence goes to show that it was
Kant's explicit doctrine.

Consider what Kant's problem was. He believed that if the
reality to be known consisted of separate things-in-themselves,
which are what they are independently of the mind that knows
them, then while we might have empirical knowledge of them, we
could have no *a priori* knowledge of them; we could never say what
they all must be, but only that, so far as we had experienced them,
they had certain characteristics. For this view there is much to be
said.

Kant, however, does not doubt that we have *a priori* knowledge
in mathematics, and also in the ultimate principles of physical
science, such as that every event must have a cause. He therefore
adopts as a hypothesis the view that the *a priori* elements in knowledge must be due not to the nature of the reality known but to the
nature of the knowing mind. This is the Copernican revolution, by
which he supposes that something in the objects *as known* is due to
the mind, just as Copernicus supposed that something in the motion of the stars *as observed* is due to the motion of the observer.

This hypothesis is obviously worthy of consideration, and if it
should solve otherwise insoluble problems (as Kant holds it does),
it would be worthy of adoption.

After much reflection [47] Kant was able to separate off space and
time, as forms of sensibility, from the categories, or pure concepts
of the understanding. If it be granted (1) that we have *a priori*
knowledge of space and time, and (2) that what can be known *a
priori* must be due to mind and not to things, it seems reasonable to
say that space and time are due to the nature of our sensibility
(rather than to the nature of our power of thinking).

We are then left with the problem of the categories, especially

47. *Prol.,* § 39 (IV, 323).

the category of substance and the category of cause. These are not seen, or sensed, or necessarily involved in all sensation, as are space and time. We can *see* that a body occupies space and lasts through time. We cannot *see* that it is a substance or a cause, we only *think* that it is.

If the categories necessarily apply to all objects, they are (on the Copernican theory) due to the nature of the knowing mind. As they are not bound up with our sensibility, they must be bound up with our understanding; for sensibility and understanding are the only two ways we have of knowing. As understanding is active, while sense is passive, we must look for the categories in the *activity* of understanding, that is, in what understanding does to any and every object which it knows. As there are different categories, we must find one activity which manifests itself (independently of the differences in objects) in different ways. So only shall we be able to have an intelligible list of the categories as a system.

All this (as an attempt to formulate the Copernican hypothesis) is most reasonable and indeed inevitable, if we admit that thought is active and sense is passive.

At first Kant seems to have considered whether the categories could be connected with the activity of thought in "comparing, combining, and separating." [48] But he became aware that the one activity of understanding which contained all the rest, and differentiated itself into different forms in order, be it noted, to bring the manifold of ideas under the unity of thought—was judgment.[49]

Here again Kant's thinking was perfectly straightforward and (if we grant his presuppositions) sound. We cannot know anything by means of mere sense, we must have conception as well. If, for example, we are to know a house, it is not enough to have a series of isolated sensations. We must unify our sensations under the concept of house, and to do so is to judge. Without judgment there is no knowledge, and no object of knowledge; there is only a series of sensations.

We can therefore say *a priori* that every object, to be an object, must be such that it is capable, not only of being sensed, but of being judged.

48. *Reflexionen,* ii, 513.
49. *Prol.,* § 39 (IV, 323). Cf. A69 = B94, "All activities of understanding can be reduced to judgement."

It was no foolish pedantry or natural muddleheadedness that made Kant proceed to seek for the categories in the forms of judgment. He was looking for something in judgment which was not determined by the object or by the matter judged, something which was contributed by the mind out of its own nature. The doctrine of Aristotelian logic was that the forms of judgment were so contributed by the mind that these forms were the basis of all inference, and held good for any and every possible matter that could be judged. Hence if an object, to be an object, must be capable of being judged, it must also be capable of conforming to all the forms of judgment, for these are necessary forms belonging to the nature of judgment itself, altogether irrespective of the matter judged.

This doctrine had held unquestioned sway over the minds of men for more than two thousand years. It was the one principle of philosophy which no man doubted. It stood on the same level of certainty as the propositions of Euclid or the principles of arithmetic. It was more venerable than the Catholic Church. What wonder if Kant decided that to found his philosophy on this was to found it upon a rock?

He could not know that the floods of modern thought were to undermine and overwhelm the rock upon which he built, that the philosophical logicians would try to make the forms of judgment fluid, and the mathematical logicians would attempt to make them infinite in number.[50] I do not believe that for this he is to be blamed, for one man cannot do all the thinking of the human race.

The Aristotelian doctrine is not in itself an unreasonable doctrine—indeed if it had been, it could not have dominated men's minds so long—and it clearly implies that every object to be an object *must* conform to all the forms of judgment. It does so, however, on one supposition, and *on one supposition alone*—that the forms of judgment are forms of those synthetic judgments by which (primarily if not solely) objects are determined, as well as of those analytic judgments which, in clarifying our concepts, may have no reference to an object at all. Personally, I do not believe that any other possibility ever crossed, or ought to have crossed, Kant's mind.

Once we accept the Aristotelian logic and realize that the (unschematized) categories are simply the forms of judgment as de-

50. *A Modern Introduction to Logic.* Stebbing, p. 45.

termining an object given in intuition in general, Kant's conclusion
—that the categories are necessary concepts of an object in general (whatever be its given matter)—is an inevitable conclusion.

It must, of course, be remembered that for Kant the categories
are not innate ideas but ways in which the mind must judge, or
ways in which thought must unite the manifold of sense in one
consciousness, or again ways in which all objects of thought must
be united. Furthermore, there are many other difficulties still to be
faced. The question of *how* the categories can apply to objects is
considered in the Subjective Deduction. The question of the connection between the pure categories (as forms of objective judgment) and the schematized categories (which involve time) has to
be dealt with in the chapter on Schematism. And the principles
founded upon the categories still require to have each its separate
proof.

The main work has, however, been done, and I venture to say
that it has been done well. It is commonly asserted that the table
of judgments has been doctored by Kant for his own ends. If this
is true at all, it is, at the least, grossly exaggerated. A glance at the
first sentence in Chap. VIII of Mr. Joseph's *Logic* [51] will show that
the list of forms which has "for long been commonly accepted" is
identical with the list given by Kant with one exception—the so-
called infinite judgment: and even that has a respectable pedigree,
going back as far as Aristotle himself.

VI

I venture in conclusion to make certain assertions:

(1) If we put ourselves at the point of view of formal logic, the
forms of judgment are the forms of *all* judgment.

(2) If we distinguish between analytic and synthetic judgments,
precisely the same forms are to be found in both. To deny this is
nonsense.

(3) To attribute this nonsense to Kant can be justified only by
overwhelming evidence.

(4) There is in the evidence examined nothing to compel such

51. P. 171.

attribution, although there is a great deal to suggest that the orthodox view is a natural misunderstanding.

(5) There is much in the evidence directly contrary to such attribution.

(6) If we accept formal logic and Kant's presuppositions, the Metaphysical Deduction (so far as it goes) is reasonable and even necessary—provided we suppose that the *same* form is present in analytic and in synthetic judgments.

(7) If we make Kant start from the nonsensical view, the Metaphysical Deduction becomes feeble in the extreme and is not even alleged to be plausible by those who insist on interpreting it in this way.

(8) The orthodox view is erroneous, or at least it rests upon evidence which I have been unable to find. The case against it is sufficiently strong to justify us in asking that the evidence should be produced.

KANT'S CLASSIFICATION

OF THE

FORMS OF JUDGMENT

Arthur O. Lovejoy

§

A detailed study of Kant's relation to the German logicians of his
century may seem to some to be the last recourse of a *Kant-For-
schung* in search of a not yet wholly exhausted subject of erudition.
In reality, however, an acquaintance with this class of facts is peculiarly indispensable for any intelligent reading of Kant or any just
judgment of his work. It is, for one thing, a necessary aid and
means of control in the exegesis of the *Kritik der reinen Vernunft;*
for the import of otherwise obscure passages sometimes becomes
intelligible enough upon a consideration of the form in which certain problems were left, or the terms in which they were discussed
by Kant's predecessors. There is nothing, moreover, which does so
much to enable us to anatomize Kant's mental processes at some of
the critical turns in his argument, to see just what logical motives
are playing upon his mind, to follow the windings of his thought
without bewilderment, to notice not only when he falls into confusion, but also why. Such an understanding of Kant's procedure and
motives from the inside is important not simply because it puts us
in a better position to judge of the coherency and value of this or
that argument in the *Kritik,* but still more because it provides the
material for determining the justice of the still widely prevalent
view that Kant was a singularly penetrating and powerful reasoner,

a master of the dialectician's game of *"distinguo."* A reputation for this sort of masterfulness in argument—such as Aristotle once had, and for a time, and in a lower degree, Spinoza—if it is undeserved, may be a very serious obstacle to the progress of philosophic insight. There are those who suspect that Kant's reputation is at the present time, especially in Germany, an influence that obstructs and diverts and confuses the course of contemporary philosophical inquiry. And finally, there is reason to think that there has been a certain amount of misrepresentation of historical realities in the current accounts of the precise points of difference between Kant and the philosophers of the preceding generation, and an excessive widening of the gap which is supposed to separate the critical method from earlier modes of philosophical procedure. For all of these reasons, an accurate knowledge of the logic of the school of Wolff is a thing eminently desirable. Yet the subject has hardly even yet been so fully and competently studied as its importance might have led one to imagine that it long since would have been.

A valuable contribution to such study has, however, recently been made by Dr. P. Hauck in an article on Kant's table of the different classes of judgments.[1] The role which this classification of judgments plays in the system is well known; it is by means of it that Kant discovers his twelve categories, whose application to objects constitutes the prerequisite condition of the possibility of experience. The list seems fetched in as a *deus ex machina* at a point where Kant's thought would otherwise have come to a stop, for the lack of any means of determining just what and how many the categories are. Now the *machina* in this case has commonly been supposed to be the Wolffian logic. Kant himself intimates that, in the main, he takes the scheme over from the formal logicians as a finished product; and even the friendliest commentators on the *Kritik,* recognizing the abruptness of the introduction of the table of judgments and its artificial character, have usually observed that Kant was misled here by a too great confidence in the fundamental significance of the distinctions of formal logic, and by a too ready and uncritical acceptance of the results reached in that field by his predecessors.

Now what Dr. Hauck shows is that this is precisely the fault with which Kant cannot be charged; that so far from taking over

1. *Kantstudien,* XI, 1906, pp. 196f.

his table of judgments ready-made, he radically alters what he found
in the classifications of the logicians to whom he refers; and that
this alteration is motivated by the supposed requirements of the
"transcendental" logic, so that it is really the table of categories that
shapes the table of judgments, rather than the contrary. The books
from which Kant's ideas on the subject took their departure are
well known. They are Meier's *Vernunftlehre* (1752), first of all;
and besides that, Lambert's *Neues Organon,* Baumgarten's *Acroasis
logica,* and Wolff's *Philosophia rationalis.* A comparison of the
division of judgments in these books, with respect to the several
fundamenta divisionis, with Kant's classification, shows how widely
he departed from the models before him. Thus, as Dr. Hauck points
out, Meier and Baumgarten, under the head of the "quantity" of
judgments, give a twofold division, based upon the nature of the
subject, one of the classes being further subdivided, as follows: I.
Judicia singularia (having a singular subject). II. *Judicia com-
munia* (having a general term as subject): 1. *judicia universalia;*
2. *judicia particularia.* But Lambert had shown the now familiar
fact that, so far as the quantity of the proposition is concerned,
propositions having singular subjects belong in the same class with
universal propositions of which the subject is a general term; since
in either case the predicate is affirmed or denied of the whole of
the possible denotation of the subject. Lambert, therefore, gives the
now accepted dual division into universal and particular propositions, with "singular" judgments constituting a subdivision of the
former. Kant expressly recognizes the propriety of Lambert's revision of the scheme. And he would have got a dual division by following *either* Lambert or Meier. But instead, he departs from both,
while taking material from each, and reaches a triple division by
treating the three classes in Meier's scheme as strictly coordinate.
Analogous innovations of Kant's own are shown in his divisions
with respect to quality, relation, and modality.

   I do not wish merely to recapitulate Dr. Hauck's important paper,
which is doubtless familiar in its entirety to all who are interested
in the subject. But it appears to me that the author does not see
the full bearing of the facts which he brings out, nor appreciate
the real significance of the historical data which he has so well exhibited. Dr. Hauck seems to be one of those whose natural powers
of vigorous insight have been hypnotized by Kant's reputation. He

remarks that "schon die Achtung vor der Grösse Kantischen Denkens" ought of itself to lead us to conclude that these alterations in the table of judgments are based upon profound and valid reasons; and he seems, in fact, to regard Kant's innovations as decidedly meritorious, even from the point of view of the formal logician. "Wäre Kant nicht gewesen, und ein anderer hätte in demselben Masse in die formale Logik eingegriffen, so wäre er der Nachwelt als ein bedeutender Logiker erschienen." To argue from the "reverence" due Kant's thought to the correctness of his method and conclusions, appears to me to be one of the forms of *a priori* reasoning which the *Kritik der reinen Vernunft* does not succeed in justifying. And I think it worthwhile to try to point out the actual meaning of Dr. Hauck's facts, as he does not do, while acknowledging throughout great obligations to his research.

First of all, one ought to note the way in which these facts illuminate Kant's curious lack of what may be called logical self-consciousness—the ability to have always clearly in mind just where one is in an argument and how one came there—and his consequent tendency to play misleading, but doubtless quite unconscious, tricks upon his reader. Hauck's argument—for the details of which the reader must refer to his paper—that Kant did not deduce his categories from his table of judgments but merely fixed his table to remove the appearance of arbitrariness from the predetermined scheme of categories, seems to me convincing. But if so, the whole section of the *Kritik* containing this table and the discussion and explanation of it is an elaborate, however unintentional, pretense. "Transcendental philosophy," says Kant grandly, in introducing the subject, "has the advantage, but also the duty, of discovering its concepts according to a fixed principle." This fixed principle the division of judgments in formal logic is to provide. But it now turns out that the principle, as applied, does not come from any formal logic then recognized; that it is a factitious construction got up *après coup* for the express purpose of giving a sanction to just the scheme of categories which the philosopher appears gravely and innocently to be deducing *from* it.

Let us, however, consider Kant's classification in detail, with the narrow-minded spirit of the formal logician. Has Kant's classification of judgments, in those respects in which it departs from the

results of his predecessors, any value? Does it even comply with
the elementary requirements of respectable classification?

I. *Quantity.*—Kant's division of judgments with respect to quantity it will be remembered, runs as follows: Universal, Particular,
Singular.

Yet, as has been remarked, he recognizes that, "in using judgments in syllogisms, singular judgments may be treated like universal ones," as Lambert had shown him. How, then, does he
justify his treatment of singular judgments (i.e., those having a
singular subject) as a coordinate class? He does not neglect to offer
a reason for his alteration. "If," he says, "we compare a singular
with a general judgment, looking only at the quantity of knowledge
conveyed by it (*der Grösse nach*), that knowledge stands to the
other (conveyed in a universal judgment) as unity to infinity, and
is therefore essentially different from it. It is, therefore, when we
consider a singular judgment, not only according to its own validity
but according to the quantity of knowledge which it conveys, that
. . . we see how well it deserves a separate place in a complete table
of the varieties of thought in general, though not in a logic limited
to the use of judgments in reference to each other." But what is
this differentiation of judgments *der Grösse nach?* Obviously, to
begin with, the "quantity" of judgments in Kant's sense is not what
formal logic has ever meant by quantity. In the latter sense, there is
a complete dichotomy among judgments: in every case the predicate
either is or is not affirmed or denied of the whole denotation, or
range of possible being, indicated by the subject. Here, then, there
can only be the usual twofold classification. What Kant signifies
by quantity is not this specific relation of subject and predicate but
"the amount of knowledge conveyed by the judgment." This simply
means that the singular proposition tells us something about only
one object, while the universal proposition tells us something about
an indefinitely large number of objects. But now, taking this Kantian
sense of "quantity," and sticking to it, do we get a tripartite division? Is there any decisive and non-arbitrary reason why we should
have, from this point of view, neither more nor less than three
"quantities" of judgments? Obviously not. A dual division here
might be reasonably significant—judgments referring to one, and
judgments referring to more than one object. But certainly when

we go beyond this general distinction of unity and plurality, there is no assignable reason for stopping with the mention of any particular number of degrees of plurality. "Some *S* is *P*," for example, a particular judgment, tells us something about a number of objects more than one, and less than the indefinite whole number of objects constituting the extension of the class *S*. The particular judgment is, therefore, without doubt, clearly and significantly distinguished from both the singular and the universal. But just as clearly and significantly distinguished from it is the judgment: "Most *S*'s are *P*'s"; that is, a number of objects more than one, and more than the half of the indefinite whole number of objects included within the class *S*, belong to the class *P*. And similarly we might make a separate class for propositions of the type: "Two thirds of *S* is *P*." Nay, more; the essential distinction which Kant draws in favor of the separate classification of "singular" judgments is not that they refer to a specific proportion of a possible class of objects, but that they refer to *one* object, while universal judgments refer to an infinity. In strictness, therefore, Kant should have a separate category of quantity, in *his* sense of quantity, for every number in the series between one and infinity. For, really, the relation of part of a class to the whole of a class has nothing whatever to do with Kant's criterion of division here. Judgments are to be distinguished, for him, not according to how great a proportion of a genus they tell us about, but *how many things* they tell us about.

The meaning of this is obvious. Kant has simply slipped over from "quantity" in the logician's special (and rather arbitrary) sense, to quantity in the purely mathematical or arithmetical sense. But he is not aware that he has done so, and he does not carry out the proper consequences of doing so. He happens to need a triple division—partly, one is compelled to believe, because he is wedded to the triad, and partly because he has already before his mind the purely mathematical categories (which have no bearing upon the logical quantity of propositions) of unity, plurality, totality. This particular triad itself lacks a proper *fundamentum divisionis*. Unity is a category of number, plurality is a category of indefinite number, but totality is a category of proportion. Its proper place (if we are to refrain from going into arithmetically definite proportions) would be in a scheme running thus: some (of a possible collective unity), most, all. And even here it would be easy to interpolate additional indefinite degrees of approximation to totality. The series beginning with unity and plurality, if it have any proper third member, must find it in "infinity." Apparently one reason which prevented Kant from putting this in place of totality, was that he already felt the need (which was to become so dominant in Hegelianism) of conceiving of the third category in each of his triads as swallowing up and uniting the characters of the other two.

It appears, then, that in dealing with the quantity of judgments, Kant (*a*) passed over from the logical to the strictly mathematical notion of quantity, without realizing that he had thereby come into a realm where the special distinctions and divisions of the formal logic are no longer in place; (*b*) he did not see what was implied by this transition but arbitrarily adhered to a triple classification; (*c*) he was led to do this last because he had already preconceived a triad of mathematical categories of quantity, which triad itself appears to be an improper classification, in that it lacks a clear and uniform basis.

II. *Quality*.—Kant is perhaps the first logician in history to conceive of a class of judgments neither affirmative nor negative, yet to be classified along with these by the same criterion of quality. At all events the Wolffian writers are innocent of any idea so ingenious. They adhere to the familiar dichotomy which so obviously appears to exhaust the possibilities of the case. Here again, however, Kant must needs have his tripartite division. He gets it, as before, by taking one of the species of one of the two apparently exhaustive genera, and erecting it into a third, co-ordinate genus. The logicians preceding him had been accustomed to call attention to a certain class of judgments affirmative in form, but having negative predicates (*termini infiniti*). An example of these "infinite judgments" is the proposition: "All dumb animals are non-rational." The effect of such a judgment, manifestly, is to imply the division of all subjects of discourse (or, as it is usually more loosely taken, of all animals) into two classes, rational and non-rational, which are together completely exhaustive, and to assert that dumb animals belong in the class "non-rational," the denotation of which is presumably the more extensive, while its connotation is the less definite or (when the proposition is taken strictly) is purely negative or privative. It is this species of affirmative judgment that Kant makes into a third class of equal rank. He does not fail to offer his defense of such a surprising addition to logic. These infinite judgments constitute a distinct "quality" from a point of view peculiar to the transcendental logic. That logic always asks: "How much is gained by a given affirmation with reference to the sum total of knowledge?" Now, in the case of an infinite judgment, "it is true that, so far as the logical form is concerned, I have really affirmed something by saying that the soul is non-mortal; for I thus place the soul in the unlimited sphere of immortal beings." All I have said, however, "is that the soul is one of the infinite number of beings which remain when I take away" from the sphere of possible being "all that is mortal. By this the infinite sphere of all that is possible becomes limited only in so far as all mortal things are excluded from it, the soul being then placed in the remaining part of its original extent. This part, however [here is Kant's point], even after its limitation, still remains infinite, and several more parts of it may be taken away without extending thereby in the least the concept of the soul [*ohne dass darum der Begriff von der Seele wächst*]." Hence these judgments are, "with respect to their contents," neither affirmative nor negative, but "limitative only."

Now what, once more, is the basis of division that Kant is employing here? Confessedly, not the usual one of "form," as determined by the presence or absence of a negative with the copula. Nor is it the psychological criterion by which the affirmative mental attitude towards given content conceived in certain relations might be distinguished from the attitude of negation or rejection towards the same content. Kant's not very luminous explanation refers rather (*a*) to the size of the genus within the denotative limits of which the subject is left by one of these "infinite judgments." That genus, he says, is infinite. There is, one may observe, no need that it should be. If I divide all mankind dichotomously into the two classes of those over two feet tall, and those not over two feet tall—or all beings into temporal and non-temporal—there is no reason to think that the extension of my negative genus is in either case greater than that of its positive counterpart. So far as their *possible* extension goes, both genera seem to be infinite, or indefinite. So far as our knowledge of their actual extension goes, the two negative predicates apparently determine narrower genera than do the positive. There thus does not appear to exist any such difference between judgments as Kant supposes. You cannot distinguish "limitative" or "infinite" judgments from affirmative and negative ones merely by the size of the genera to which they assign their subjects. For many ordinary affirmative judgments (by form), and *all* negative judgments having positive predicates, assign their subjects to classes that may be as large as, or larger than, those of the corresponding infinite judgment. Negative judgments, notably, are of equivalent logical force to affirmatives with negative predicates, as is recognized in the elementary inferential process of obversion. To say "No dumb animals are rational" is, as everyone knows, the same as saying "All dumb animals are non-rational"; when you "ask how much is gained" by the former proposition "with respect to the sum total of knowledge," you find that just exactly as much, and as little, is gained in it as in the latter. If, therefore, Kant were to adhere throughout his division to his own criterion of quality—as applied in the definition of his third class of judgments—we should find some negative judgments, and some affirmative ones, falling into the same class with the so-called "infinite," and we should thus, at best, come back once more to a dual classification—a classification, too, in which we should lack any clear means for drawing the line between the two classes. But, of course, what Kant has done is to take the division into affirmative and negative as he finds it—based, as it is, upon the ordinary formal distinction of "quality"—and then to proceed to make parallel with these a third variety which he has differentiated by means of a wholly disparate and inconsistent distinction.

Partly, however, Kant (*b*) seems to have in mind the fact that "infinite" predicates ascribe no positive quality, no definite connotation, to their subjects. But here the same difficulty arises: negative propositions (with positive predicates) are, in this regard, in the same case as the "infinite" or "limitative" ones; both are species of the one genus. According to the criterion of division now suggested to us by Kant's language, we should get another twofold classification: I. Judgments which assign a definite, positive, and concrete attribute to their subjects. II. Judgments which assign to their subjects no such attribute. The first class would include: (1) Affirmative judgments with positive predicates; (2) negative judgments with negative predicates. The second class would consist (1) of affirmative judgments with negative predicates ("infinite judgments"), and (2) of negative judgments with positive predicates.

In the case of the category of quality, then, Kant has fallen into the exceedingly elementary error of confusing the basis of division which he should use for distinguishing species with that by which the genera are distinguished; and, by thus shifting his *fundamentum divisionis* in the middle of his classification, he contrives to introduce a third kind of judgment. So long as he is held down strictly to one basis, he gets only a dual division, no matter which of the alternative and ambiguous senses of his criterion be taken. It is to such distressing confusions of ideas that the great philosopher descends in order to save his triads.

III. *Relation.*—The idea of classifying judgments with respect to "relation" is, as Hauck notes, apparently original with Kant. His predecessors have, however, a classification, based upon other grounds, which contains the elements of Kant's third triad. They divide judgments, namely, into simple and complex; and under the latter they give, as species, hypothetical judgments and disjunctive judgments (and, in some cases, still others). Changing the term "simple" into "categorical," Kant again arranges the three species included in a Wolffian dual division in a row as co-ordinate genera.

The basis upon which the Wolffians make their division is obviously rather trivial, since it is the alogical one of purely grammatical complexity. But this is merely an inadequate expression of a natural and proper (though still essentially formal) distinction of propositions into categorical and conditional, the two forms of the latter being the hypothetical and the disjunctive. In the last analysis —as is shown by the possibility of resolution—all judgments may be called either categorical or conditional, as you please; but the dual classification and subclassification just indicated has a certain convenience, and it is clear and consistent. We have, then, propositions in which the predicate is affirmed of the (nominal) subject (of the principal clause) with no express limitation, or with such limitation, which latter may be (so far as its expression goes) of more than one form. There is, however, as every elementary student of logic knows, no real difference between the proposition, "A is either B or C," and the assertion conjointly of the pair of propositions: "If A is B, it is not C; and if it is not B, it is C." Kant's classification must, then, be considered a poor one, since it ignores the possibility and superior logical propriety of regarding the hypothetical and the disjunctive judgments as merely two forms of conditionality. But there is no such confusion here as in the former cases: there is no actual cross-classification, no using of genera as species of other genera that are at the same time classified as co-ordinate with the first.[2]

IV. *Modality.*—The term "modality" Kant derives from Baumgarten; his classification in its essentials is to be found otherwise (and, as we shall see, more lucidly) expressed by Lambert (1764). In this case, and in this case only, Kant found a tripartite division already provided by an earlier logician. Lambert (cited by Hauck) distinguishes our judgments as possible (*mögliche*), actual (*wirkliche*), and necessary (*notwendige*), the three being exemplified by the following propositions:

1. A *is capable* of being B (*kann B sein*).
2. A *is* B.
3. A *must be* B.

Kant's innovation here, then, consists in the introduction of a new terminology—"problematical, assertoric, and apodictic," being substituted for Lambert's expressions. In the *Logik* (which, while its published form dates from the critical period, probably expresses an earlier formulation of Kant's ideas on the present matter) the new terms are expressly identified in meaning with Lambert's: "Die problematischen Urteile sind mit dem Bewusstsein der blossen Möglichkeit, die assertorischen mit dem Bewusstsein der Wirklich-

---

2. In his *Logik* (Kinkel's ed., p. 115) Kant denies the possibility of reducing hypothetical judgments to the categorical form. This odd logical doctrine he supports by another characteristically blundering argument. "Some say that it is easy to transform a hypothetical into a categorical proposition. But this cannot be, for the two are by their nature wholly different from one another. In the categorical judgment, there is nothing problematical, but everything is assertoric; in the hypothetical, on the contrary, only the consequent is assertoric. . . . There is an essential difference between the two propositions, 'All bodies are divisible,' and 'If all bodies are composite, they are all divisible.' In the first proposition I make the assertion without qualification; in the second, only under a condition, expressed as problematical." Nobody, of course, ever did say it is "easy" to reduce a hypothetical proposition to a categorical one *of different import*. All that logicians generally have maintained is that, e.g., the proposition "If all bodies are composite, they are all divisible," is exactly equivalent in its logical force to the proposition "All *composite* bodies are divisible." Kant's ability, as illustrated in this example, to get lost intellectually even on the straightest of roads, is to me a perpetual marvel. As for the equation of "categorical" with "assertoric" and of "hypothetical" with "problematic" in the passage quoted, that appears to be the *fons et origo* of the confusion about modality to be noted in the next section of the text.

keit, die apodiktischen endlich mit dem Bewusstsein der Notwendig-
keit des Urteilens begleitet."

Now, Lambert's distinction rested upon a clear and significant
principle; the only criticism that can be brought against it is that
his triple division could, like Kant's third triad, be advantageously
transformed into a dual one, with two species included in one of
the genera. The basis of Lambert's classification consists in the *relation of the subjects and predicates of propositions from the standpoint of our knowledge of the "compossibility" of concepts.* According to a familiar and fundamental principle of the Wolffian
doctrine, different pairs of ideas stand in quite different relations
to one another with respect to their possibility of coinherence, i.e.,
the possibility of conceiving one as a predicate of the other. Some
concepts are known by us simply as compossible; that is to say, it is
conceivable that one should be predicated of the other; there is between them no intrinsic "repugnancy to coexist." Any proposition
is at least "possible," if its subject and predicate can thus be conceived as compossible. For example, there is nothing impossible or
self-contradictory about the judgment, "There are canals on Mars";
whether it can be known to be true is another matter. All judgments,
then, are possible in so far as they are not self-contradictory; and a
possible judgment has this relation to our knowledge, that it *cannot be known in advance, and from a mere analysis of the concepts
involved, to be untrue.* An actual judgment (by which both Lambert and Kant mean, of course, "actual without being also necessary") is one which, being possible, is also empirically found to be
true. And a necessary judgment is one of which the truth may be
known from the impossibility of conceiving the subject, in accordance with the terms of its own definition, when the predicate is
negated of it. Propositions, in short, are necessary in so far as they
can be known to be true *a priori,* by the test of the inconceivability
of the opposite. These distinctions are all entirely luminous, and
they are important for logic and for metaphysics. Since, however,
all actual judgments must also be (merely) possible, the two might
properly be classified together; or again, since both actual and necessary judgments differ from possible ones in being known as true,
the two former might be grouped in a single genus. In either case,
from the two different points of view, we should get a dual classification; the second, which is the more instructive, would run as fol-

lows: I. Judgments known as *possible* but not known to be true. II. Judgments known to be true: (1) merely *actual* truth, ascertained empirically; (2) *necessary* truth, ascertained *a priori* by the criterion of the inconceivability of the contradictory.

Now Lambert does not express this so fully, nor, possibly, so clearly, as I have done; but the essential point of the distinction should have been perfectly plain to anyone at all acquainted with the Wolffian logic, since the categories (in the sense defined) of possibility, actuality, and necessity may be said to make up the very backbone of that system. Kant, however, takes from his predecessor this luminous and consistent division, and forthwith involves it in the most preposterous confusion as anyone may (after the foregoing explanation) see by turning to the passage on the subject in the *Kritik*.[3] We are first of all given an almost meaningless definition of modality; it has nothing to do with the content of propositions, but *"nur den Wert der Copula in Beziehung auf das Denken überhaupt angeht."* This, if it means anything, appears to mean (*a*) that the modality of a judgment consists in the (subjective) degree of confidence with which it is affirmed. This would appear to be one of the several notions in Kant's mind; but it does not, of course, fit the categories included under modality, nor is it congruous with the rest of the discussion. There follow some illustrations of problematic and assertoric propositions. In these examples and his remarks on them, Kant (*b*) identifies modality with the relation of conditionality between one truth and another. Thus he tells us that "the two judgments, the relation of which constitutes the hypothetical judgment, are always problematical"; the consequent is not affirmed to be true except upon the condition of the truth of the antecedent, which is itself not affirmed. Now, in the Wolffian sense, a proposition does not need to be conceived as depending upon the hypothetical truth of another proposition, to be defined as "possible"; any simple proposition is, as we have seen, "possible," if free from internal contradictions. Kant's second sense of modality is thus quite irrelevant to the Wolffian distinction. Taking Kant's conception of modality now in this second sense, two things need to be said about it. First, it reduces at least the first two categories of modality to identity with, respectively, the second and third (for the problematical judgment) and the first (for the

3. A, 74-76; B, 99-101.

assertoric judgment) category of "relation." Secondly, it does not properly permit of the classification of apodictic judgments in the same scheme with the problematical and assertoric, as now defined. For, on the one hand, the apodictic judgment is not differentiated from the other two by virtue of the conditionality or unconditionality of the assertions contained in it. The apodictic character of a judgment, for Kant, consists purely in its necessity for our thought, its inevitability, and its capacity to be known *a priori;* and these characters evidently may belong to either categorical or conditional propositions. From Kant's own point of view all *a priori* propositions are in a true sense "problematical"; for they do not refer to real existence, and they only enable us to say: *"If* I have any experience of a certain sort, it will conform to certain laws." On the other hand, since the apodictic proposition simply "represents the assertoric as determined by the laws of the understanding, and therefore as capable of being affirmed *a priori,"* it would follow that the apodictic ought to be classified as a species of the assertoric.

Finally, Kant sometimes means by "modality" precisely the distinction underlying the classification of Lambert and the Wolffian logic generally. When, as the last citation indicates, he is speaking of apodictic propositions, he manifestly has this, and only this, meaning in mind. The same sense is indicated by one of the discrepant observations about the "problematical" variety: these propositions "express logical (not objective) possibility only," while the apodictic "express logical necessity." The term modality itself implies this meaning; the *modi* of a proposition, as the term is used by Baumgarten, consist in its *necessitas vel contingentia,* the *convenientia aut repugnantia* of its terms. For the kinds of modality in this sense, it is obvious that the Wolffian expressions are incomparably clearer and less ambiguous than the Kantian. The infelicity of the nomenclature which he prefers to invent for himself is perhaps partly the cause, as well as partly the effect, of the profound confusion of Kant's ideas concerning the modal distinction.[4]

We see, then, that Kant means by modality three different and

4. If we were to consider Kant's account of the "transcendental" categories and "postulates" of modality, we should find this diversity of meanings still further increased. E.g., the "objective" possibility of a thing is said to require that we should have had "an example of it from experience" (A, 291; B, 347); thus possibility would be verifiable only *a posteriori.* We are further told (*loc. cit.*) that a concept may not be possible without being impossible.

incompatible things; that one of these meanings is such as to reduce the categories of relation to those of modality, or vice versa; and that, for the indication even of the proper distinctions of this sort, he coins a new terminology that is both unnecessary and misleading. In the case of this fourth group of judgments, moreover, Kant's confusions and obscurities are peculiarly inexcusable, and they have been, in their historical influence, especially harmful, because of the fact that they obfuscate a significant logical distinction that had been made entirely clear by his immediate predecessors.

ON KANT'S REPLY

TO HUME

Arthur O. Lovejoy

§

It is one of the accepted traditions of the history of philosophy that Kant made an original—and, as some would add, a conclusive— "reply to Hume" upon the question of the *a priori* validity of the law of the universal and uniform causation of events. To Kant himself, his argument about causality seemed the very core of the *Kritik der reinen Vernunft;* just as Hume's criticisms upon the "idea of necessary connection" were what waked Kant from his dogmatic slumbers, so Kant's own argument for the rehabilitation of that idea was, in the eyes of its author, his great point of originality. What forever differentiated him from Leibniz and Wolff and all "dogmatic" speculators, Kant felt, was the fact that he had learned from Hume the great insight that all judgments about causation are synthetical and therefore incapable of being demonstrated by any appeal to the principle of contradiction, by any analysis of the explicit or implicit content of the concepts contained in the judgment. And what, on the other hand, raised him above the mere "skeptic" and barren denier of the validity of such judgments, was the fact that he had discovered a new, a "critical," way of establishing their *a priori* rights—or at least, of establishing the necessity of the general principle of causality. But for the supposed uniqueness and originality of his position with regard to the logical status of

The passages from Wolff and Kant in this essay appeared in German in the original. They are replaced here by English translations.—ED.

this principle, Kant's famous antithesis of "dogmatism" and "criticism" would lack its main point.

Now concerning Kant's special argument about causality I desire, in this paper, to make three facts evident regarding, primarily, the relation of this part of Kant's system to the doctrines of his predecessors:

1. That the argument fails to establish any essential difference between Kant's "critical" view about causality and the "dogmatism" of his German predecessors, for the reason that one of the two leaders of the "dogmatists," Leibniz, fully anticipated Hume's skeptical insight, while the other, Wolff, invented, long before Hume wrote, a new argument upon the subject, from which the substance of Kant's own argument appears to be derived, or with which, at all events, it is in essence identical.

2. That Kant, in adopting the Wolffian device for proving the validity of the principle of causality, at the same time combines therewith an addition of his own, which is not only incongruous with the stock upon which it is grafted but also, in itself, irrelevant to the problem in connection with which it is introduced; and that, such being the case, it is impossible for anyone to analyze or understand aright the course of Kant's reasoning upon the problem without first carefully discriminating these two distinct and incompatible factors in what Kant presents as a single argument.

3. That, in any case, Kant's reasoning really reduces the law of universal causation to the type of judgment which his own definitions would require us to call "analytical"; that is to say, his reasoning falls back upon the Principle of Contradiction, in its proper Leibnitian sense for its form and method; and therefore it does not, as Kant supposed, constitute a generically new type of argument which should show us how judgments may, in the Kantian phrase, be "synthetical" and yet valid *a priori* for all possible experience.

In order to establish these contentions, it will be necessary for us to come to somewhat close quarters with the details of Kant's ratiocination on the subject, as contained in the proof of the "Second Analogy of Experience." And in so doing we shall be attempting something that—perhaps out of consideration for their readers—historians of philosophy, and even special writers about Kant, rather often neglect to do. The readers of philosophical manuals are commonly told with much emphasis that Kant refuted Hume; but an examination of a number of recent books of this sort indicates that the nature of that refutation is somewhat rarely divulged. It amounts to nothing to say that <u>Kant showed that whatever is a condition of the possibility of experience as such must be valid *a priori* for all possible experience,</u> unless one also shows precisely how Kant contrived to connect the special principle of causal uniformity with this general truism—why he held the realization of that principle to be one of the conditions of the possibility of experience. And since Kant's only reasons for such an opinion are to be found in the argument of the Second Analogy, no one who fails to present a careful and thoroughgoing analysis of that involved, difficult, and highly elusive piece of reasoning can be said to have dealt with Kant's theory of causality at all.

I

But—as Kant himself used to say, after devoting several pages to a subject—nun laßt uns zu unserer Aufgabe fort gehen. We are, first of all, to examine into the originality of Kant's argument, and into the degree in which his doctrine of causality diverged from that of the "dogmatic" Leibnitio-Wolffian school. The first essential, therefore, is to determine precisely what had been the view of the "dogmatists" themselves about judgments of causality. <u>The principle that every phenomenon in time must have an antecedent determinate cause upon which it follows according to a fixed rule, was involved, for both Leibniz and Wolff, in that general principle of Sufficient Reason, which in the doctrines of both played a part second only to the Principle of Contradiction itself.</u> Leibniz, it is true, usually had in mind, when he spoke of the former principle, final rather than efficient causation; the principle referred primarily to the teleological action of the creative mind in choosing among all the logically possible worlds that one in which the maximum of good was present. But a number of passages, some of which I shall presently quote, make it clear that Leibniz understood his favorite maxim to imply also the universal law of the efficient causation of all temporal phenomena. And Wolff, in so many words, identifies the law of universal causation and the Principle of Sufficient Reason. Consequently, the views of both philosophers about the logical character of the judgment of causality are to be determined by ascertaining what they held to be the grounds and the scope of the validity of the Principle of Sufficient Reason, in its application to phenomena in time. Now upon this point Leibniz and Wolff differ explicitly; and the difference between them corresponds very closely to the difference between the doctrines of Hume and of Kant in regard to the same issue.

The utterances of Leibniz upon this point vary somewhat, but his main opinion is unmistakable: the Principle of Sufficient Reason, in the sense in which it is equivalent to the principle of the universality and invariableness of the causal nexus, cannot be derived from the Principle of Contradiction, is incapable of any apodictic proof, and gets its justification, which is practically adequate but logically incomplete, only from the fact of its uniform realization in past experience and its indispensability in the guidance of present conduct. Thus in his controversy with Clarke, when the English theologian asks for a proof of this much vaunted principle, Leibniz confesses that, in the strictly logical sense, he has no proof to give. It is not a metaphysical verity; the only, but the sufficient, reasons for accepting it are that it has never yet failed of empirical verification, and that it is necessary in all reasoning about practical matters. "Is this," he asks (Gerhardt VII, 419f.) "a principle that needs proving? Is not everybody accustomed to make use of it on a thousand occasions? It is, indeed, true that on many other occasions it has been forgotten through carelessness. . . . I have often challenged people to cite me a single instance running counter to this great principle, one uncontested case in which it has failed. But they have never been able to do so, and they never will. On the other hand, there is an infinite number of cases in which it has succeeded—or rather, it has succeeded in every known case in which it has been employed. This ought reasonably to make us conclude that it will still succeed in the cases that are not yet known— following the rule of experimental philosophy, which proceeds *a posteriori*, even though such procedure should not be justified by the pure reason, or *a priori*." Similarly, in a brief paper without date or title (Gerhardt VII, 300), Leibniz insists that, while the principle is of capital importance, it does not constitute a necessary judgment, since its grounds are purely *a posteriori*. "This axiom ought to be esteemed one of the greatest and most fruitful within the whole range of human knowledge; and a great part of meta-physical, physical, and moral science is founded upon it. In truth, without it we should be equally unable to prove God's existence from that of created things; and to reason from cause to effect or from effect to cause; and to reach any conclusion whatever in regard to affairs of state (*in rebus civilibus quicquam concludi*)." Yet this maxim, "of however great force, nevertheless does not establish the necessity of anything, nor take away contingency; since the contrary conclusion always remains possible *per se,* and involves no self-contradiction." And finally, in the *Nouveaux Essais* (IV, ch. 6, 10, 12) the spokesman of Leibniz recognizes that judgments of this type—since the relation between their subject and predicate is known, not by the *"convenance ou disconvenance des idées"* but by *"l'expérience seule"*—cannot attain to metaphyscal necessity, but only to a *"certitude morale."* It is a fact, then, that, as Mr. Bertrand Russell rightly observes, "Leibniz perceived as clearly as Hume and Kant that causal connections are synthetic." It should be added that, upon occasion, Kant himself recognized this fact about his re-lation to Leibniz. In his Reply to Eberhard [1] he maintains that his own philosophy is the true continuation of the Leibnitian, just be-cause Leibniz had seen the Principle of Sufficient Reason to be syn-thetic (i.e., independent of the Principle of Contradiction) but had not gone on to discover, as Kant believed that he had himself dis-covered, any new apodictic justification for such synthetic judg-ments. This, however, is tantamount to the admission that, so far as the problem of causality is concerned, Leibniz belongs, in the Kantian classification, not among the "dogmatic" but among the "sceptical" philosophers. The temper of Leibniz was, to be sure, essentially affirmative; he had nothing of Hume's ambition to startle by sensational paradoxes, and he was content, therefore, with the "moral" certainty of the law of causal uniformity. But if we are to consider not the temperaments of philosophers but their doc-trines, Leibniz and Hume belong together; and Kant's reproach against the former, as well as against the latter, is not that he ac-cepted too much as knowledge *a priori,* but that he accepted too little.

---

1. Über eine Entdeckung, nach der alle neue Kritik der reinen Vernunft durch eine ältere entbehrlich gemacht werden soll, 1790. In *Werke,* ed. Rosenkranz, I, 478-479.

It is Wolff, then, who is the representative of the "dogmatic" way of dealing with the problem of causal connection? Or, on the other hand, are we to say that Wolff, too, errs in Kant's eyes rather by being too much of a skeptic — by failing to discover any *a priori* justification of the causal law? In reality, Kant is entitled to indict Wolff upon neither score. It is true, certainly, that Wolff regretted the failure of Leibniz to attempt any sort of logical proof for the Principle of Sufficient Reason, and that he himself undertook to supply the deficiency. It is true, also, that he incidentally proposes a *reductio ad absurdum* of the position of those who deny that principle—thus appealing, for the support of the Principle of Causality, to the Principle of Contradiction, and making the former appear, in Kant's sense, as an analytical judgment. But the important thing is —though Kant and his many commentators seem to have forgotten it—that the proof upon which Wolff especially insists, recurring to it twice in his chief metaphysical treatise,[2] rests upon the same principle as Kant's own "transcendental" proof of the validity of the law of causal uniformity. In other words, both Wolff and Kant —in contrast to Leibniz and Hume—attempt an apodictic proof of the Law of Sufficient Reason; and Kant's proof is little more than elaborated form of Wolff's, *plus* two curious inconsistencies of which Wolff was innocent.

Leibniz, says Wolff,[3] "had given no proof of the Principle of Sufficient Reason, even though Clarke demanded one of him." But "a sufficient proof will appear when we show below (§ 142) that it is through this principle alone that the distinction between reality and dreams, between the real world and Schlaraffenland, arises." In the subsequent passage referred to, Wolff develops his argument, which, omitting some redundancies, I give in his own words: "Because everything has its sufficient reason for existing, there must also always be a sufficient reason why changes in simple things succeed one another in one way and not in another, why the parts of composite things stand next to one another in one way and not in another, and also why their alterations follow each other in one way and not in another. The order that is found in the proper execution of a proof is of this kind. Now, since an order of this kind

2. Vernünftige Gedanken von Gott, der Welt und der Seele des Menschen, auch allen Dingen überhaupt, 4 Aufl., 1729, §§ 30, 31, 42.

3. *Op. cit.*, § 30.

is not found in a dream (where there is no ground in virtue of experience why things are juxtaposed or why alterations in them follow one another), one recognizes clearly from this that truth is separated from dreams by means of order. And <u>the truth is, accordingly, nothing else than the order of the alteration of things,</u> while a dream is absence of order in the alteration of things." After illustrating his point by a concrete example, Wolff continues: "When one compares truth with dreams and thereby attends to what distinguishes them from each other, one will be able to ascertain no other difference as the one previously cited; namely, that in truth, but not in dreams, everything is mutually grounded. Thus, in the former case, the alterations have an order, while sheer lack of order is to be found in a dream. Whoever considers this thoroughly will sufficiently recognize that there can be no truth with the principle of Sufficient Reason. Yes, it is moreover clear that one recognizes the truth when one understands the ground why this or that can be; that is, the rules of order that are to be encountered in things and their alterations." [4]

The argument which Wolff thus very crudely but perfectly clearly expresses is, in brief, that <u>the principle that every real "change" or event must have a determinate antecedent upon which it follows according to a rule, gets its validity from the fact that, without the use of it, the distinction—which it is certain, as a fact of experience, that we actually make—between purely subjective phenomena and the world of objective realities, would be impossible. And this is precisely the line of argument to which Kant resorts when he finally reaches, in the "Second Analogy of Experience," his central problem.</u> The thesis of the Second Analogy, it is scarcely necessary to recall, is (First Edition): "Everything that happens (begins to exist) presupposes something which it follows according to a rule." The gist of the exceedingly prolix and repetitious proof which follows is contained in the following sentences:

"The apprehension of the manifold in appearance is always successive. The representations of the parts succeed one another. Whether they also succeed one another in the object is a second point of reflexion that is not contained in the earlier one. . . . In

4. Vernünftige Gedanken von Gott, der Welt usw., 1 Aufl., Halle 1720. The argument continues to appear in subsequent editions up to (at least) the fifth (1733); in the Latin Ontologia it is only rather obscurely suggested. The italicized passages are to be compared especially with those in the Kant citation below.

so far as appearances are at the same time objects of consciousness
as representations, they are not at all distinguished from apprehension (that is, from reception into the synthesis of imagination); and
one must accordingly say: the manifold of appearances is always
successively produced in the mind. . . . One soon sees that appearance, as opposed to the representations of apprehension, can only
be represented as the object of apprehension which is distinguished
from them when it (the appearance) stands under a rule which
distinguishes it from every other apprehension and makes necessary
a kind of connection of the manifold. . . . If one posits that nothing
precedes an occurrence upon which that occurrence must follow according to a rule, all succession of perception would be solely in
apprehension (that is, merely subjective); but would not thereby be
objectively determined (precisely which would be the preceding and
which the succeeding perception). . . . Thus it follows that we never
attribute succession (of an occurrence that something happens that
did not previously exist) to the object, even in experience, and distinguish that perception from the subjective succession of our apprehension except where there is a basic rule that necessitates us to
observe this order of perceptions rather than another. . . . If we
investigate what the relation to an object gives our representations
in the way of a new characteristic and what the dignity is which
they thus receive, we find that it [the relation] does nothing further
than to make the connection of representations necessary in a certain manner and to subject them to a rule; that, conversely, objective
reference is given them only because the existence of a certain order
in the temporal relation of our representations is necessary. . . .
That something happens, therefore, is a perception that belongs to
a possible experience that becomes real when I look upon the appearance as determined through its position in time and thereby as
an object which can always be found according to a rule in the
connection of appearances. But this rule of determining something
according to temporal succession is: the temporal succession under
which the occurrence always (i.e., necessarily) follows is to be
found in what goes before. Thus the Principle of Sufficient Reason
is the ground of possible experience—namely, of objective knowledge of appearances with reference to their relation in temporal
order. . . . Thus, should my perception contain knowledge of an
occurrence (since something really happens), these must be an empirical judgment in which one thinks that a succession is deter-

mined; that is, that it presupposes another appearance in time which it necessarily or according to a rule follows. In the absence of this, if I posit what precedes and the occurrence does not necessarily follow upon it, I would have to regard it as only a subjective play of my imagination. And should I imagine by it something objective, I would have to call it a mere dream." [5]

Kant's language is, for the most part, more technical; it was as characteristic of Wolff to avoid technical phraseology as it was of Kant to multiply such phraseology *praeter necessitatem*. Yet the identity of the main argument in the two passages is unmistakable: Kant fully follows Wolff in resting the case for the *a priori* validity of the causal law upon the supposed fact that without it we should have no criterion for distinguishing the purely subjective from the objective, in the changes of things. And at one or two points Kant even seems to be influenced by a vague reminiscence of the rather infelicitious popular language of Wolff. The question of direct borrowing by Kant is, of course, one which cannot be profitably discussed. Every probability, I confess, seems to me to favor the hypothesis that Kant was reproducing as a novelty of his own a piece of reasoning with which he had long since become acquainted in the principal German metaphysical treatise of the best-known German philosopher of the time in which Kant grew up. That Kant should have made so gross a mistake in all innocence will seem probable enough to any who recall the extraordinary confusions of memory of which Kant was capable, in later life, in regard even to his personal affairs. But whether it be a case of borrowing or of coincidence, the essential fact is clear: that the substance of the argument upon which Kant relied to refute Hume's skepticism about causality, had already been advanced by the most notorious of the so-called "dogmatists" over sixty years before the *Kritik* was published—and some twenty years before the appearance of Hume's *Treatise*.[6]

5. Kr. d. r. V., 1781, pp. 189, 191, 194, 196, 200, 201.
6. It is scarcely credible that, in the huge mass of Kant-philology, so significant a fact can have nowhere been noted. But the fact is, at all events, ignored in such representative special studies as Wartenberg's *Kants Theorie der Kausalität* (1899); Koenig's *Die Entwickelung des Causalproblems* (1888); Arnsperger's *Wolff's Verhältnis zu Leibniz* (1879); and Laas' *Kants Analogien der Erfahrung* (1876), in which the lack of originality in Kant's arguments is especially insisted upon.

The genealogy of the argument of the Second Analogy may, indeed, be traced beyond Wolff. In various writings Leibniz attempted to deal with the question raised by Descartes, how dreams, hallucinations, and other illusory perceptions are to be distinguished from objective realities, and how, in general, we are to define the marks of objectivity. He observes upon this point that "the more connection (*liaison*) we find in the things that happen to us, the more are we confirmed in our opinion of the reality of the things that we perceive" (Gerhardt I, 373). "The reality (*verité*) of sensible things consists in nothing but the connexion des phenoménes qui devait avoir sa raison; and it is this that distinguishes them from dreams. . . . The true criterion of reality in the case of objects of sense is the connection of the phenomena, that is to say, the connection of what happens in different times and places, and in the experience of different men, who are themselves, in this regard, very important phenomena to one another" (Nouveaux Essais I, 4, ch. II, § 14, Gerhardt V, 355). It seems, indeed, to have been a commonplace among the Leibnitians that the criterion which differentiates the valid and objective from the purely subjective perception lies in the fact that the former belongs to a context characterized by the causal connectedness and the fixed order of its temporally successive (and also its spatially co-existent) parts. Leibniz himself, however, did not turn the argument about, so as to find a proof for the validity of the law of sufficient reason in just the fact that it is used as such a criterion—the (supposed) fact that without its help the distinction between objectively valid and purely subjective sense-presentations could not be made. It was Wolff who converted this old Leibnitian idea into a new (and exceedingly questionable) argument in defense of the second of the two great Leibnitian principles. And in this, as we have seen, Kant follows him.

II

It is, however, true enough that Kant likewise gives Wolff's argument a new turn of his own; but one must add that it is distinctly a turn for the worse, and also that, even so, it does not essentially differentiate Kant's reasoning about causality from that of his

predecessor. To understand the argument of the Second Analogy
at all, it is essential to analyze the interworking of the old and the
new factors in Kant's thought.

Kant, namely, connects the argument—in his more detailed and
involved efforts to make it clear—with a peculiar psychological
observation of his. It occurs to him as a significant and paradoxical
fact that all our perceptions, whether they be of objects that change
or of objects that are stationary and immutable, are themselves temporally successive. And reflection upon this fact brings to light what
Kant regards as an important psychological conundrum: *How is it
that we are able, in a series of apprehensions that are constantly
successive, to recognize that some of these successions in apprehension correspond to and represent successions in the objects apprehended, and that others do not?* How can we get behind the subjective succession so as to discriminate the mutable from the immutable, the moving from the stationary, object; and what is the
criterion that we employ in making this discrimination? Kant's
illustrations of this situation are, no doubt, familiar. "For instance,
the apprehension of the manifold in the phenomenal appearance of
a house that stands before me is successive. The question then
arises, whether the manifold of the house be successive by itself,
which, of course, no one would admit." That is, I see first the basement, then the walls, then the roof; the question is, why do I not
suppose that these parts themselves somehow temporally *come after*
one another? Certainly, in other cases I do infer from the successiveness of my perceptions to the successiveness of the objective
phenomena. For example, I see a ship moving down stream; I perceive its successive positions at one point in the stream after another; and I conclude that the ship has changed its position. If, in
the case of the house, I regard the successively perceived parts as
stationary, why do I not regard the successive perceptions of a ship
as representing a row of stationary ships? Or *vice versa*, if I regard
the latter series of perceptions as representing a moving and changing object, why do I not regard the former in the same way?

Here is Kant's great psychological puzzle, upon the momentous-
ness of which he manifestly flatters himself not a little. The answer
which he gives for it is this: I distinguish the successive perceptions
which represent a succession in the object from those which do not,
by virtue of a verifiable difference in the two cases, namely, the dif-

ference that, in the case of my successive perception of the really moving object the *order* of my perceptions is fixed and irreversible, whereas in the case of the stationary object the order is found (upon repetition of the observation of the object, Kant seems to mean) to be reversible at will. "If, in a phenomenon which contains an event, I call the antecedent state of perception A and the consequent B, B can only follow A in my apprehension, and can never precede it. I see for instance a ship gliding down stream. My perception of its place below follows my perception of its place higher up, and it is impossible that the ship should be perceived first below and then above." But with my perception of the parts of a stationary manifold it is different. For example, "in the case of the house, my perceptions could begin at the roof and end in the basement, or begin below and end above; they could apprehend the manifold of the perceived object from right to left, or from left to right. There was therefore no predetermined order in the succession of these perceptions, determining the point where I had to begin in apprehension in order to connect the manifold empirically; while in the apprehension of an event there is always a rule which makes the order of the successive perceptions necessary." Since, without the recognition of this rule, we could not make the distinction between the two kinds of experience, therefore all experience of the objective kind must conform to the rule, which is therefore certain and necessary *a priori*. That is to say, all events must conform to the rule of causal connection, for the reason that otherwise we could not know them to be events at all (in the sense in which an event is different from a moment in the subjective succession of states of consciousness). Kant's argument really attempts to reduce the proof of the law of causal connection to an example of Leibniz's Principle of Contradiction: an event is *by definition* (i.e., by virtue of that which has been shown to be the sole essential mark distinguishing it from an experience that is not an experience of an event) a phenomenon that follows another phenomenon according to a rule; hence, by what is (in Kant's sense—though he fails to see the fact) a purely analytical judgment, it follows that "every event presupposes something upon which it follows according to a rule"—*quod erat demonstrandum*.

Just how, now, does this reasoning differ from Wolff's? The essential differences are two; and in both, Kant not merely diverges from his original but also gives his argument a form inconsistent with the main line of proof which he supposes himself to be following.

1. Kant is attempting, as we have seen, to rest the case for the validity of the Principle of Sufficient Reason upon the supposed necessity of assuming that principle as the basis of the distinction between merely subjective, and objectively valid, perceptions of change, between veridical representations and "mere dream." But in the unlucky turn which Kant gives the argument, the principle really comes to figure rather as the basis of the distinction *between perceptions of change and perceptions of permanence, no matter whether the perceptions be "objective" or purely illusory.* This is not what Kant means to argue; but it is precisely what he actually does argue. For what his reasoning comes to is this: that we can distinguish—and, indeed, can conceive of—a moving or changing object, in contrast with the stationary or unchanging—only in so far as we consciously think the succession of perceptions in the former case as following one another according to the law of causal uniformity. In other words, except by a reference to the Principle of Sufficient Reason, we cannot differentiate an experience of moving things from an experience of the unmoved, the variable from the constant. But manifestly we *do* make this distinction both in our dreams and out of them, both in our most "objective" and veridical judgments of perception and in our private imaginings and hallucinatory representations. It is, at all events, not the common experience that in dreams one is incapable of picking out, within the universal successiveness of one's subjective representations, those series of perceptions that are representations of moving objects, and those that are not. In the "subjective play of my imagination," I do not ordinarily find any difficulty in discriminating those sequences of images that "contain an event" from those that—though themselves successive—image only objects that are thought as permanent and stable. Throughout the whole range of our perceptual experience—true or false, objective or subjective, waking or dreaming —we have perceptions alike of motion and of rest, of change and of fixity. Consequently even if we should attach any value to Kant's argument that we could not know that the ship moves while the house is stationary, without a knowledge of the principle of causal connection—we should still be compelled to say that this argument

<!-- handwritten margin note: Doesn't he use changing vs. permanent objects only as nent objects unter a (perhaps unter as twate) example? -->

is neither identical nor compatible with the other argument to which we have seen him giving expression. The same principle manifestly cannot be both (a) the basis of the distinction between objective and subjective perceptions of change, and (b) the basis of another distinction which runs cross-wise through *both* objective and subjective perceptions of change. There are, then, two threads of argument in Kant's proof of the Second Analogy—the Wolffian and his own. The two are hopelessly inharmonious, but Kant never suspects the fact. It is clearly, as his language shows, the Wolffian sort of argument that he really intends to present; but with characteristic confusion of thought he allows this argument, unobserved, by a subtle metamorphosis resulting essentially from verbal ambiguities, to transform itself into something quite incongruous with the proof that he intends.

It is easy, moreover, to discover through just what misapprehensions Kant was led to make this unfortunate transition. In the first place, his seemingly profound problem—that of explaining how a "succession of perceptions" can ever afford a perception of a stable, or non-successive, object—is a problem which exists only for Kant's imagination. In actual perception (not, of course, in mere sensation), so long as our attention to a given object be continuous, objects are directly *given* as moving or stationary, as altering or retaining their original sensible qualities. All that is necessary in order that a series of sensations should yield a perception of an object characterized by fixed position, is the mind's ability to fixate attention upon an object of which the individuality is assumed to be continuous, to perceive the successive spatial relations of that chosen object of attention to other visible or tangible objects, and to remember and compare these perceptions from moment to moment. Given this much, I can, in the language of common sense, *see* the ship move, see that the house is stationary—even though it be a dream-house, or a vessel seen in the imagination of a shipwrecked sailor. And the fact that my perceptions in both cases alike are temporally successive, creates no difficulty and is, psychologically speaking, irrelevant; and there is therefore no occasion for appealing to anything so remote from immediate experience as the Principle of Sufficient Reason for a criterion for distinguishing perceptions of things that move from perceptions of things that stand still.

Kant was still further helped toward this confusion of two distinct and incompatible arguments by his failure to remark that he was using the expression "in the object" in a highly ambiguous sense. His error, indeed, consisted precisely in transforming the question—Wolff's question—: "Does this my perception of a succession of states of a given object constitute a perception of a truly *objective succession?*"—into the very different, though verbally similar, question: "Does this succession of my perceptions constitute a perception of succession *in the object?*" Now, in the ordinary sense, a succession may take place "in the object," without necessarily being, or being regarded as, in any epistemological sense "objective"; without possessing, or even seeming to possess, any objektive Gültigkeit. For all perception deals with objects, and with objects that, as we have seen, are given as either moving or not moving, as undergoing qualitative change or as qualitatively constant. And, as the last paragraph has shown, it is just this implication of *objects* in perception that is the explanation of the fact that, within the successiveness of perceptions, we are able to distinguish perceptions of constancy from perceptions of change. Involved in the power of perception is the necessity of thinking of an object that has some sort of separate and continuous identity. Thus a subjective succession of perceptions is distinguished from (i.e., is not confused with) a perception of succession "in the object," simply because perception is perception of objects, and an object is that which—whatever its metaphysical status—is over against the subject and is somehow taken as identical with itself through the changes of its own states. The marks of this identity of which we commonly make use would, no doubt, be found to be wholly empirical and relative, and to be reducible to certain essentially practical tests. With that matter, however, we are not here concerned; we need to bear in mind merely these three points: that what is implied in our distinguishing successive perceptions of succession from successive perceptions of permanence is not the idea of the uniform casual connectedness of the former sequences but the idea of the (practical) identity or fixableness of the object perceived; that this implication is so immediate that the power to distinguish between objects that change and objects that do not may be regarded as directly given in perception as such; and that this whole question, concerning permanence or impermanence in the object of perception, is by no means the same as the question concerning the objective validity of our perceptual judgments. Even our least "objective" perceptions—if they are perceptions at all, and not merely a flux of unconnected sensations—are perceptions of objects thought as having some sort of provisional continuity and individuality through successive moments.

(2) Yet Kant's reasoning, based upon the supposed difficulty of discriminating a perception of succession from a succession of perceptions, does, after all, prove something. When, however, we note precisely what it is that it proves, we find Kant in a still worse case. For the thing proved has nothing to do with the law of causality or the Principle of Sufficient Reason, has no bearing whatever upon the thesis of the Second Analogy. In so far as Kant adds to or transforms Wolff's argument, his reasoning becomes irrelevant to the thesis with which he is dealing.

For the real fact of consciousness which is brought out by Kant's reflections concerning the differentia by which, in the succession of our perceptions, we distinguish the permanent from its contrary, is this: that when we conceive of an object as moving or changing, or as having moved or changed, we necessarily imply that the (actual or potential) sequence of our perceptions in observing the object was fixed or irreversible; whereas, when we conceive of an object (or rather of a system of objects, e.g., the several parts of a house) as stationary or unchanged, we necessarily imply that we might (so far as the object is concerned) have observed its parts in any other sequence, as well as in that which we actually followed. In other words, by the logical implications of the concept, a "changing object" is that system of successive presentations of which the succession must, in any given case, be observed by us, if it is observed at all, in one single order, which is independent of the action of our will, of any shifting of our attention. The stable object, *per contra,* is, by a similar implication, that system of successive presentations, of which the succession in perception is conceived as depending, in any given experience, upon the movement of the attention of the subject, upon the fixation of attention upon different objects: which, in turn, implies that the order of our observation, in the supposed instance, might, so far as the object is concerned, have been different. This, I say, is what Kant's arguments, and his illustrations of the irreversibility of the sequence of our perceptions of a moving ship and the indeterminateness of the sequence of our perceptions of the parts of a house, go to prove; and the point, so far, although fairly obvious, is perfectly well taken. It makes explicit something that is contained in the *meaning* of the complex concept of a changing single object, as over against a "permanent manifold." The determinateness of the sequence of perceptions of a single object undergoing change or movement is implied by the fact that we are, by hypothesis, dealing with *one object;* for then, necessarily, whatever differences appear from moment to moment in the presented content must belong to the object or to its relations with other objects, since there is assumed to be no new fixation of attention on the part of the subject. In other words, it is found that perception implies an individuated object: and so long as the direction of attention upon one perceptible object is known or assumed to be constant, any inconstancy in the successive perceptions must be independent of the attention of the subject; and hence, in the given experience, the *order* of those perceptions must be independent of changes in the order of the subject's acts of attention. On the other hand, when the object in successive moments of attention is not assumed to be the same—or, what is the same thing, when there is known or assumed to be a change in the fixation of attention—then the dissimilarities in the successively presented contents of perception are conceived as not belonging to any one of the objects successively attended to, and the order of the succession of the perceptions is conceived to be determined purely by the order of changes in the subject's attention. This last implies that if, on another occasion, the subject should perceive the same system of objects, nothing in the assumed nature of the objects would prevent the subject from apprehending them in quite a different order. In fine, then, Kant shows us this: that we cannot conceive or define any one object as changing without implying that the sequence of perceptions which would have been had by any subject fixedly attending to that object would have been determined by something "in the object," and could not at the time have been had by the subject in any reverse order.

But all this has no relation to the law of universal and uniform causation, for the manifest reason that a proof of the *irreversibility* of the sequence of my perceptions in *a single instance* of a phenomenon is not equivalent to a proof of the necessary *uniformity* of the sequence of my perceptions in *repeated instances* of a given *kind* of phenomenon. Yet it is the latter alone that Hume denied and that Kant desires to establish.

Kant's own chosen illustrations may be used, once more, to show the nature of his confusion here. What, according to Kant, enables me to discriminate the house as a stationary object from the ship as a moving one—when in either case my perception involves a succession of subjective states—is the fact that, in the case of the ship, "my perception of its place below follows my perception of its place higher up, and it is impossible in the apprehension of this phenomenon that the ship should be perceived first below and then above"; while in the case of the house, my perceptions of the several parts may come indifferently in any order. Now this "impossibility of seeing the ship first below and then above" obviously applies only to the successive—or the continuously changing—positions of a single identical ship on a single occasion. It does not apply at all to all phenomena of the same kind, i.e., to the behavior of all moving ships. After the given event, I necessarily assume that —inasmuch as I conceive the object, and not merely my subjective attention, as having changed—I could not by an act of will have had the perceptions at that time, in any other order; but this does not in the least imply that all *like* perceptions will repeat that order. Yet if the thesis of the Second Analogy—that "every event follows upon an antecedent event according to a rule"—is meant to have any relevancy to Hume's problem, it should mean that every event has some determinate antecedent and that it can be certainly known *a priori* that the same kind of antecedent will in all instances be followed by the same kind of consequent.

It is, indeed, true that the distinction just made, between the sequences of perception that are "determined by" or depend upon the voluntary movement of our attention, and those that are determined by, or independently given in, the object, already assumes the principle of causality. Certainly, a self-conscious mind can and must distinguish those changes in its experience, those scene-shiftings in the content of its perceptions, which are to be taken as due to its own movements, to the acts of the subject, from those other changes that are merely given from the outside; and in this sense, and to this degree, the applicability of the category of causality to experience is a necessary implication of the fact of self-consciousness. But this is not Kant's argument; and moreover, the point could not be used to prove what Kant desires to prove. That I invoke the notion of causation in distinguishing changes in perception produced by alterations in my own attention, from externally given changes with which my volition appears to have nothing to do, by no means goes to show that in that realm of externally caused or non-volitional changes, all phenomena must follow one another according to a rule of uniform and "necessary" connection. It merely shows that those external phenomena are disconnected from, and independent of, that species of causal process which I know inwardly as intentional or purposive control of attention. Whether or not those outer changes follow one another nach einer Regal or not, is a thing that still remains to be found out.

The nature of this *non-sequitur* in Kant's reasoning—this irrelevancy of his proof to his conclusion—is especially well illustrated in the paragraph (1st Edition, pp. 197–198) in which this whole argument about the necessity for an objective determination of "real events" in the Reihenfolge der Zeit is given in a condensed form. If, says Kant, I am to regard a series of changes in my representations as constituting a perception of change, eine Begebenheit, I must ascribe to any such change in der Zeit eine gewisse bestimmte Stelle. This, however, I remark, is equally true of changes in representations that I do not attribute "to the object" at all; if I look (to use Kant's illustration again) at the basement of the unchanging house at one moment, and at the roof at the next moment, each of those moments in the "subjective succession of my apprehensions" has a temporal place no less definite and inalienable than the moments occupied by the "objective" changes of the ship's position as I observe her floating down stream. It is, then, not the temporal Bestimmtheit of the changes regarded as external which distinguishes them from those changes which I am accustomed to regard as merely subjective shiftings in my perception of unchanging objects; for, as regards their position in time, both sorts of change are equally definite. It is rather that I conceive that the sequence of changes of perceptual content in the one case *might have been* (so far as the object was concerned) different from what it actually was, if the order of attention on the part of the subject had been different; whereas, in the case of the succession of perceptions which are taken as representing an actual succession of states in the object—e.g. in the perception of the successive positions of the moving ship—I assume that no change on the part of the subject merely, could (so long as it attended to the object at all) have altered the given sequence of the perceptions. The externality or "objectivity" of an event does, unquestionably, imply the *givenness* of the order of moments constituting it, *for* the subject of the perception; and this means the independence of that order with reference to the subjective order of changes of attention; and this means, in turn, the impossibility of *having had the perception in any other order,* in the given case. Thus, as I have said, we may admit that Kant proves—when one helps him out a little in his argument—that the contrast between a perception of succession, and a succession of perceptions of the non-successive, does turn upon the contrast between a given and irreversible sequence of perceptions, and a sequence determined entirely by the action of the subject, and so potentially reversible. Kant, however, in the paragraph cited, not only jumps abruptly from the idea of the *definiteness of the temporal position* of an event to the idea of the *irreversibility,* in the given instance, of the sequence to which it belongs—but from this in turn to the idea of the necessary *uniformity* of the sequence in all cases in which the same kind of event appears as antecedent. Here are his words: "The determinate place in time [of the appearance] in its temporal relation can be gotten only because something is presupposed in the preceding situation which it always (that is, according to a rule) follows—from which it then follows, first of all, that I cannot reverse the sequence and can place it before that which happens. Secondly, [it follows] that, when the state of affairs that goes before is posited, this determinate occurrences follows inevitably and necessarily." The italicized words express precisely enough what Kant was called upon to prove, if he was to answer Hume; but to the proof of them the argument about the irreversible "given-ness" of the order in which my perceptions of changes in objects come to me, is wholly incompetent. The sentence I have just quoted, then, seems to me one of the most spectacular examples of the *non-sequitur* which are to be found in the history of philosophy.

We have thus seen—to recapitulate—that as soon as Kant leaves the main line of the Wolffian reasoning, he makes use of arguments that are irrelevant to the subject with which he is dealing and inconsistent with his proper position. He does not himself perceive their irrelevancy because of two rather gross confusions of ideas into which he falls: (1) He fails to see that the distinction between barely subjective and objectively valid perceptions of succession is not identical with the distinction between the successive perception of succession "in the object" and the successive perception of permanence; and he therefore illicitly substitutes the latter for the former. (2) He also fails to see that to prove that the conception of an object as changing necessarily implies that the series of perceptions in an observer of the object is in any given instance irreversible and independent of the observer's subjective changes of attention—that this is by no means equivalent to a proof that similar changes in objects must at all times follow one another in a fixed and invariable order, such as is indicated by the law of causal uniformity.

We may, however, fairly regard those phases of Kant's proof which are at once the most original and the most illogical, as temporary aberrations from the argument at which he really aims—the argument of Wolff. For, as has already perhaps been sufficiently illustrated, Kant always, in the final formulation of his proof, comes round to the Wolffian contention that the Principle of Sufficient Reason can be shown to be valid by showing its indispensableness to the distinction between purely subjective presentations of temporal phenomena and objectively real phenomena. When Kant wishes to express in a single sentence the essential point of his defense of the axiom of causality, he puts it thus: "Also ist das Verhältnis der Ursache zur Wirkung, die Bedingung der objectiven Gültigkeit unserer empirischen Urteile in Ansehung der Reihe der Wahrnehmungen, mithen der empirischen Wahrheit desselben." Taking this Wolffian contention, then, as Kant's essential one, it remains only to consider how far this contention can be justified, and whether even in it there can be found any convincing reply to Hume's doubts.

The answer to this question need not be long. For the sake of clearness, the argument not very lucidly set forth either by Wolff or Kant may be reduced to the two propositions which appear to constitute its logical essence; and we may consider the force of each of these in turn. (1) The only criterion for distinguishing between purely subjective and objectively valid judgments of perception

consists in the fact that the latter deal with phenomena in which
the law of uniform causality holds good, while the former deal
with phenomena in which it does not hold good. Such is the initial
—the minor—premise of the argument. If the word "only" be
stricken out, the proposition contains some glimmer of truth. We
do make a practical distinction [7] between merely subjective presentations and objective perceptions—one that is nowise synonymous
with the metaphysical distinction between phenomena and things-
in-themselves. What the essence of this practical sort of objectivity
is neither Wolff nor Kant at all helps us to understand; Leibniz
threw more light upon the subject than either of them when he
spoke of "the connection of what happens in different times and
places, and in the experience of different men, who are themselves,
in this regard, very important phenomena to one another." Practically the most important criterion of the "objectivity" of a perception, at the time that I am having it, is its agreement with the experience of other men about me. But it is true that if the test of
social currency cannot be applied, I am likely to test the perception
by seeing whether it conforms to the rules of causal sequence uniformly exemplified in the phenomena of my past experience. For
example, late at night I think I hear the sound of a bell ringing in
the house; to discover whether this was a veridical perception or an
illusion I look to see whether any bell in the house is still visibly
vibrating. I.e., I test my perception by assuming a certain invariable
connection between certain phenomena and certain others. In this
sense, the principle of uniformity in the connection of cause and
effect is assumed by us as one of the minor criteria of objective
validity—as one of the means of distinguishing "the subjective play
of my imaginations" from a true and "workable" perception. So a
dream, be it never so vivid while it lasts, is afterwards recognized
as a dream, partly because things happened in it in a way that does
not correspond with the prevailing order of my experience, and
partly because I cannot connect the experiences which I had in it
with the general context of uniformly connected experiences that
I had before and have had since.

We may, then, recognize that there is a certain amount of rather
unimportant truth contained in the first proposition implied by

7. It is needless to say that the question of the metaphysical reality of the
object, as *Ding-an-sich*, is involved in neither Wolff's nor Kant's argument.

Wolff's and Kant's argument. The second proposition may be regarded as the major premise of a syllogism of which the first is the minor; and it may be expressed thus: (2) Whatever principle is employed as a criterion for distinguishing subjective illusion from objectively valid judgments of perception, must necessarily be true *a priori* of all possible (objective) experiences. The conclusion, then, to fill out the syllogistic form, would of course run: the law of causality is thus necessarily true *a priori* of all possible (objective) experiences.

The argument, when thus put in order, is not destitute of intelligibility nor of a certain plausibility. It becomes fallacious only after we have stricken out—as we found it necessary to strike out—the word "only" from the minor premise. If it were indeed true that all events that can be called objective must be connected with other events according to a uniform rule, and if they could be recognized as objective only in so far as they exhibit such a connection—then, truly, I could know *a priori* that all possible experiences of objective events will conform to this law of causal connection. The proof of the law would still be "analytical," since the truth of the minor premise obviously could be established only by virtue of a definition of what one means by objective; but if the definition agreed with the common meaning and corresponded to a real aspect of experience, this premise, and therewith the whole argument, would be convincing. But since it is not true that perceptions that are in the ordinary sense called objective can be known to be such only by the criterion of the presence or absence of connection "according to a rule" in the changes perceived—then the argument falls to the ground. If one is content, indeed, to say that one chooses to mean by "objective event" nothing more or less than an event following the rule of uniform causality, one is entitled to hold to the argument; it then becomes, not untrue, but merely empty and tautological. But, although one test of objectivity in phenomena that is commonly applied does depend upon the assumption of the law of uniform causation, we have seen that it is not the sole nor the essential test of the kind of objectivity that is practically significant for us. I know that in the future I shall be willing to call any event objective—even though it be an unmitigated miracle, a sheer violation of all known or conceivable rules of uniformity—provided that my vivid perception of it is corroborated by the perception of other men. And therefore, knowing this, I am unable to know (at least so far as the argument now in question is concerned) by any *a priori* certainty that all future objective events must comply *also* with the requirements of Kant's Second Analogy. There is nothing in Kant's argument which tends to show that my habitual assumption that events that are objective will also follow uniform rules of sequence, is anything more than a practical postulate, bred of an illogical but natural habit of expecting nature to repeat herself, and encouraged by past success in prophecies based upon that expectation. This is to say that there is nothing in the argument which in any way replies to Hume.[8]

The present paper, if it has made out its case, has shown, in the central argument of the *Kritik der reinen Vernunft,* both the curious confusion in Kant's thinking and its lack of genuine originality. In concluding, I think it worthwhile to add that the proof of a lack of originality could, if space permitted, be extended to other parts of Kant's system. It is easy, for example, to show that Kant's whole antithesis of "dogmatism" and "criticism" involves, when subjected to analysis and to historical comparisons, a misrepresentation of historic facts regarding the nature of the philosophical method employed by his predecessors and the degree of his own divergence from them. The prevalent superstition that between the method of philosophizing in vogue before Kant's time, and that in vogue since, there is a great gulf fixed, has done no little injury to the interests of philosophy. In his conception of philosophical methodology, in his formulation of the ultimate criteria of truth, and in several of his special arguments, Kant not only is far less unlike some of his precursors than he himself and most historians of philosophy since have supposed; he is also frequently far less clear and instructive than they. So far as epistemology and the theory of method in metaphysics are concerned, we need not merely to go "back to Kant" but also "back of Kant"—to Leibniz on the one hand, to the English school on the other—to get a clearer and simpler and more just formulation of the fundamental logical prob-

8. The present paper shows that Kant's attempt to reply to Hume consisted chiefly in reviving an unconvincing argument employed by Wolff many years before Hume wrote. It has already been shown by others, by means of a direct comparison of Hume's own position with Kant's, that Kant neither understood nor refuted the Scotch philosopher. V. especially Dr. L. Stein in *"Der soziale Optimismus,"* pp. 126-154, and Dr. I. Mirkin in *"Kantstudien,"* 1902.

lems and a better, if still an insufficient, light upon the real nature and limits of our valid processes of judgment. And so, first of all, in the interest alike of philosophy and of a more accurate history of the development of concepts—it is amazing, but it is true, that such a thing still requires to be said—we need a fuller and far more precise understanding of the relation between Kant's doctrines and those of his German predecessors.

Index

Acroasis logica (Baumgarten), 271
Actual judgment, 280
Actual truth, 281
Adickes, 25, 27, 28, 51, 53, 56, 89; on transcendental deduction, 26
Affirmative judgments, 277
Analogies of experience, 252. *See also* Second analogy.
"Analytic and Synthetic as Categories of Inquiry" (Hartman), 232
Analytic judgments, 125, 257-261; *a priori,* 228; forms of, 248, 250, 251, 255, 263; logical criterion of, 232; phenomenological criterion of, 233
Analytic-synthetic distinction, 203, 205-208, 215, 228, 229, 232, 239, 253, 267
Apodictic judgment, 282
A priori: concepts, 43-45, 48, 50, 51, 57, 59, 85; and empirical judgments, difference, 250; knowledge, 225; propositions, 282; rules, 84
Aristotelian logic, 250, 266
Aristotle, 193, 249, 255, 270; and forms of judgment, 250
Arnauld and Nicole, *Port Royal Logic,* 219, 233
Arnoldt, *Krit. Excurse,* 41
Assertoric judgment, 282

Augustine, 160, 163
Augustinianism, 160, 161

Baumgarten, 88, 109, 114, 120, 122, 125, 127, 250, 279, 282; *Acroasis logica,* 271
Beck, Lewis White, 203, 204; on synthetic-analytic distinction, 205
Being and Time (Heidegger), 148, 150
Berkeley, 176, 184
Bruno, Giordano, 176

Cassirer, E., 99-101
Causality, 173, 240, 284-286, 289, 301
Clarke, 287
Cohen, H., 135; *Kants Begründung der Ethik,* 146
Commentar zu Kants Kritik der reinen Vernunft (Vaihinger), 232
"Concerning Scientific and Nonscientific Philosophy" (Riehl), 133
Couturat, M., 110
Critique of Judgment (Kant), 149
Critique of Practical Reason (Kant), 145, 149, 154, 173, 181, 184
Critique of Pure Reason (Kant), 13, 17, 25, 28, 47, 62, 63, 65, 69, 73, 86, 89-103, 122, 128, 131,

Critique of Pure Reason (cont.)
132, 134, 139, 140, 142-144, 149,
151-154, 158, 159, 161, 163, 164,
166, 167, 170, 172, 178, 186, 195,
216, 225, 240, 257, 260, 262, 269,
272, 281, 284, 292, 307
Cusanus, 176, 177, 181, 182

Definition, 216, 241; accidental, 219;
analytic, 217; analytic nominal,
220; analytic real, 221; essential,
219; nominal, 217-220; real, 217,
218, 220; synthetic, 217, 222;
synthetic nominal, 220; synthetic
real, 221; and analytic judgments,
225, 227, 228; and progress of
knowledge, 223, 224
Democritus, 172
Determinism, 172, 196
Die Akademische Preisschrift (Kant),
262
*Die Transcendentale Deduktion der
Kategorien* (Vaihinger), 63
Doctrine of schematism, 139
Dogmatism, 95, 107, 129, 196, 285,
307
Dreams of a Spiritseer (Kant), 153,
154, 164

Eberhard, 98, 115, 117, 114, 125,
225, 226, 235, 236, 288; *Philo-
sophisches Magazin,* 122; and syn-
thetic judgments *a priori,* 126
Empirical concepts, 59, 60, 82, 83
Epicurus, 172
Erdmann, B., 24, 27, 60, 64, 68;
Kants Kriticismus, 24
Euclid, 266

Fatalism, 172, 196
Fichte, 195
Finitude of human knowledge, 137,
140, 151, 154
Fischer, K., 54
Formal logic, 250, 254, 267, 268;
and origin of concepts, 254
Forms of judgment, 247, 262

Freedom, 174, 194-196; and divine
causality, 197; and temporality,
197

God, as *ens realissimum,* 178; as
first cause, 193
Goethe, 156

Hartman, R. S., "Analytic and Synthetic as Categories of Inquiry,"
232
Hauck, P., 270-272, 278, 279
Heidegger, 100, 101, 135, 138, 146-
151, 156, 157; *Being and Time,*
148, 150; concept of finitude, 155;
and doctrine of schematism, 139;
and finitude of human knowledge,
136; fundamental ontology, 155;
*Kant und das Problem der Meta-
physik,* 100; and metaphysics, 134
Heimsoeth, H., 102-104
Hobbes, 177
Horae Subsecivae (Wolff), 115
Hume, 239, 245, 246, 289, 303, 307;
criticism of rational structure of
empirical knowledge, 240, 241;
idea of necessary connection, 284,
285; *Treatise Concerning Human
Nature, 292*

Idea of Negative Magnitude (Kant),
119
Identity, implicit, 231; explicit, 231
Imagination, 13, 16, 31, 34, 35, 52,
71, 78; productive, 18, 37-40, 48-
52, 54, 56, 87, 100, 222; reproductive, 54, 57, 86-88; transcendental, 38, 49, 87, 143, 150, 152,
154
Inaugural Dissertation (Kant), 182,
186, 195
Infinite judgments, 276, 277
Intuition, 34, 140, 222, 256, 257;
and synthetic judgments, 258; and
understanding, 141

Jacobi, F. H., 143
James, William, 106
Joseph, *Logic,* 267
Judgments, *per attributa,* 124, 125; of perception, 304, 306

Kant: *Critique of Judgment,* 149; *Critique of Practical Reason,* 145, 149, 154, 173, 181, 184; *Critique of Pure Reason,* 13, 17, 25, 28, 47, 62, 63, 65, 69, 73, 86, 89-103, 122, 128, 131, 132, 134, 139, 140, 142-144, 149, 151-154, 158, 159, 161, 163, 164, 166, 167, 170, 172, 178, 186, 195, 216, 225, 240, 257, 260, 262, 269, 272, 281, 284, 292, 307; *Die Akademische Preisschrift,* 262; *Dreams of a Spiritseer,* 153, 154, 164; *Idea of Negative Magnitude,* 119; *Inaugural Dissertation,* 182, 186, 195; *Logik,* 279; *Lose Blätter,* 23, 53, 89; *Metaphysics of Morals,* 186; *Metaphysische Anfangsgründe der Naturwissenschaft,* 257, 260; *Monadologia physica,* 171, 180; *Opus Postumum,* 23, 183; *Progress of Metaphysics,* 119; *Prolegomena,* 24, 68, 107, 120, 243, 257, 259, 260, 262; *Reflexionen,* 23, 53; *Reply to Eberhard,* 119; *Streitschrift gegen Eberhard,* 250
Kant und das Problem der Metaphysik (Heidegger), 100
Kants Begründung der Ethik (Cohen), 146
Kants Kriticismus (Erdmann), 24
"Kants Lehre vom analytischen Urteil" (Koppelmann), 234
Kehrbach, 27
Kierkegaard, 156
Kingdom of ends, 100, 145, 154, 170, 178, 190, 191
Koppelmann, "Kants Lehre vom analytischen Urteil," 234
Krit. Excurse (Arnoldt), 41

Laas, 118, 119
Lambert, 279, 280, 282; *Neues Organon,* 271
Law of contradiction, 96-99, 210. *See also* Principle of contradiction and Principle of non-contradiction.
Law of sufficient reason, 179. *See also* Principle of sufficient reason.
Leibniz, 95-97, 105, 110, 117, 118, 121-123, 129, 165, 172, 177, 179, 181, 182, 192, 250, 262, 284, 285, 305, 307; and analytic judgments, 120; and analytic-synthetic distinction, 110, 114; doctrine of definition, 113, 114; *Nouveaux Essais,* 288; and phenomenality of space, 185; and principle of contradiction, 108, 109, 286, 287, 289, 295; and principle of sufficient reason, 109, 286-289; and virtually identical propositions, 95, 98, 99
Lewis, C. I., 236, 241, 242
Logic (Joseph), 267
Logik (Kant), 279
Lose Blätter (Kant), 23, 53, 89
Lovejoy, A. O., 95-99, 207-209
Lutoslawski, 66

Malebranche, 163, 172, 177, 182
Material substance, 188
Materialism, 189
Mathematical judgments, status of, 242-246
Mathematics: and *a priori* knowledge, 245; and intuition, 244; and synthetic propositions, 244, 245
Meier, G. F., 250; *Vernunftlehre,* 271
Mellin, 261
Mendelssohn, 132, 181
Metaphysical deduction, 70, 73, 78, 81, 83, 85, 206, 207, 247, 249, 253, 256-258, 263, 264, 268
Metaphysics of Morals (Kant), 186
Metaphysische Anfangsgründe der

Metaphysische (cont.)
Naturwissenschaft (Kant), 257, 260
Modality, 209, 279-283
Monadologia physica (Kant), 171, 180
Moral law, 145, 146, 154

Necessary truth, 281
Negative judgments, 277
Neo-Kantianism, 135, 150
Neo-Platonism, 175, 193
Neues Organon (Lambert), 271
Newton, 177, 182, 184, 185
Nouveaux Essais (Leibniz), 288

Occasionalism, 162, 172
Opus Postumum (Kant), 23, 183

Parmenides, 107
Paton, H. J., 17-22
Philosophia rationalis sive logica (Wolff), 116, 117, 271
Philosophie des Selbstbewusstseins (Thiele), 26
Philosophisches Magazin (Eberhard), 122
Philosophy of Leibniz (Russell), 111
Plato, 144, 160, 161, 163
Platonic dialogues, 63, 66
Platonism, 161
Port Royal Logic (Arnauld and Nicole), 219, 233
Possible judgment, 280, 281
Predeterminism, 196, 197
Principle of contradiction, 112, 118, 120, 121, 124, 126, 127; principle of contradiction in Leibniz and Wolff, 108, 109. *See also* Law of contradiction and Principle of non-contradiction.
Principle of non-contradiction, 252; principle of non-contradiction and analytic judgments, 253; and synthetic judgments, 253. *See also* Principle of contradiction and Law of contradiction.

Principle of sufficient reason, 291, 296, 297, 299. *See also* Law of sufficient reason.
Prolegomena (Kant), 24, 68, 107, 120, 243, 257, 259, 260, 262
Progress of Metaphysics (Kant), 119
Pure concepts, 82, 83

Quality, 208, 275-279
Quantity, 208, 273-275; mathematical notion of, 275

Rationalism, 171
Realism, 167
Reflexionen (Kant), 23, 53
Reicke, 64, 68
Relation, 208, 278, 279, 283
Reply to Eberhard (Kant), 119
Riehl, 54, 132, 133; "Concerning Scientific and Non-Scientific Philosophy," 133
Russell, B., 110, 288; *Philosophy of Leibniz*, 111

Schopenhauer, 147, 152
Schultz, 226, 237
Second analogy of experience, 83, 106, 210, 211-213, 237, 240, 285, 286, 290, 293, 294, 297, 299, 301, 307. *See also* Analogies of experience.
Sensibility, 13, 16, 20, 34, 52
Singular judgments, 274
Smith, N. K., 63
Space, 128, 174, 175, 177, 178, 186, 187, 191, 192, 194; and God, 181-184; and soul, 188; subjectivity of, 104
Spinoza, 172, 177, 181, 192, 195, 270
Spinozism, 187, 193, 196
Spiritual substance, 188
Spontaneity, 13, 15, 141, 165, 166, 169, 170
Streitschrift gegen Eberhard (Kant), 250

Subjective deduction, 267
Subjective sources of knowledge, 13, 15, 16, 19-21, 26, 32-40, 51, 65
Synthetic *a priori* knowledge, 227
Synthetic judgments, 234, 237, 259, 261, 288; *a priori,* 95-98, 101, 102, 107, 109, 130, 159, 170, 204, 210, 216, 225, 250, 285; forms of, 248, 255, 260, 263; and intuition, 258

Thales, 108
Thiele, G., *Philosophie des Selbstbewusstseins,* 26
Thing-in-itself and appearance, distinction, 102, 104
Time, 174, 175, 186, 194, 198; and God, 192; subjectivity of, 104
Transcendental aesthetic, 31, 32, 41, 53, 83, 139, 181, 213, 214
Transcendental analytic, 31, 53, 142, 153, 213
Transcendental deduction, 13-15, 17-19, 22-24, 26, 31-33, 40, 47, 50, 55, 60, 63-65, 67-70, 72-75, 81, 84, 86, 90, 91, 138, 152, 206, 262, 263
Transcendental dialectic, 107, 142
Transcendental doctrine of method, 251
Transcendental idealism, 159
Transcendental logic, 139, 250, 254, 271

Treatise Concerning Human Nature (Hume), 292

Vaihinger, H., 13-22, 62, 63, 65, 66, 68, 69, 71-77, 82, 83, 86, 89-91; *Commentar zu Kants Kritik der reinen Vernunft,* 232; *Die Transcendentale Deduktion der Kategorien,* 63
Vernünftige Gedanken von den Kräften des menschlichen Verstandes (Wolff), 116
Vernunftlehre (Meier), 271
Vorländer, 27

Whitehead, fallacy of the perfect dictionary, 239
Wolff, 105, 110, 114, 117-121, 123, 127-129, 250, 262, 278, 280, 284, 285, 289, 292, 293, 295, 298, 299, 305, 306; and analytic judgments, 122; *Horae Subsecivae,* 115; *Philosophia rationalis sive logica,* 116, 117, 271; and principle of contradiction, 108, 109, 286, 287; and principle of sufficient reason, 109, 286, 287, 290, 304; and synthetic judgments *a priori,* 115, 122; *Vernünftige Gedanken von den Kräften des menschlichen Verstandes,* 116
Wolffian logic, 270, 281, 282